In loving memory,

to my father Samuel Goodman.

Acknowledgements

The love of cooking and the never-ending search for knowledge about the preparation of food is something that has been a part of my life for a very long time. I owe a special thanks to all of those who have both taught and encouraged me for these many years, but especially to Bonnie, without whom there would have been no beginning.

I would like to thank my husband for all his help with this book. Full credit for the beverage chapter and the wine suggestions belong to him, as his knowledge in this field is far greater than mine. He has lovingly and with patience put up with my experiments in the kitchen for twenty-five years without complaint. And for this I thank him as well.

A special thanks to Nelle Irby for her expertise in typing the manuscript for this book. I can cook, but my typing is terrible and my handwriting worse.

Proof-reading is a task that is both tedious and painstaking. I want to thank my mother for helping to proof-read the manuscript of this book.

I would like to thank the staff of the Ludington and Gladwyne libraries in Lower Merion Township who helped locate many hard to find books needed in the research of this project.

And last, but certainly not least, I want to thank the Schiffers. I am a very fortunate person to have worked with publishers such as Peter, Nancy and Herbert. They guide and advise with kindness and understanding that is unique in their field. They have been a joy to work with on this book.

COOKING FOR THE '80's

FROM

Les Cuisiniers

by

Hermie Kranzdorf

Schiffer Publishing Ltd

Box E, Exton, Pennsylvania 19341

Other books by this author:

Co-author of *Chef Tell Tells All.*

Library of Congress Catalog Card Number: 80–52023
ISBN 0-916838-31-5

Printed in the United States of America

This Edition Prepared for Distribution by
Schiffer Publishing Limited, Box E, Exton, Pa. 19341

Table of Contents

Photograph by Maurice Tannenbaum

Author's Notes

The *italics* used throughout this book serve a twofold purpose: used directly under the recipe title, their function is one of description of or comment about that particular recipe. Second - and most important - they are used to indicate various stopping or do-ahead points in the recipe. Storage, reheating and freezing instructions are also *italicized* for each recipe.

Every cook has his or her own particular idiosyncrasies and preferences when it comes to food. Cookbook authors are even more guilty in that respect. Since they may make a difference in how the recipes turn out, I should like to list for you my own preferences which are pertinent to this book.

The butter used in the recipes is always sweet unsalted butter. Salt is a preservative added by manufacturers to give the butter a longer shelf-life. The salt will disguise a rancid taste if the butter is no longer fresh. I prefer to use unsalted butter and to add whatever salt the recipe calls for separately. You have much better control over exactly how much salt you use this way.

I use regular pasteurized cream for both cooking and eating. The flavor of dairy products that have undergone an ultra-pasteurization process is altered somewhat. To me, they have a chemical rather than a fresh taste. At least one large supermarket chain (A & P) carries its own brand of regular pasteurized products that work quite well.

I do not object to the use of margarine for cooking purposes. Butter does taste better, but margarine will work. As a matter of fact, most recipes state whether margarine can be substituted successfully for butter. Use an unsalted margarine if possible. There are many such brands on the market.

Flour is always unbleached regular flour unless stated otherwise. Regular flour is now pre-sifted and does not need to be sifted again unless specifically mentioned in the recipe. When using whole wheat flour, try to get some that has been stone-ground, the taste will be better. The same applies to corn meal.

The small amount of butter and flour that it takes to coat a pan or dish for cooking or baking are not included in the ingredients list of the recipes. Use whatever it takes to coat the pans well without worrying about specific amounts.

In recipes that call for the addition of coffee included in the dessert section, I always use instant coffee powder dissolved in a little liquid. Regular brewed coffee is never strong enough in flavor and if boiled down it will take on a bitter flavor. This is one case where instant is better.

I cook and bake with extra-large eggs. Please take this into account if you are substituting different sized eggs, especially for baking.

I prefer to cook with coarse or kosher salt as it has, at least to me, an even saltier and better flavor than regular table salt. For baking, however, I do use table salt. It is more finely ground and free flowing and therefore is more easily incorporated into the other ingredients.

The amounts of salt and pepper that you add to your food is really one of personal preference. For the most part, no specific measurements for salt and pepper are given in the recipes. Taste your food both as you cook and before serving and then season to your own particular taste.

There is nothing better than freshly ground pepper for cooking. I like to add one part of whole allspice along with seven parts of peppercorns to my pepper mill. This combination gives food a tremendously aromatic smell and the allspice is just barely discernible in taste. I am indebted to to Richard Olney for this idea many years ago.

Fresh herbs, if available, are always preferable to dried. Amounts given for parsley, dill and chives in this book are always for the fresh herb, as they are readily available in most parts of this country. Other than these three herbs, all amounts are listed for dried herbs, unless the recipe particularly specifies otherwise. To change from one to the other, a three to one ratio usually works well. It takes one tablespoon of a fresh herb to equal the potency of one teaspoon of an herb that has been dried.

An easy way to grind whole dried spices or herbs is to use a small electric coffee mill. I find that I use mine for spices far more than I do for coffee.

There is nothing like the taste of fresh lemon juice with food and I never use the bottled variety. Fresh oranges, lemons and even limes are available all year long - use them if possible. Citrus juices specified in the recipes always mean fresh.

It is perfectly acceptable to substitute canned stock or even bouillon cubes for home-made stocks in many of the recipes in this book. I recognize that most people do not have time to start from scratch and make a pot of stock every time they need a small amount for cooking. I certainly don't always have the time myself. When you do have the time, however, make stocks in as large a quantity as possible. They freeze beautifully and taste better than canned. When substituting for fresh stock, just be very careful with the addition of salt to your food, as most commercial products are extremely salty. Always taste before adding any additional seasonings. Many canned soup products are concentrated into a double-strength form - dilute before using as instructed on the package label.

I like to make my own home-made demi-glace for flavoring sauces. There are, however, a few commercial products that can be used for both color and flavor. Maison Glass in New York City makes a good glace de viande which lasts almost forever if kept in the freezer.

I like to cook with wine and do so in many recipes. Wine lends both flavor and depth to many things. Please do not use the so-called "cooking wines" available in supermarkets. They are extremely salty and do not have a particularly good flavor. Buy yourself an inexpensive bottle of white chablis and one of red burgundy to use for cooking. If the wine is refrigerated and the bottles are kept tightly corked, they will keep for a very long time.

Do not be afraid to use water when you cook. If a sauce begins to stick or you need more liquid to deglaze a pan, reach for the water first. It will not alter the taste of your sauce and can always be cooked down without any harm if you add too much. Throw in too much wine or stock and you change the taste - but not so with water.

A word about oven temperatures and baking times - every oven is different. Just because you set the oven to 350 degrees does not guarantee that this is the actual temperature inside. Get to know your own oven and how to control it properly. It is for this reason that the recipes in this book give an approximate cooking or baking time and then use the words "or until done" with a brief explanation of how the food should look or feel when it is finished.

Not all ovens heat evenly. As a matter of fact, most do not. Ovens tend to develop hot spots where food burns easily and cool spots where cooking seems to take forever. Learn to turn your food - especially cakes while they are baking, so that they will cook more evenly.

Another problem I have found recently is the varying amounts of energy we receive in our homes at different times of the day. During "peak" periods we receive less, while at "off" hours, more. A stove or oven, be it either gas or electric, will never heat quite as high as we may prefer during these peak periods. Food may therefore take longer to cook than expected. Rather than rely completely on times given in any recipes, not just mine, think of them as a guide and try to use your own judgement as to when food is properly cooked.

One last important fact - remember that no recipes are sacred. Those in this book were certainly not handed down from the Mount, so do not be afraid to alter them to suit your own particular tastes and preferences in food.

Cooking can be a creative, rewarding and enjoyable experience for everyone. Cooking is fun and love for me...and I hope for you, too.

Introduction

We are all now living or will have to learn to live in an environment made cooler not by nature, but by man himself. The world is no longer able to consume energy at the tremendously wasteful rate that it has in the past. Our federal government has suggested guidelines that both request and direct its citizens to conserve fuel and energy.

So now, without choice, we work for a good part of the year in office buildings and factories that are cooler. When we eat in a restaurant or attend a function in a public building we again feel cooler. And if we follow these guidelines at home, we also live in a much cooler climate than many of us might prefer or enjoy.

This new pattern of both working and living in a cooler environment is one that looks as if it will continue for a long time into the future. There are several things we can do to make ourselves more comfortable while still colder. Besides wearing that extra sweater all day and using an extra blanket at night, we can also learn to adjust some of our eating patterns. When we are cold, we need food that is hot and hearty - food to warm our souls as well as our bodies.

If we were to take a look at the history of the world we would realize that this is certainly not the first adjustment that man has had to make to a changing climate. Vilhjalmur Stefansson, in his book *The Fat of the Land,* said that the first known anthropoids lived in the hot and humid land forests and jungles that covered much of what is now Europe, Asia and Africa. These forerunners of man were primarily vegetarians, existing on a diet of roots, nuts, fruits and tubers. Occasionally they would catch a few animals and eat them. But mainly they existed on what food they found growing in the jungles.

Then slowly, through the centuries, the climate of certain hugh land areas began to change and dry out. Over the millenniums lush forests turned into dry praries. Man, in order to survive, had to learn to hunt. He ate less and less vegetables to sustain himself and more and more fish and animals. What had begun as a vegetarian diet became primarily an all protein or meat diet.

Then about twenty thousand years ago (but a moment in time as far as mankind is concerned) still another change began to take place. Systematic and planned agriculture first began to develop. Man learned that by planting and growing his own foodstuffs, he could sustain many more people than if he merely hunted. This meant that man now ate less protein than he had in his recent past and he began to consume more starches and carbohydrates.

As each of these changes took place in the history of mankind they surely caused him many physical and digestive problems. Through natural selection, the vegetarian slowly adjusted to the meat diet of the hunter. Next the protein consuming hunter had to adjust to the varied diet that we know today. We are probably still living through that second period of adjustment even now, for twenty thousand years is but a short span in the history of this world.

Doctors and nutritionists today are still unsure of which proportions of what food each of us needs to maintain ourselves in so-called "good health." As well they should be, for no one knows why some people are healthy while others are not when both eat essentially the same diet. Every year brings its share of "fad" diets, each only to be replaced the following year by the next new and definitive discovery. Most new diets seem to cause more confusion than actual weight loss or good health. No one really knows for sure what we should or should not be eating.

There are certain types of foods that give us a sense of warmth and well being. Eskimos have existed well in an extremely cold environment for a very long time on an all protein and fat diet. Now I certainly do not advocate that we follow their regime, for sensible if not proper nutrition suggests that we follow a diet that is balanced in all the essentials. No food group should be eaten exclusively nor eliminated entirely from our diets.

I do know one thing for sure, when I am cold, I like to eat foods that make me feel warmer. So does everyone. Therefore, the concepts, menus and recipes presented in this book are primarily those that are hearty in nature yet healthy and well-balanced. Food that is both warm and satisfying at the same time—sensible and timely food that is for "Cooking in the '80's."

Appetizers

There is an endless variety of foods that can fit into the general classification of appetizers. Many recipes from other sections of this book are eminently suitable to use as a first course.

A small portion of pasta makes a delightful beginning. For example, pasta with curried scallops, or mushrooms and peas, etc. Salads are a light and lovely way to start a meal - consider using any of the salad recipes.

Fish, to my mind, is always the perfect first course, especially for company dinners. Many of the fish recipes work beautifully as appetizers as well as entrées. Try bass in an asparagus sauce, or any of the shellfish recipes - just keep the portions small.

And of course, soups as well as pâtés and terrines are also appetizers - the variety is indeed limitless.

SAUTEED SCALLOPS WITH PARSLEY AND CHIVES

Fresh scallops in a mild cream and herb sauce are perfect for any meal and make a wonderful appetizer as well as entrée. They only take a few minutes to cook and are absolutely delicious. This recipe will work equally well with bay or sea scallops.

3 Tbsp. chopped shallots
3 Tbsp. butter
1½ pounds scallops
3 Tbsp. white wine
3 Tbsp. dry vermouth
salt, white pepper
3 Tbsp. heavy cream
scant 1 tsp. lemon juice
1½ Tbsp. chopped parsley
1½ Tbsp. chopped fresh chives

Sauté the shallots in half the butter in a frying pan for just a minute or two. Add the scallops, white wine, vermouth and a little salt and pepper to the pan.

Cook for just a few minutes, until the scallops lose their opaqueness and turn white. Remove the scallops from the pan with a slotted spoon and reserve.

Add the cream and lemon juice to the pan and simmer the sauce for a few minutes.

Drain off any juices that have formed around the scallops and add this liquid to the pan. Cook to reduce the sauce so that less than one-half cup remains. Taste and correct the seasonings.

Add the scallops back to the pan and continue to cook for just a minute. You only want to heat the scallops, not to cook them further.

Add the parsley, chives and the remaining butter to the pan. Remove the pan from the heat and stir until the butter melts.

Serve immediately. Wonderful with a rice pilaf. Serves three to four as an entrée or six as an appetizer.

COQUILLES au GRATIN

This is an elegant first course for any meal. The truffle is not necessary to the taste of the dish but it does make it look pretty. Use it or not, depending on your finances at the moment.

2 cups Mornay Sauce, page 62
4 Tbsp. butter
2 shallots, chopped
6 mushrooms, sliced
salt, pepper
1 pound bay scallops
½ cup white wine
juice of ½ lemon
1 chopped truffle
¼ cup grated Parmesan cheese

Prepare the Mornay Sauce and reserve.

Heat two tablespoons of butter in a frying pan and add the shallots. Sauté for one minute.

Add the sliced mushrooms, salt and pepper. Continue to cook, stirring, for two or three more minutes.

Add the scallops, white wine and lemon juice to the pan.

Cook until the scallops turn white. This only takes a minute for tiny bay scallops.

Strain the contents of the pan, reserving the liquid. Divide the scallop and mushroom mixture into six small ramekins or scallop shells.

Add the diced truffle to the ramekins, if using.

Combine the liquid from the scallops and the Mornay Sauce. Stir to mix them well.

Spoon the sauce over the scallops in the ramekins.

Sprinkle the tops of the ramekins with the grated cheese and dot with the remaining two tablespoons of butter.

The recipe can be prepared to this point early in the day and refrigerated. Increase the baking time by five minutes if you do so.

Place the ramekins in a 400 degree oven for about ten minutes, or until they are hot and browned.

Serve immediately. This recipe serves six.

If bay scallops are unavailable, substitute sea scallops, cut into thirds.

Alternate: This dish can also be made with half scallops and half shrimp. Add the peeled and diced raw shrimp to the shallots along with the white wine and the lemon juice. Cook for a few minutes before adding the scallops and then continue with the rest of the recipe. Or just add some diced pre-cooked shrimp right along with the scallops.

SEAFOOD TIMBALES

This is a perfect dish for those special occasion meals. Do not let the instructions frighten you, the recipe is easy to prepare. A food processor is necessary, however, because a blender cannot purée the fish finely enough.

8 Tbsp. butter
½ cup water
salt, white pepper
½ cup flour
2 eggs
2 cups flounder or fluke fillets
½ cup mushrooms, diced
½ cup diced raw shrimp
½ cup bay scallops
½ cup lobster meat, diced
1 cup heavy cream, chilled
1 tsp. chopped truffle, optional
Beurre Blanc Sauce, page 63
2 Tbsp. chopped parsley

Place four tablespoons of butter, the water and a pinch of salt into a saucepan and bring it to a boil.

Add the flour to the liquid all at once and stir, over heat, until the mixture is smooth and dry. It will form a ball around your spoon.

Remove the saucepan from the stove.

Beat in the eggs, one at a time, mixing well until each is incorporated before adding the next egg.

Set the mixture aside to cool a little while you prepare the fish.

Cut the flounder into large dice and place in a food processor. Purée.

Add the cooled flour mixture to the fish and process until it is well blended.

Remove the fish mixture from the processor and chill well.
Heat the remaining four tablespoons of butter in a frying pan. Add the mushrooms and cook them for a few minutes, until they give up most of their liquid.

Add the shrimp, lobster and scallops. Season with salt and pepper and sauté for just a minute or two. Cool this mixture also.

When the flounder mixture is very cold, gradually stir in the cup of chilled heavy cream.

Add the cooled shellfish mixture to the flounder mixture. Mix in the truffle, if using, and correct the seasonings.

Butter eight small timbale molds. Fill each about two-thirds full with the fish mixture.

The timbales can be prepared to this point early in the day and refrigerated.

Place the timbales into a pan filled with an inch of warm water. Bake them in a 350 degree oven for twenty to twenty-five minutes or until they are done. The tops of the timbales will be puffed and feel firm and springy to the touch.

Unmold the timbales onto individual plates. To unmold, loosen the edges with a small knife. Place a plate on top of the timbale and turn both the plate and the mold upside down. Jiggle sharply to loosen.

Spoon the Beurre Blanc Sauce around the timbales, sprinkle with the chopped parsley and serve immediately.

This recipe serves eight.

The timbales can be kept for a little while after they are baked. Loosen the timbales, but leave the molds in place, do not remove the fish.

When you are ready to serve the fish, return the timbales to the water bath. Cover them lightly and reheat the timbales for a few minutes in the oven. Then turn out as the recipe instructs.

FISH QUENELLES

A food processor is necessary for this recipe. The quenelles are easy to make and are a very impressive appetizer. They can be done ahead of time as they reheat quite well in the Sauce Badania.

5 ounces bread	5 ounces butter
water, for soaking	salt, white pepper
10 ounces pike or fluke fillets	Fish stock for poaching, page 59
4 egg whites	Sauce Badania, page 60

Soak the bread in a little water until it is soft, then squeeze it very dry.

Cut the fish into chunks. Place them in a food processor and grind well.

With the motor on, add the egg whites through the top of the machine.

Stop the machine and add the bread, the butter, the salt and pepper. Process until well mixed.

Correct the seasonings and remove the fish from the machine.

Bring the fish stock to a boil.

Form the fish mixture into small oval or quenelle shapes, using a tablespoon.

Poach the quenelles in the fish stock. Allow about eight to ten minutes after the quenelles rise to the surface of the stock, then lift one out and taste to see if it is done enough.

Remove the quenelles with a slotted spoon once they taste cooked. They should be firm. Do not let them cook until they fall apart.

Serve the quenelles with a Sauce Badania, page 60.

This recipe will serve eight or more.

The poached quenelles can be kept covered overnight in the refrigerator. Wrap them well. Reheat the quenelles in the Sauce Badania.

Quenelles can be frozen but the texture will change and they will not be as firm. I do not recommend freezing them.

If you do not have any fish stock, the quenelles can be poached in a Court Bouillon, page 62. Double the recipe. Cook for thirty minutes and strain before adding the quenelles.

The quenelle mixture can also be used as a stuffing for fish.

Alternates: Chicken or veal can be substituted for the fish in this recipe. Poach the quenelles in chicken stock and serve with a Sauce Mornay, page 62.

QUICHE

Quiche is really an economical and multi-purpose dish. It is great for brunch and equally good for lunch or dinner with a hot bowl of soup and a salad. Quiche also makes a good late night supper after the theatre or movies.

Quiche can be prepared ahead and frozen before baking. Place in the oven frozen and add an extra ten to twenty minutes to the baking time.

I prefer not to freeze quiche as I find the crust is never quite as flaky and the filling becomes too watery. The crust can be baked blind early in the day. The filling can also be prepared and refrigerated separately early in the day or even a day ahead. It is very simple just to pour the readied filling into the crust and bake the quiche right before serving time.

CRUST FOR QUICHE – HAND-MADE METHOD

I like to use half butter and half margarine to make a crust for a quiche. The dough is much easier to handle than if you used all butter. With a cream and egg filling, it will taste rich enough. You can, however, use all butter if you like.

All crusts for a quiche should be baked blind before they are filled, as this will prevent your quiche from having a soggy bottom.

1¼ cups flour
pinch salt
4 Tbsp. butter, room temperature
4 Tbsp. margarine, room temperature
2 to 3 Tbsp. ice water

Mix the flour and salt in a bowl.

Cut the butter and margarine into small dice right on top of the flour.

Either with your fingers, two knives, or a pastry cutter, work the butter into the flour until it is very crumbly.

Make a well in the center of this mixture. Slowly add the ice water, working it in until large lumps begin to form.

Turn the dough out onto a floured board and work it into a large ball with your hands.

Wrap the dough in waxed paper and let it rest in the refrigerator for at least thirty minutes.

The dough can be prepared to this point and refrigerated for a day or two.

Roll the dough out to fit a quiche pan, if possible, one with removable sides. It will make it much easier to serve the quiche.

If you have an extra ten minutes at this point, place the crust back into the refrigerator. It will shrink less if put into the oven chilled.

Place a piece of aluminum foil on top of the crust. Press it down into the pan, covering all the dough.

Put either lead weights (especially made for this and great to have - they last forever) or dried rice or beans on top of the foil.

Set the pan onto a baking sheet and place it into a 375 degree oven for twelve to fifteen minutes.

Remove the pan from the oven and lift out the foil and the weights.

Place the crust back into the oven for an additional five minutes. Watch carefully. If any large air bubbles form in the bottom of the crust while it is baking, simply prick them with a fork and they will deflate.

Remove the crust and let it cool just a little. Then proceed with your quiche recipe.

CRUST FOR QUICHE - FOOD PROCESSOR METHOD

1¼ cups flour
pinch salt
4 Tbsp. butter, chilled
4 Tbsp. margarine, chilled
2 to 3 Tbsp. ice water

Place the flour and salt into a food processor fitted with the metal blade. Turn on and off once, to mix.

Cut the chilled butter and margarine into small pieces and place them on top of the flour in the machine.

Turn the machine on and off a few times for just a few seconds each time. The mixture should form small crumbs.

Remove the plunger from the top of the machine. With the machine on, add the ice water through the top, just until the dough begins to form into small lumps.

Be careful not to overwork your dough at this point. If you have processed it into one large lump, you have gone too far. Be more careful next time as the crust will be tough.

Stop the machine and turn out all the bits and pieces of dough onto a floured board. Form them with your hands into a large ball.

Flatten the dough and wrap it in waxed paper. Chill the dough in the refrigerator for at least thirty minutes before rolling out your crust.

The dough can be prepared to this point and refrigerated for a day or two.

I know it may sound complicated at first, but if you get used to using your machine properly you can make very good crust in just a matter of seconds. Just remember to keep the butter, margarine and water very cold and to "under" rather than "over" process the dough.

Follow the same instructions for rolling and baking the crust as given in the hand method recipe.

HAM AND LEEK QUICHE

2 leeks, white part only
3 Tbsp. butter
salt, white pepper
4 ozs. ham, diced
2 eggs plus 1 egg yolk
1½ cups heavy cream
1 partially baked crust, page 18

You will need a quiche pan, preferably with a removable bottom, nine by one and one-quarter inches.

Wash the leeks well and cut them in small rounds.

Heat the butter in a frying pan. Add the leeks, salt and pepper and sauté, stirring, until the leeks begin to get tender. This will take about ten minutes.

Add the diced ham and continue to sauté for another minute or two. Remove the pan from the heat and let the ham and leek mixture cool a little.

Mix the eggs and the egg yolk with the cream.

Stir the leek and ham mixture into the eggs and cream. Taste and correct the seasonings.

Pour the filling mixture into the prepared crust.

Bake in a 400 degree oven for about twenty-five minutes or until the crust is brown and the filling is set and golden. This recipe serves eight to ten.

SMOKED SALMON QUICHE

¼ pound smoked salmon or nova
1 medium onion, chopped
2 Tbsp. butter
salt, white pepper
4 ounces cream cheese
1 egg plus 2 yolks
1½ cups light cream
2 to 3 Tbsp. chopped dill
1 partially baked crust, page 18

You will need a deep quiche pan, preferably with a removable bottom, nine by one and three-quarter inches.

Cut the salmon into small dice and reserve.

Sauté the onion in the butter until it is soft. Add a little white pepper.

Add the salmon to the onion and sauté for just a minute. Set this mixture aside to cool a little.

Beat the cream cheese until it is soft. You can use the flat beater of your mixer. Do not use a food processor, it will purée the mixture too much.

Beat the egg and the yolks into the cream cheese.

Add the light cream and beat until the mixture is very smooth.

Stir in the reserved salmon mixture and the dill. Taste to check the seasonings. Add salt and more pepper if needed.

Pour the filling into the crust and bake in a 375 degree oven for thirty-five minutes or until the filling is set and the top is lightly browned.

Let the quiche cool a little before slicing. This quiche is best when served at room temperature.

This recipe serves eight to ten.

SHRIMP QUICHE

This recipe makes a very pretty presentation. The tails of the shrimp extend over the edge of the pastry in a decorative pattern - leaving no doubt as to what kind of quiche you are serving.

Of course, if you like, you can remove the tails and place all the shrimp inside the quiche.

½ pound shrimp
2 eggs
salt, white pepper
1 cup heavy cream
1 Tbsp. chopped parsley
¼ cup grated Swiss cheese
1 partially baked crust, page 18

You will need a quiche pan, preferably with a removable bottom, nine by one and one-quarter inches.

Cook the shrimp according to the directions on page 95, for boiled shrimp.

Clean and shell the shrimp but leave just the tails attached to about eight of them.

Arrange the shrimp with the tails attached around the edge of the pastry, placing the tails over the rim of the crust.

Cut the rest of the shrimp into dice and scatter them over the bottom of the crust.

Mix together the eggs, salt, pepper, cream and the parsley. Check and correct the seasonings. Pour the filling into the crust.

Sprinkle the top of the quiche with the grated cheese.

Bake in a 375 degree oven for thirty minutes or until the filling is set and the top lightly browned.

Let the quiche cool for ten minutes before slicing.

This recipe serves eight to ten.

Alternate: Mix the grated cheese directly into the filling instead of sprinkling it on top of the quiche.

VEGETABLE QUICHE

This is a great way to use up all those bits and pieces of leftover vegetables. Economical and delicious at the same time - one of my daughter's favorites.

- 2 to 2½ cups cooked diced mixed vegetables, such as string beans, carrots, broccoli, cauliflower, mushrooms, zucchini, peas, etc.
- 1 partially baked crust, page 18
- 1½ cups light cream
- 3 eggs
- 1 scant tsp. salt
- white pepper
- dash nutmeg
- 2/3 cup grated Swiss cheese

You will need a deep quiche pan, preferably with a removable bottom, nine by one and three-quarter inches.

Steam or cook all the vegetables so that they are still crisp. Drain well and dice all the vegetables.

Place the diced vegetables into the bottom of the prepared crust.

Mix the cream, eggs, salt, pepper and nutmeg together. Pour this mixture over the vegetables.

Sprinkle a thick layer of grated cheese on top of the filling.

Bake the quiche in a 375 degree oven for forty to forty-five minutes or until the crust is brown and the top of the quiche is puffed and beginning to brown.

Remove the quiche from the oven and let it sit ten minutes before slicing.

This recipe serves ten to twelve.

This quiche can be made a few hours ahead of time and reheated for a few minutes right before serving.

Alternate: The cheese can be mixed right into the filling instead of being used as a layer on top.

PISSALADIERE

Pissaladière is a funny name for a version of "French Pizza" - a tomato, anchovy and onion pie with no cheese. Instead of a yeast dough, this recipe uses a quick pastry crust.

Crust:

1½ cups flour
½ tsp. salt
½ cup butter (or half margarine)
2 to 3 Tbsp. ice water

Mix the flour and the salt.

Work in the butter until tiny particles are formed (see Quiche Crust, pages 18–20 for technique).

Add enough ice water to form a dough. Form the dough into a ball.

Wrap the dough in waxed paper and chill for at least thirty minutes.

Roll the dough out into a large round shape. Place it onto a greased and floured baking sheet.

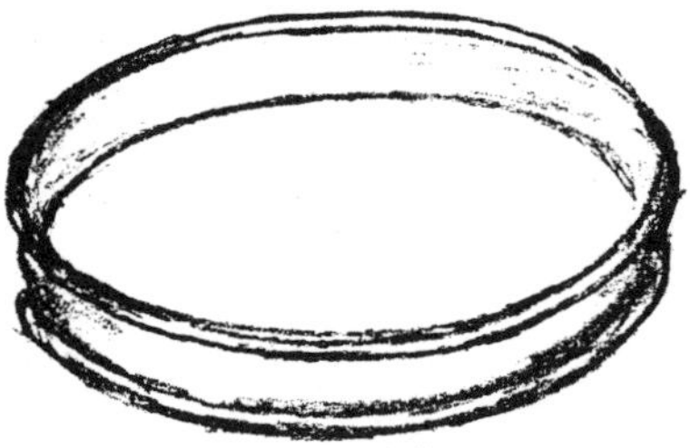

Using a round ten inch circle or flan ring as a guide, cut the dough evenly into a circle and remove the extra pieces.

Prick the crust with a fork and bake it in a 400 degree oven for twenty minutes.

Filling:

2 large onions
5 to 6 Tbsp. butter or oil
salt, pepper
pinch sugar
2 tomatoes
½ tsp. oregano
1 to 2 Tbsp. chopped parsley
1 small tin anchovies
10 to 12 black olives, pitted and halved

Slice the onions very thinly and sauté them in three tablespoons of butter or oil. Sprinkle with salt, pepper and the sugar. Continue to cook slowly until the onions are very tender.

Spread the cooked onions onto the prepared crust.

Slice the tomatoes and place them on top of the onions. Sprinkle the tomatoes with salt, pepper, oregano and parsley.

Rinse the anchovies and dry them well. Form a lattice pattern with the anchovies on top of the tomato slices.

Place a black olive half in the center of each lattice square.

Drizzle the top of the Pissaladière with the rest of the butter or oil and place it into a 400 degree oven for fifteen minutes.

Serve hot or warm, cut into wedges.

This recipe serves eight to ten.

If anchovies are too salty for your taste, soak them in a little milk (after rinsing) for a half-hour. Then dry them well and proceed with the recipe. The milk will draw out some of the salt.

CURRIED BEEF IN PASTRY

Curried Beef in Pastry makes a perfect cocktail party appetizer - just spicy enough to pique the appetite. No one would ever believe its origin is Chinese. Use Madras curry powder if possible for this recipe, it is the best of the tinned variety.

The Curried Beef in Pastry can be completely prepared up to a day ahead of time and kept in the refrigerator until ready to bake. It can also be reheated, if necessary.

Crust:

1½ cups flour
½ tsp. salt
9 Tbsp. butter (or part margarine)
3 to 4 Tbsp. ice water
1 egg, beaten lightly

Mix the flour and salt.

Cut in the butter until tiny particles are formed (see Quiche Crust, pages 18–20 for technique).

Add enough ice water to form a dough. Form the dough into a ball.

Wrap it in waxed paper and let the dough rest in the refrigerator for at least thirty minutes.

The egg is needed when the pastry is assembled.

Filling:

1 small onion, chopped
1 to 2 Tbsp. oil
½ pound ground beef
salt and pepper
1 small clove garlic, crushed
1½ tsp. curry powder
pinch sugar
2 to 3 Tbsp. ketchup
½ tsp. cornstarch
2 tsp. water
1 Tbsp. dried bread crumbs

Heat the oil in a frying pan. Add the onion and cook for a few minutes.

Add the beef, salt and pepper and continue to cook and stir until the beef is browned. This will take about four to five minutes.

Add the garlic, curry powder, sugar and ketchup. Cook and stir for another minute or two.

In a small bowl, mix the cornstarch with the water to form a paste.

Add the liquid cornstarch to the meat mixture and cook for one more minute.

Remove the pan from the heat and stir the bread crumbs into the meat mixture.

Taste to correct the seasonings, then chill the filling.

The prepared filling can be refrigerated for a few days, or it can be frozen.

Assembly:

Roll out half the crust into a long rectangle.

Place the filling, using one heaping teaspoonful at a time, into mounds across one long side of the rectangle, one inch in from the edge. Space the mounds about one inch apart.

Moisten a small circular area of the crust around the filling using a pastry brush dipped in water.

Fold the long end of the rectangle over, lengthwise, to cover the filling.

Press down the circular area with your fingers to seal around the mounds of filling.

Cut out the filled pastry into rounds with a cookie cutter or a glass.

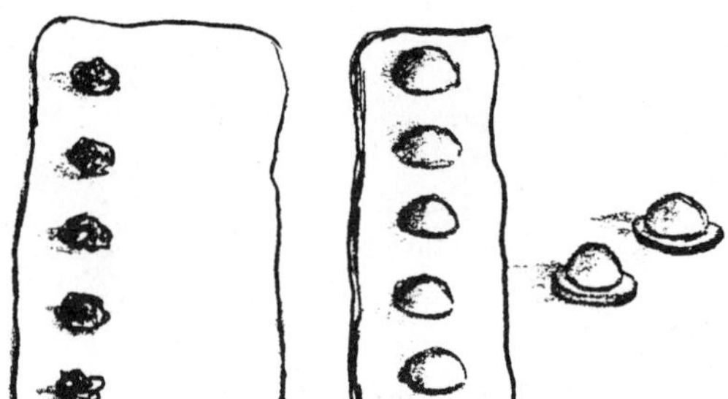

Repeat until all the filling and dough are used.

Place the rounds onto a greased baking sheet.

Brush the tops of the rounds with the lightly beaten egg, using a pastry brush.

Bake in a 375 degree oven until the crust is browned, about thirty-five minutes.

This recipe makes about sixteen rounds.

Alternate version: Roll the dough out into two rectangles. Fill each rectangle with half the filling. Fold in the sides and roll up, sealing the long end with water. Bake at serving time. Cut into slices after baking. This version is messier to eat but much faster to make if you are in a hurry.

STRUDEL

Filo, phyllo or strudel leaves can be bought ready for use, in refrigerated packages. Try not to buy frozen leaves as they are much harder to handle.

The whole secret of working with strudel leaves is to keep them covered at all times and to work quickly. Use a dry towel to cover the leaves if they are fresh and a slightly damp one if they are a little dried out.

Always use melted butter and a thin sprinkling of bread crumbs between the layers of dough. It will keep the leaves separate as they bake and make your pastry much flakier.

CABBAGE STRUDEL

Cabbage strudel has been one of the most popular appetizers in my classes. Just one taste and even tried and true cabbage haters will like this dish.

1 small head cabbage or
  ½ large head
salt
¼ cup butter
1 Tbsp. sugar
black pepper
8 strudel leaves
½ cup melted butter
½ cup toasted bread crumbs

Core and shred the cabbage. Sprinkle it liberally with salt. Mix well and let the cabbage sit at room temperature for a few hours.

Squeeze the cabbage very well in a towel to eliminate the extra liquid.

Heat the quarter cup of butter in a large skillet. Add the sugar and the cabbage and stir well.

Cook slowly, stirring often, until the cabbage becomes soft and golden-brown. This should take about thirty minutes.

Add lots of freshly milled black pepper and salt to taste. The filling should be nice and peppery.

The cabbage filling can be refrigerated, covered, for a few days.

Keep the strudel leaves covered with a dry towel until each one is needed.

Place one leaf in front of you on a second dry towel.

Brush the leaf with the melted butter, using a pastry brush. Sprinkle with a thin layer of bread crumbs.

Repeat two more times, using butter and crumbs between each layer. Place the fourth leaf on top, leaving it plain.

Using one-half of the filling, make a lengthwise row about two inches from the top edge of the strudel.

Fold the top edge over the filling, then fold in the sides. Roll the strudel towards you, using the towel for leverage.

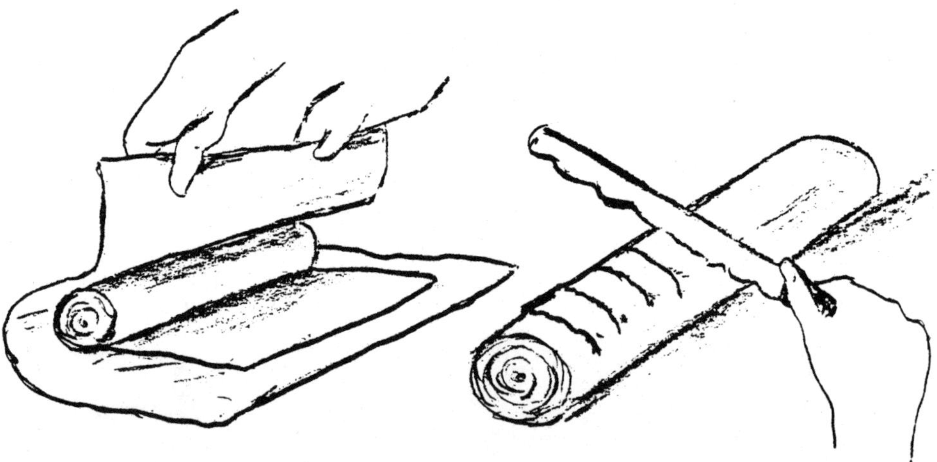

With your knife, slice the top of the strudel about one-third of the way down into serving sized pieces.

Place the strudel roll onto a buttered baking sheet and brush the top well with butter.

Repeat with the remaining filling and leaves.

Bake the strudel in a 375 degree oven for about twenty-five minutes or until the crust is well browned.

Slice, using the cuts as your guidelines. Serve hot.

This recipe makes two strudel rolls, or twenty to twenty-four pieces.

A finely chopped onion can be added to this recipe if you like. Sauté the onion in the butter first, before adding the cabbage, then proceed with the rest of the recipe.

Margarine can be substituted for the butter in this recipe.

The unbaked strudel can be readied early in the day, covered very well and refrigerated until baking time.

The strudel can also be frozen unbaked. Do not thaw, allow an extra ten minutes of baking time.

MUSHROOM AND LIVER STRUDEL

½ pound chicken livers
4 Tbsp. butter
salt, pepper
1 small onion, chopped fine
1 pound mushrooms, chopped fine
8 ozs. of cream cheese, diced
8 strudel or filo leaves
½ cup melted butter
½ cup toasted bread crumbs

Remove any membranes from the chicken livers and separate them into lobes. Rinse and dry the livers.

Heat two tablespoons of the butter in a small frying pan.

Sprinkle the livers with salt and pepper and sauté them, turning often, over high heat for just a few minutes. The outside of the livers should be brown and the inside still pink. Set them aside to cool.

Cook the onion in the two remaining tablespoons of butter for a few minutes.

Add the diced mushrooms and some salt and pepper to the onions. Cook, stirring occasionally, until the mushroom mixture is dry. Let it cool for a minute.

Mash the chicken livers coarsely with a fork. Add them to the mushroom mixture along with the cream cheese. Mix well.

Taste the filling to check the seasonings.

Fill, roll and score the strudel following the same directions as given in the cabbage strudel recipe.

Repeat with the rest of the leaves and the filling.

Bake the strudel in a 375 degree oven until brown and crisp, about twenty-five to thirty minutes. Let the strudel rest for five minutes before slicing. Serve warm.

This recipe makes two strudel rolls, or twenty to twenty-four slices.

The unbaked strudel can be prepared a few hours ahead of time and kept well covered in the refrigerator. The filling can be prepared up to a day ahead of time and kept refrigerated.

SPINACH AND CHEESE STRUDEL

3 ten-ounce packages frozen spinach
2 Tbsp. butter
1 onion, finely chopped
salt, pepper
8 ounces Ricotta cheese
½ cup grated Gruyere cheese
2 eggs
dash nutmeg
1 to 2 Tbsp. flour, if needed
8 strudel leaves
½ cup melted butter
½ cup dried bread crumbs

Cook the spinach in boiling salted water until it separates and is thawed. Refresh under cold water and drain well. When cool, squeeze the spinach dry and chop it finely.

Sauté the onion in the two tablespoons of the butter. Season with salt and pepper and add the chopped spinach.

Cook, stirring, for a few minutes, until the spinach is dry. Cool a little.

Mix the spinach with the two cheeses and the eggs. Add the nutmeg and taste to correct the seasonings. If the filling seems too loose, add a little flour.

Fill, roll and score the strudel following the same directions as given in the cabbage strudel recipe.

Repeat with the rest of the leaves and the filling.

Bake the strudel in a 375 degree oven until it is brown and crisp, about twenty-five to thirty minutes.

Let the strudel rest for five minutes before slicing. Serve warm.

This recipe makes two strudel rolls, or twenty to twenty-four slices.

The unbaked strudel can be prepared a few hours ahead of time and kept well covered in the refrigerator. The filling can be made up to a day ahead and refrigerated.

INDIVIDUAL CHEESE CUSTARD

Almost any cooked vegetables can be used in this custard. Try finely diced asparagus spears or string beans. Also good are diced cooked mushrooms or peas. The custard is even good plain, without any vegetables.

If you would like to serve the custard with a sauce, try it with a Sauce Mornay or an Hollandaise.

1 cup milk
¼ cup grated Swiss cheese
¼ cup grated Cheddar cheese
2 eggs
4 drops Tabasco
salt, white pepper
½ cup cooked diced vegetables

You will need six small custard cups that have been well buttered. Preheat the oven to 350 degrees.

Scald the milk and remove it from the heat.

Stir the grated cheeses into the milk.

Beat the eggs together just to mix. Then whisk the eggs into the scalded milk.

Add the Tabasco and season to taste with salt and pepper. Stir in the finely diced vegetables.

Pour the custard into the prepared cups. Place the cups into a pan filled with about one inch of hot water.

Bake the custard in a 350 degree oven for forty-five minutes or until they are puffed and firm.

Remove the custard cups from the water bath and let them sit for about five minutes.

Loosen the sides of the custard with a knife, then turn them out onto individual plates to serve. Serve hot.

This recipe makes six individual custards.

HOT CHEESE SOUFFLE

I do not usually put a collar on hot soufflé dishes. They are a mess to take off and more times than not, are unnecessary. If you use a large enough dish and do not fill it quite up to the top, your soufflé should rise no more than two inches over the rim. It will look pretty and hold well at this height.

You can use almost any type of hard cheese that you like for this soufflé. Swiss Gruyere or a mild Cheddar are excellent. Part Parmesan (but not all) is also good mixed with the Gruyere.

3 Tbsp. butter
1/3 cup flour
¾ cup milk
4 eggs, separated
½ cup grated cheese
white pepper
dash nutmeg
1 extra egg white
½ tsp. salt

Butter and flour a six cup soufflé mold and set it aside.

Melt the three tablespoons of butter in a small saucepan and add the flour. Cook and stir for a minute or two, then remove the pan from the heat.

In a separate saucepan, bring the milk to a boil. Add the hot milk to the cooled roux, stirring constantly.

Bring the mixture back to the boil and simmer for just a minute. Remove the soufflé base from the heat and let the mixture cool down a little.

Add the egg yolks to this soufflé base, mixing them in well. Stir in the grated cheese, pepper and nutmeg.

The soufflé base can be made ahead to this point and refrigerated. Let it then sit out for at least one hour to warm up to room temperature before adding the egg whites - never add the beaten whites to a cold soufflé base.

Beat the egg whites until they are foamy. Add the salt and continue to beat until the whites are very stiff.

Stir, do not fold at this point, about one-quarter of the whites into the soufflé base. Then fold the rest of the whites in carefully.

Pour the soufflé mixture into the prepared dish. Bake in a 375 degree oven for about thirty minutes.

Bake five minutes less if you like a soufflé with a very soft runny center or five minutes longer if you prefer your soufflé firmer.

Serve immediately. This soufflé will serve six.

BAKED POTATO SKINS

Never throw away the potato skins from baked potatoes - they make a terrific appetizer. You can fill them with many things. Just plain butter and salt are good - follow this recipe for baking times.

For each half of a baked potato skin you will need:

1 tsp. butter
¾ Tbsp. grated Cheddar cheese
¾ Tbsp. grated Swiss cheese

To bake potatoes for this dish, wash and dry the potatoes well. Prick the potatoes to keep them from exploding in the oven.

Bake the potatoes without any covering in a 400 degree oven for one hour, or until the potatoes feel done when you squeeze them a little.

After baking, cut the potatoes in half lengthwise. Scoop out the pulp with a spoon. Be careful not to break the skins. Do not throw out the potato pulp. Use it to make Pommes Macaire or the Layered Potato Cake.

Dot each skin with the butter. Mix the two cheeses together and spread them on the inside of the skins.

Place the skins onto a baking sheet. Bake in a 400 degree oven for twenty minutes. The skins should be crisp and the cheese melted.

Cut each potato skin in half, lengthwise, or serve whole. Serve hot, allowing at least one half of a potato skin per person.

STUFFED MUSHROOMS

12 large mushrooms
1 tsp. chopped shallots
1 Tbsp. butter
salt, pepper
2 Tbsp. soft bread crumbs
1 Tbsp. grated Swiss cheese
1 tsp. chopped parsley

Wash the mushrooms and dry them well. Remove the stems from the caps and chop the stems finely.

Sauté the shallots in one-half of the butter for just a minute. Add the chopped mushroom stems, season with salt and pepper and cook until the mushrooms are dry. Remove from the heat.

Add the bread crumbs, grated cheese and parsley to the cooked mushrooms and mix well. Check and correct the seasonings.

Fill the mushroom caps just level with the rims. Dot with the remaining butter.

The mushrooms can be prepared to this point and refrigerated for up to a day.

Bake in a 375 degree oven for twenty-five to thirty minutes. The mushrooms should be tender and the tops browned.

Serve hot. This recipe makes twelve stuffed mushrooms.

Alternate: You can add a tablespoonful of chopped ham to the stuffing mixture along with the cheese.

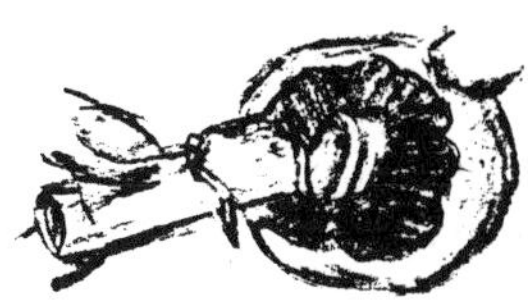

WALNUT MUSHROOMS

This recipe is fast and easy. Walnut Mushrooms make a nice snack for a cocktail party.

3 Tbsp. chopped walnuts
1 tsp. finely chopped shallots
2 Tbsp. butter, softened
3 Tbsp. dried bread crumbs
1 Tbsp. chopped parsley
¼ tsp. Madras curry powder
salt, pepper
12 large mushroom caps

Mix all the ingredients together, except the mushrooms, to form a thick paste.

Wash the mushrooms, dry them well and remove the stems. Save the stems for another dish.

Place some of the filling in each mushroom cap and smooth it level with the rim of the cap.

This is enough filling to stuff twelve mushrooms, each having a two-inch diameter.

The mushrooms can be prepared to this point and refrigerated for up to a day.

Bake in a 375 degree oven for twenty-five to thirty minutes. The mushroom caps should be tender and the tops browned.

Serve immediately. This recipe makes twelve stuffed mushrooms.

Margarine can be substituted for the butter in this recipe.

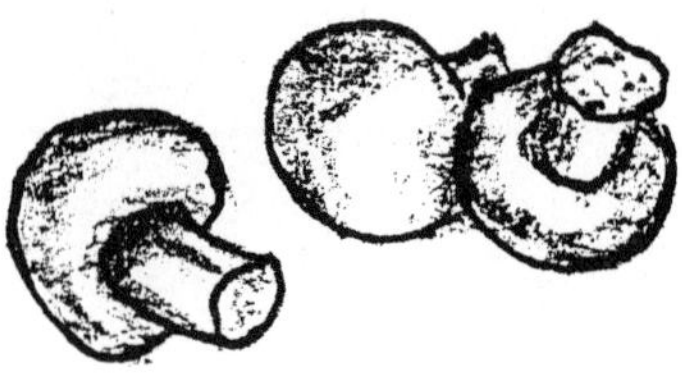

Pates and Terrines

Pâtés and terrines are wonderful do-ahead appetizers. Meat pâtés, especially, should sit and mellow for at least three days before serving and they will keep very well for a week.

Pâtés may be frozen if necessary, but their texture will change and they will not be nearly as good as they are when fresh.

BASIC FORCEMEAT

A food processor is a necessity for making pâtés and terrines, for it makes simple work of a forcemeat. Forcemeat is the base for several meat pâté recipes. It consists of equal parts of veal, pork and fatback along with heavy cream and seasonings. This forcemeat acts as the base which binds your pâté together.

You will notice that in the forcemeat recipe, ice cubes are added to the meat. The reason for this is to keep the meat very cold so that the mixture will not separate when you add the heavy cream. Be careful not to overwork your forcemeat in the processor, it is always better to err on the side of "under" rather than "over" working this mixture.

¼ pound pork
¼ pound veal
¼ pound fatback
½ cup ice cubes
½ cup heavy cream
1 to 2 Tbsp. brandy
salt, pepper
spices - see individual recipes

All the meats and the fatback should be ground or well chopped before thay are placed in the food processor.

Place the meats and fatback into the food processor and process for just a few seconds.

Place the ice cubes on top of the meat and remove the plunger from the machine.

Turn the motor on, then pour in the cream and the brandy.

Stop the machine and add the salt, pepper and seasonings. Process just until blended.

The ingredients should be mixed well, but be careful not to over-process at this point.

Remove the mixture from the machine. If there are any large pieces of ice left, discard them.

Chill the mixture in the refrigerator until needed.

ROUGH COUNTRY PATE

1 recipe forcemeat, page 35
Seasonings for the forcemeat:
- 1 tsp. thyme
- 1 tsp. ground allspice
- ¼ tsp. nutmeg
- salt, pepper

½ pound mushrooms
2 Tbsp. butter
salt, pepper
1 pound ground veal or pork
1 pound cooked ham, diced
2 to 3 Tbsp. brandy
¼ cup pistachios, shelled
1 package bacon - to line the mold

Make the basic forcemeat and flavor it with the thyme, ground allspice, nutmeg, lots of salt and freshly ground black peppercorns. Chill the forcemeat a little.

Chop the mushrooms into small dice.

Heat the two tablespoons of butter in a small frying pan and sauté the mushrooms along with some salt and pepper until the mushrooms are dry.

Mix the prepared forcemeat with the ground veal or pork, the diced ham and the brandy.

Add the cooked mushrooms and the pistachios. Mix well and correct the seasonings.*

Butter an eight cup terrine mold. Line the mold, crosswise, with bacon slices. The butter will keep the bacon in place so that it does not slip down when you fill the mold.

Fill the mold with the meat mixture. Bang the mold sharply on a flat surface to settle the contents. Level the top of the pâté.

Cover the top of the pâté with overlapping bacon strips. Cover with aluminum foil and place the mold in a bain-marie.

Bake the pâté in a 350 degree oven until the meat is done inside, about one and one-half to two hours.

There are two ways to tell if your pâté is done:

Poke a hole straight down through the center of the pâté, using a large meat fork or a meat thermometer and leave it there for about twenty seconds. Then remove and carefully touch the fork against the top of your lip, or the area between your lip and nose. If the fork feels cold in the center and hot at both ends, your pâté needs to cook longer. It should feel equally hot all over when the pâté is fully cooked.

Also check the juices that run out of the hole that you have poked. If they are pink, the pâté is not cooked. If they run clear or yellow, it is done.

Drain off the excess liquid from the pâté while it is still hot.

Let the pâté cool down a little then turn it out of the mold. Allow the pâté to cool to room temperature then wrap it well.

Refrigerate for at least three days before serving.

This pâté will serve twelve to sixteen.

Meat pâté is nice when served with a crock of mustard or some little sour cornichon pickles. Onions à l'Orientale, page 182, makes an excellent accompaniment to any of the meat pâtés as well.

Rough Country Pâté is also good with Cumberland Sauce, page 66.

Alternates: There are many variations of country pâté that can be made from this recipe simply by substituting a few of the ingredients.

For a chicken and veal pâté, use one pound of ground veal rather than the pork in the mixture. Add a half-teaspoon each of oregano and savory to the seasonings for the forcemeat and eliminate the nutmeg. Instead of ham, cook one pound of diced raw chicken in a half-cup of red wine until the liquid is absorbed. Fold the cooked chicken into the basic mixture, then follow the rest of the recipe.

Or make a hare or rabbit pâté. Grind part of the meat and mix it in instead of pork or veal. Dice and cook the rest with red wine as you would the chicken. Add a teaspoon of rosemary to the basic forcemeat.

Or try venison. Leave the fillet of venison whole and place it in the center of the pâté. It will look pretty and taste good, too. Flavor with rosemary. Some chopped truffles never hurt any pâté, either.

*To check your seasonings, take a small spoonful of the pâté mixture and sauté it in a little butter or oil and then taste. Remember, it takes more spice to flavor a cold pâté than one which is hot.

GALANTINE OF DUCK

1 recipe basic forcemeat, page 35
Seasonings for the forcemeat:
1 tsp. ground allspice
1 tsp. thyme
salt, pepper
2 ducks
¼ pound diced tongue or veal tenderloin
½ cup red wine
¼ cup pistachios, shelled
1 tsp. chopped truffles
2 Tbsp. Port wine or brandy
salt, pepper
1 to 2 Tbsp. oil
½ cup water

Prepare the basic forcemeat, seasoning the mixture with allspice, thyme, salt and pepper.

Bone one duck from the back

To bone the duck, first remove the wishbone.

For this recipe, you need to leave the wings intact, turning the last wing joint back onto itself.

Slit the duck down the back and bone by using your knife to scrape against the bone, not the meat, as you work.

Cut through the wing and thigh sockets from the inside to release them from the main rib cage structure.

Remove the rib cage. Be careful not to cut through the skin of the duck at the front of the breastbone area where this skin is very thin.

Scrape the meat from the thigh bones and remove the bones, leaving the drumsticks in place.

Remove any extra internal fat from the duck.

Remove all the meat from the second duck.

Grind an equal amount of this duck meat as you have of forcemeat - about two cups. Use a meat grinder, not a food processor.

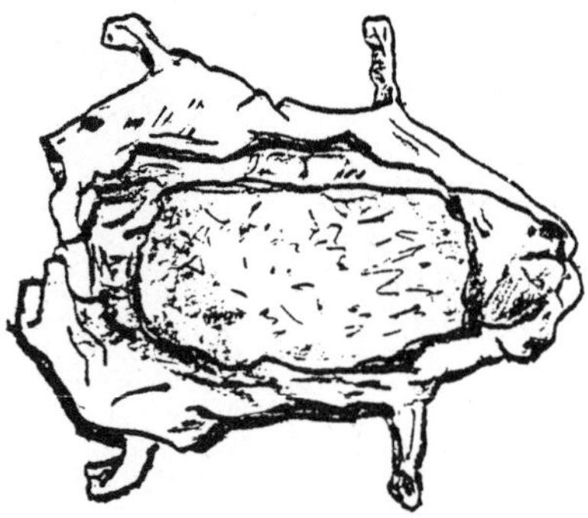

 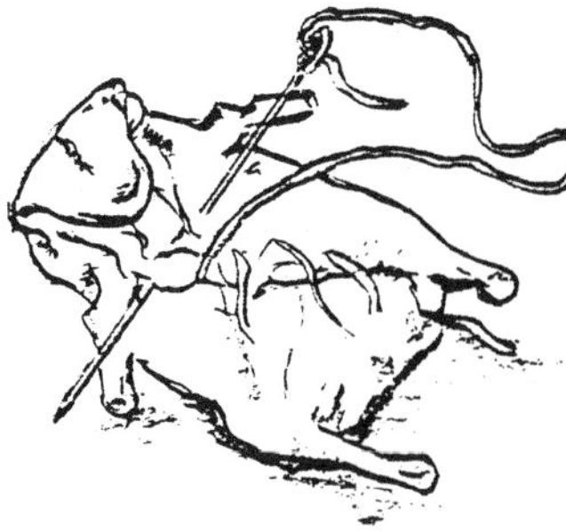

Dice the veal or the tongue meat. Place the meat in a small saucepan with the red wine and cook over high heat until all the wine is evaporated. Cool a little.

Mix the prepared forcemeat with the ground duck meat and the veal or tongue. Add the pistachios, truffles and Port wine or brandy and mix well. Correct the seasonings.*

Stuff the filling into the boned duck. Sew the skin up the back. Sprinkle the duck with salt and pepper.

Oil the bottom of the roasting pan. Place the duck, breast side up, in the pan. Add the one-half cup of water.

Roast the duck in a 375 degree oven for one and one-half to two hours, basting often. Test to see if the duck is done. It should be hot all the way through and the juices should run clear. See the Rough Country Pâté recipe, page 37 for technique.

Remove the duck from the oven and let it cool. Remove the strings, wrap well and refrigerate.

The galantine will keep well for three or four days in the refrigerator.

To serve, first cut off the wings and the drumsticks, then slice as you would any pâté

This galantine serves twelve or more.

This duck galantine is nice with a cold fruit such as poached or spiced peach halves.

*Sauté a little of the filling in a spoon of butter or oil and taste to check the seasonings. This dish is served cold, so make sure that it is spicy enough.

TERRINE OF DUCK WITH GREEN PEPPERCORNS

This terrine has an unusual and delightfully spicy flavor from the green peppercorns. It must mellow for at least three days before serving and will keep very well, refrigerated, for a week.

You can leave the fat in the terrine around the duck as the recipe states. This is the way it is served in Europe.

Or you can pour the fat out of the terrine while the duck is still warm and the fat still liquid. If so, you may paint the duck with a light coating of aspic. See the quick aspic recipe, page 58.

1 duck
salt, pepper
3 Tbsp. brandy
½ pound veal
½ pound pork
½ pound fatback
1 duck liver
1 or 2 cloves garlic, crushed
¼ tsp. allspice
¼ tsp. nutmeg
1 or 2 eggs
3 Tbsp. green peppercorns
¼ cup pistachios, shelled, optional

Bone the duck as described in the Galantine of Duck recipe, page 38.

Remove any visible fat and sprinkle the inside of the duck with salt, pepper and one tablespoon of the brandy.

In a food processor, grind the veal, pork, fatback and the duck liver.

Add the garlic, allspice, nutmeg, salt, pepper, the remaining brandy and one egg. Process again, being careful not to overwork.

If the mixture seems very dry, add the second egg.

Remove the meat mixture from the processor and mix in the green peppercorns. If you are using pistachios, add them in now also.

Fill the duck skin with this mixture and sew it up the back using a trussing needle and string.

Place the duck, string side up, into a well greased terrine mold just large enough to hold the duck tightly.

Using a layer of buttered foil or parchment paper, seal the terrine well. Then place a lid over the sealed terrine.

Place in a 375 degree oven and cook for one and one-half hours or until the duck tests done.

Remove the lid and cool the duck in the terrine until it is lukewarm. Place a weight on top of the duck while it is still in the terrine and refrigerate until it is very cold. Remove the weight.

Cover and keep the duck refrigerated in the mold for at least three days in order to allow enough time for the flavors to mellow.

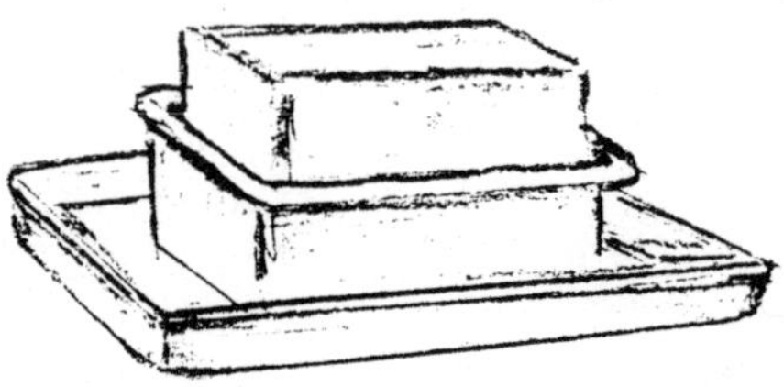

To serve the duck directly from the terrine, remove the strings - they are on top - and slice.

To unmold and serve, warm the bottom of the terrine a little, the fat will melt enough to loosen the duck.

Lift the duck out of the terrine and remove the strings. Scrape off the extra fat, slice and serve.

This duck terrine serves ten.

SWEETBREAD TERRINE

This is another terrine that must be made ahead of time. It will keep well for up to a week in the refrigerator.

The recipe sounds complicated but it can be broken down into several steps and completed over a period of days.

Prepare the sweetbreads and cook the spinach one day. The next day (or even two days later) finish the terrine. It is delicious and well worth the effort involved.

1 or 2 pairs sweetbreads
1 small onion, diced
1 carrot, diced
1 stalk celery, diced
2 Tbsp. butter or oil
salt, pepper
½ cup Madeira
1½ cups chicken stock
4 bay leaves
½ tsp. thyme
2 ounces bread crumbs
1 ten-ounce package frozen spinach, or 1 pound fresh
12 ounces pork
6 ounces fatback
2 eggs
pinch nutmeg
3 or 4 Tbsp. Cognac
¼ cup pistachios, shelled
thinly sliced fatback for lining mold

Wash the sweetbreads by rinsing them several times in cold water.

Place them in a large pot of cold salted water. Bring the water to a boil and then simmer for five minutes.

Drain the sweetbreads and refresh them under cold water.

When they are cool enough to handle, remove any large connective tissue and gristle.

In a frying pan, sauté the onion, carrot and celery in the butter or oil.

Add the sweetbreads and season them with salt and pepper. Braise, turning, until the sweetbreads are lightly browned on both sides.

Deglaze the pan with the Madeira, scraping well.

Add the chicken stock, one bay leaf and half of the thyme. Simmer for twenty minutes.

The recipe may be completed to this point and the sweetbreads stored in the refrigerator in their cooking liquid for up to three days.

When ready to proceed, remove the sweetbreads and strain the cooking liquid into a small saucepan. Reduce the liquid until a half-cup remains in the pan.

Add the bread crumbs to the reduced liquid and stir well. Set this mixture aside.

Blanch the spinach in boiling salted water. Refresh under cold water, drain, squeeze dry and chop.

Grind the pork and the fatback using a meat grinder or chop them into small dice before adding them to the food processor.

Place the pork, fatback, the bread crumb mixture, the eggs, salt, pepper, the remaining thyme, nutmeg and Cognac into a food processor. Process only for a few seconds.

Remove this mixture from the machine and mix in the spinach and the pistachios.

Line a two quart terrine with the fatback. Place one-half of the meat mixture into the terrine. Bang the terrine mold down well on a flat surface to settle the contents.

Place a layer of sweetbreads in the center of the terrine, lengthwise.

Cover the sweetbreads with the other half of the forcemeat and bang down again to settle the contents of the mold.

Place three bay leaves on the top of the meat for decoration. Cover the terrine with aluminum foil and place the mold into a bain-marie.

Bake the terrine in a 375 degree oven for about one and one-half hours or until done. The meat juices should run clear and the terrine should be equally hot all the way through.

Let the terrine rest for ten minutes then drain off the extra fat.

Once the terrine is cool, turn it out. You can remove the fatback, or leave it in place if you prefer.

Wrap well and refrigerate the sweetbread terrine for at least three days to allow time for the flavors to mellow before serving. The cooked sweetbread terrine will keep for one week, if refrigerated.

This terrine serves twelve.

MOLDED LIVER PATE

- 2 pounds chicken or calves liver
- 1 cup Madeira or Port
- 1 onion, chopped
- 1 cup butter
- salt, pepper
- pinch of allspice
- ½ tsp. thyme
- 2/3 cup heavy cream

Dice the livers and marinate them in the Port or the Madeira for a few hours. Turn the livers a few times while marinating.

Drain and reserve the liquid.

Sauté the onions in one-quarter cup of the butter until they are soft.

Add the livers to the pan. Season them with salt, pepper, the allspice and the thyme.

Sauté the livers, turning, for a few minutes until they are browned on the outside but still pink on the inside.

Remove the livers with a slotted spoon and place them into a food processor. (If using a blender, do it in two batches.)

Deglaze the pan with the reserved Port or Madeira, scraping well. Pour the liquid over the livers in the processor and purée.

Add the cream and the rest of the butter and purée again. Correct the seasonings.

Line a small mold with a damp piece of cheesecloth. Or just butter the mold very well.

Place the pâté into the mold, smoothing it down well. Cover and chill. If you prefer, you can pour the liver mixture into a large crock and serve it directly from there rather than using a mold.

This pâté will keep for a few days if refrigerated.

When ready to serve, turn the pâté out of the mold. Serve with hot toast and cornichons.

This recipe will serve twelve or more.

If you want to be really fancy, you can glaze the unmolded pâté with a layer of aspic, recipe page 58. Decorate the top with truffle slices and pimento cutouts, then paint again with aspic and chill well until serving time.

LAYERED FISH TERRINE

This layered terrine will make fish lovers out of people who claim they hate fish. The presentation is beautiful - the pink of the salmon in the binding against the different colors of the fish layers. It is a perfect appetizer that can be done ahead of time.

4 fish fillets, each a different kind
3 Tbsp. melted butter
2 eggs, separated
6 Tbsp. flour
salt, white pepper
½ cup water
¼ pound flounder or fluke
¼ pound smoked salmon
¾ cup cold butter, plus butter for the pan
dash cayenne pepper
¼ to ½ cup pistachios, shelled

Use four different kinds of fish fillets such as red snapper, salmon, striped bass, sea bass, trout or fluke for this terrine. Do not use anything too oily such as mackerel or bluefish. The fillets should each be the same size as the pan used to cook the terrine. Remove the skin from the fillets and any bones present.

Mix the three tablespoons of melted butter, egg yolks, flour, salt and pepper in a small saucepan. Add the water and mix well.

Cook until thick, stirring constantly. Spread the mixture out on a buttered dish to cool.

An alternate method for making this paste would be to mix all the ingredients in a food processor. Blend and then cook until thick. The mixture will be smoother this way.

This paste can be prepared a day ahead, covered and refrigerated.

Grind the quarter pound of fluke in a food processor. Add the smoked salmon and process again.

Add in the cooled paste, the egg whites, the cold butter, salt, pepper and the cayenne pepper. Blend well and check the seasonings. Remove the mixture from the processor and chill a little.

Butter a deep loaf pan well. Place a layer of buttered parchment or waxed paper on the bottom. Butter the paper. Smooth a layer of the ground fish mixture along the bottom and sides of the pan.

Place one fish fillet across the pan, lengthwise. Sprinkle with salt and pepper.

Spread a thin layer of the ground fish mixture on top of the fillet. Dot with pistachios.

Repeat this process, using all four different layers of fish. Spread any remaining ground fish mixture across the top of the last fillet. Do not use any nuts on the top.

Cover the top of the terrine with a piece of buttered parchment or waxed paper. Then seal well with a piece of aluminum foil.

Place the fish mold into a warm water bath (bain-marie) and bake it in a 375 degree oven for about one hour.

Test after fifty minutes to see if the fish is done. The top will be firm and springy and the fish equally hot all the way through.

Remove the fish from the oven. Take it out of the water bath and let it rest for ten minutes. Pour off the extra liquid that has formed around the fish.

Put a weight on top of the terrine and refrigerate overnight.

The next day, unmold the terrine, wrap it in clear plastic wrap and refrigerate until ready to serve.

This terrine will keep well for up to four days.

This recipe will serve twelve.

Serve the Layered Fish Terrine with an Herb Mayonnaise, page 65, or a Cucumber Salad with Cream, page 177, or both.

TERRINE de POISSONS

This is my favorite of all the pâtés and terrines in this book.

1 medium onion, finely chopped
2 Tbsp. butter, plus butter for mold
½ pound mushrooms, finely chopped
salt, pepper
3 Tbsp. chopped parsley
juice of one lemon
3 ounces of bread
1 ten-ounce package frozen spinach, or 1 pound fresh
1 pound flounder or whiting, finely chopped
2 eggs
pinch cayenne pepper
pinch nutmeg
1 pound salmon
¼ cup pistachios, shelled
10 small sole or flounder fillets, or less as needed

Sauté the onion in the two tablespoons of butter until it is soft.

Add the chopped mushrooms, salt and pepper and cook until all the water is evaporated and the mixture is dry.

Add the chopped parsley and cook one more minute. Add the lemon juice and remove the pan from the heat.

Soak the bread in a little water to soften. Squeeze very dry.

Blanch the spinach in boiling salted water for a few minutes. Refresh under cold water, drain. Squeeze dry and then chop.

Chop the one pound of flounder. Use a food processor, a meat grinder, or chop finely by hand with a knife.

Mix together the mushrooms, the bread paste, the spinach, the chopped flounder, the eggs, salt, pepper, cayenne pepper and nutmeg. Check and correct the seasonings.

Remove the skin and any dark spots from the salmon and cut it into one-half inch cubes. Add the salmon and the pistachios to the fish mixture and mix them in carefully, by hand.

Rinse and dry the sole or flounder fillets well. You will need enough fillets to line a eight cup terrine mold. If you substitute fluke for flounder, you will probably need much less than ten fillets. Salt and pepper the fillets.

Butter the inside of the terrine mold well. Lay the fillets in the terrine, skin side up, overlapping the edges. (see page 87.)

Fill the terrine with the prepared fish forcemeat. Bang the terrine down once on a flat surface to settle the contents. Turn the fish fillets over to cover the top of the forcemeat. Patch any open spots with extra pieces of fish.

Cover the terrine with a piece of buttered parchment paper or aluminum foil. Then cover the paper with a lid and place the terrine in a warm bain-marie.

Bake the terrine in a 375 degree oven for forty-five minutes. The surface of the fish should be firm and springy to the touch, and the fish hot all the way through.

Remove the terrine from the bain-marie and let rest until it is lukewarm. Drain off the extra liquid that has formed around the fish.

Unmold the terrine onto a serving platter. Cover it well with clear plastic wrap and refrigerate overnight.

This recipe will serve ten to twelve.

Terrine de Poissons will keep well for up to four days in the refrigerator.

Serve with Mayonnaise, page 64, or a Tomato Coulis, page 65, and a Cucumber Salad with Cream, page 177.

If fresh sorrel is available, substitute it for half the spinach in the recipe. It gives the terrine a lovely flavor.

SALMON PATE WITH FOIE GRAS

This is a really extravagant pâte for special occasions only. It is reminiscent of one that was served in New York at The Palace, known as the most expensive restaurant in this country. This pâté is delicious even without the foie gras and can be made and served this way as well.

¼ pound butter, plus butter for mold
salt
1 cup water
1 cup flour
4 eggs
4 cups raw fresh salmon
¼ pound smoked salmon
white pepper
1 cup cooked shrimp, diced
1 cup cooked lobster, diced (optional)
1 cup scallops, poached
½ cup pistachios, shelled
2 cups heavy cream
1 can pâté de foie gras

Place the butter, salt and water into a saucepan. Bring the mixture to a boil and stir in the flour all at once. Continue to cook and stir until the mixture is very dry.

Remove the pan from the heat and let cool for a minute.

Beat in the eggs, one at a time, until a smooth firm mixture is formed. Let it cool. You can use a mixer fitted with a flat beater to incorporate the eggs, or it can be done by hand.

Place the fresh salmon and the smoked salmon into a food processor and grind until blended. Add the cooled flour and egg mixture, salt and pepper and process again.

Remove this mixture and place it in a bowl. Mix in the shrimp, lobster, scallops and the pistachios. If you are using bay scallops, leave them whole. If you are using the larger sea scallops, cut them into dice.

Lightly whip the cream. Fold the cream into the salmon mixture.

Butter a two quart terrine mold well. Place half the fish mixture into the mold. With your hand, make a small trench down the center of the mold.

Form the foie gras into a long narrow cylinder. Place it into the formed trench. Cover the foie gras with the rest of the fish mixture.

Bang the mold on a flat surface to settle the contents. Cover the mold with a lid or a piece of buttered aluminum foil.

Place the mold in a warm bain-marie. Bake in a 375 degree oven for one hour or until the fish tests done. It will be firm and springy to the touch.

Remove the mold from the water bath. Let the pâté sit until it reaches room temperature. Then turn out to unmold. Wrap well and chill.

Serve this pâté sliced thin, with a Tomato Coulis, page 65.

This recipe makes twelve to sixteen servings.

This salmon pâté does not have to mellow and can be used the same day that it is made. It will, however, keep very well wrapped and refrigerated for up to four days.

Stocks and Sauces

CHICKEN STOCK

You can make chicken stock without a stewing chicken if you have enough bones and giblets.

It is much more economical to buy whole chickens than to buy chicken parts, especially those already boned. Learn to cut and bone a chicken yourself. It is not at all hard to do and well worth the effort. Freeze and save the bones along with any giblets that you do not use at the time and eventually you will have enough to make a pot of soup. Your only cost will be the price of the vegetables - a real bonus for the thrifty cook.

1 stewing chicken, cut into quarters
extra bones and giblets (no livers)
1 large onion, coarsely chopped
2 large carrots, chopped
2 stalks celery, chopped
2 parsley roots, chopped
salt
white pepper
1 bay leaf
handful green parsley tops
½ tsp. thyme
2 quarts water, and more as needed

Rinse the chicken well. Place the chicken and all the rest of the ingredients into a large stockpot. Fill with cold water to cover the chicken and the vegetables.

Bring the water to a boil and skim off any scum that rises to the surface of the pot.

Lower the heat and simmer the stock for two to three hours. Add water as needed to keep the meat and the vegetables covered.

I always remove the chicken breast meat to use for another dish. After the first hour of cooking time, check the meat. When the breasts are tender, remove them and let them cool a little. Then remove the meat from the bones.

Add the bones back to the pot and continue to cook until the stock is done. You can remove the dark meat as well as the white and use this also. See the Index for suggested recipes.

Strain the stock once it has finished cooking. Allow it to reach room temperature then chill the stock. Once the stock is cold, remove the fat layer that has formed on the surface.

Chicken stock will keep, refrigerated, for a week or two. Boil it every few days to kill the bacteria and keep the stock from spoiling. Or you can freeze it - chicken stock freezes beautifully.

This recipe makes about two quarts of stock.

BEEF STOCK

Beef stock can be made simply by putting all the ingredients into a stockpot and boiling until done - you can make a perfectly nice stock that way. However, I prefer the method described in this recipe. It is a little more complicated to brown the bones and vegetables first, but your stock will have more flavor and a much better color.

2 Tbsp. oil
4 pounds beef bones
2 pounds beef short ribs or soup meat
1 large onion, chopped
2 carrots, chopped
2 stalks celery, chopped
greens of 1 or 2 leeks, chopped
3 quarts water, or more as needed
1 or 2 tomatoes, chopped
2 cloves garlic, unpeeled
6 to 8 parsley sprigs
1 bay leaf
1 tsp. thyme
½ tsp. rosemary
salt, pepper

Try to get a marrow bone or two to make a rich beef stock. Ask your butcher to saw the bones for you into two inch pieces. Veal bones, if available, can be substituted for part of the beef bones.

Add the oil to the bottom of a large roasting pan. Put the bones and the short ribs* in the pan and place the pan into a 450 degree oven.

Roast the bones and the short ribs for thirty minutes. Turn them and add the chopped onion, carrots, celery and leeks to the pan. Continue to roast for another thirty minutes. The bones should be very brown.

Remove the pan from the oven. Place the bones, soup meat, and the browned vegetables into a large stockpot using a slotted spoon.

Pour off the extra fat from the roasting pan. Put the pan back on the stove and add one cup of the water. Bring the water to a boil and scrape well to loosen the brown particles clinging to the bottom of the pan. Carefully pour this liquid into the stockpot.

Repeat if there are still many particles stuck to the bottom of the roasting pan. This both flavors the stock and makes pot washing easier.

Add the tomatoes, garlic, parsley sprigs, bay leaf, thyme, rosemary and salt and pepper to the stockpot and fill with the rest of the water.

Be careful not to add too much salt to your stock when you begin. As the stock cooks down the salt flavor becomes concentrated. Add just a teaspoon to start, you can always add more later.

Some scum will continue to rise to the surface of the stock during the first hour or two of cooking. Remove this scum as it forms. Simmer the stock for six to eight hours. Add additional water to keep the meat and vegetables covered, as needed.

Cool the stock a little, then strain, discarding the bones and vegetables. After cooking this long they will have no flavor at all.

Let the stock cool down to room temperature, then refrigerate. Remove the fat layer that forms on the surface of the stock after it has chilled.

Beef stock can be kept in the refrigerator for a week or two. Boil every few days to keep the stock fresh. Beef stock also freezes beautifully.

This recipe makes two to three quarts of stock.

*Cooked this way, the short ribs or the soup meat will not be edible, as all the flavor is boiled out into the soup. If you want to use the meat for a meal, do not add it now. Wait to add the meat until you transfer your ingredients to the stockpot, then remove the meat once it is tender.

BROWN SAUCE OR ESPAGNOLE

Brown sauce or Espagnole is used as both a base and an enrichment for many sauce recipes. With some brown sauce handy, you can prepare many "sauté" dishes with a minimum of effort. Just sauté your meat, deglaze the pan with a little wine, add some brown sauce, flavor and serve. Fast, easy and good, too.

The initial browning of the bones and the vegetables can be done in a frying pan on top of the stove or in a roasting pan in a 450 degree oven.

1 to 2 Tbsp. oil
5 to 6 pounds beef or veal bones
1 large onion, chopped
2 carrots, chopped
2 stalks celery, chopped
1 leek, chopped
4 Tbsp. flour
1 or 2 cloves garlic, whole
1 or 2 tomatoes, chopped
1 cup white wine
6 cups stock, or more as needed*
handful parsley sprigs
1 tsp. thyme
1 large or 2 small bay leaves

Heat the oil in a very large frying pan. Add the bones and cook, turning, until they are very brown.

Add the chopped onions, carrots, celery and leeks. Cook, stirring once in a while, until the vegetables take on a brown color.

Sprinkle the flour over the bones and vegetables and stir it in well. Continue to cook, stirring, until the flour is lightly browned. This will take about four to five minutes.

Add the garlic and tomatoes to the pan. Pour in the white wine, scraping the bottom of the pan well.

If your frying pan is deep enough, you can continue right in there. If not, transfer all of the ingredients from the frying pan to a stockpot.

Make sure you scrape up and transfer all the brown residue from the bottom of the pan as well. Use a little of the stock to deglaze the pan again, if necessary.

Add the parsley, thyme and bay leaf. Do not add salt.

Pour the stock into the pan, making sure all the ingredients are covered.

Bring the stock to a boil then simmer for at least three or four hours. Remove the fat and scum as it rises to the top of the pot while the stock cooks.

Replenish the pot with more stock, if needed. You can even use water if you run out of extra stock.

Strain the brown sauce. Let it chill and remove the fat layer that forms on the surface.

This brown sauce can be kept in the refrigerator for several days. Reboil every two days to kill the bacteria and keep it fresh. The sauce also freezes beautifully.

This recipe makes about one quart of sauce.

*Either veal, beef or chicken stock can be used for this sauce. Even a combination of stocks would work.

ENRICHED STOCK

Homemade stock is wonderful but none of us always has the time or the inclination to make a pot of stock every time we want to make a sauce.

This is a short cut recipe that you can use to enrich a canned stock. It will end up as a type of brown sauce that can be substituted, when necessary, in recipes calling for a brown sauce or Espagnole.

If you have any extra chicken bones or giblets around, add them to the pan first, brown a little, then add the vegetables. They will help to enrich the flavor even further.

1 Tbsp. butter
1 small onion, chopped
1 carrot, diced
1 stalk celery, diced
1 clove garlic, whole
½ cup white wine
one 10½ ounce can chicken stock
one 10½ ounce can beef stock
1 tsp. tomato paste
few parsley sprigs
1 bay leaf
½ tsp. thyme
pepper
3 cups water, or more if needed

Heat the butter in a saucepan. Add the diced onion, carrot and celery. Cook for a few minutes until the vegetables become soft.

Add the rest of the ingredients and bring the liquid to a boil. Simmer for about one hour. Skim off any fat or scum as it rises to the surface.

Strain the sauce and use it as you would a brown sauce.

The canned stocks tend to be very salty, so do not add any additional salt to this recipe.

If the sauce is too strong in taste for you, add a little water.

This recipe makes about three cups of sauce.

Storage instructions are the same as for a brown sauce.

All beef stock or all chicken stock may be used for this recipe, as well as the combination of both.

Margarine or oil can be substituted for the butter in this recipe.

SAUCE DIABLE

Enriched brown sauce can be used in place of the homemade brown sauce called for in the following recipes. The homemade will, however, taste better.

2 Tbsp. chopped shallots	1 cup Brown Sauce, page 52
½ cup white wine	few drops Tabasco
½ tsp. paprika	2 Tbsp. butter

Place the shallots and the white wine in a saucepan. Cook until the wine is reduced by half.

Stir in the paprika and cook for one minute longer. Add the brown sauce and simmer for a few minutes.

Add Tabasco to taste and remove the sauce from the heat. Swirl in the butter and serve hot.

This recipe makes about one cup of sauce.

Serve Sauce Diable with grilled or roasted chicken or pork.

MOREL SAUCE

Morels are an extremely expensive type of mushroom. It is just about impossible to buy them fresh in this country. They are imported in a dried form.

You only need a small amount of dried morels to give a wonderful flavor to sauces. They will keep indefinitely as long as they are stored in an air-tight container.

3 or 4 dried morels	1/3 cup Madeira
½ cup water	1 ounce Cognac
1 cup Brown Sauce, page 52	salt, pepper

Soak the morels in a half cup of warm water for one hour.

Remove the morels and wash off any grit that might remain. Reserve the soaking liquid. Slice the morels.

In a saucepan, heat the brown sauce with the Madeira. Add the morels and their soaking liquid. Be careful not to add any of the grit that may be present in the liquid.

Cook and reduce the liquid by one-half.

Add the Cognac and continue to heat the sauce until the raw taste disappears. Add salt and pepper to taste and serve.

This recipe makes about one cup of sauce.

The sauce can be further enriched by the addition of a tablespoon of butter after it has been removed from the heat.

Serve the Morel Sauce with cornish hens or Poulet en Croûte. Wonderful with sautéed chicken breasts or even roast beef or plain roast duck.

SAUCE ROBERT

3 Tbsp. chopped shallots
½ cup white wine
1 cup Brown Sauce, page 52
1 or 2 Tbsp. Dijon mustard
salt, pepper

Place the shallots and the white wine into a saucepan. Cook until the wine is reduced by half.

Add the brown sauce and simmer for a few minutes.

Whisk in the mustard to taste. Correct the seasonings with salt and pepper.

Serve the Sauce Robert hot with roasted or sautéed pork.

This recipe makes about one cup of sauce.

The sauce can be further enriched by adding a spoonful of butter at the end. Or add a tablespoon of chopped parsley to freshen up the taste.

TRUFFLE SAUCE

Serve this Truffle Sauce with grilled or broiled steak or any plainly cooked beef. It will add a touch of elegance to any dish.

¼ pound mushrooms, sliced thin
¼ cup red wine
¼ cup Madeira
1 cup Brown Sauce, page 52
1 truffle, chopped, plus liquid
salt, pepper
1 Tbsp. butter

Place the mushrooms in a saucepan with the red wine and the Madeira. Cook until the liquid is reduced by half.

Add the brown sauce and the chopped truffle along with any of its juices.

Simmer for a few minutes to reduce the sauce a little. Add salt and pepper to taste.

Remove the pan from the heat and swirl the butter into the sauce.

This recipe makes about one and one-half cups sauce.

Alternate: Add one-half cup heavy cream when adding the truffles. Reduce a little and serve with veal.

VEAL STOCK

Veal prices being as high as they are, veal stock is an extravagance. It is, however, the most delicate and the best stock to use for flavoring sauces. Veal stock is extremely versatile and can be added to almost every dish because of its lightness.

4 pounds veal bones, knuckle preferred
3 quarts water plus water for bones
2 pounds inexpensive cuts of veal or veal trimmings
1 large onion, chopped
2 large carrots, chopped
2 stalks celery, chopped
greens of 1 or 2 leeks, chopped
1 clove garlic, unpeeled
1 bay leaf
6 sprigs parsley
1 tsp. thyme
salt, pepper

Place the veal bones in a stockpot. Cover the bones with water. Bring the water to a boil and simmer for about five minutes.

Pour the contents of the pot into a colander and rinse the bones well to remove the scum.*

Wash the pot out well. Return the bones to the stockpot and add the meat and the rest of the ingredients. Do not add too much salt. Bring the water to a boil.

Remove any more scum as it rises to the surface while the stock is cooking. Add water as needed to keep the meat and vegetables covered.

Cook the stock at a slow boil for about six hours.

Strain the stock. When it reaches room temperature, refrigerate. When cold, remove the fat layer that has formed on the surface.

Veal stock will keep in the refrigerator for a week or two. Remove and boil every few days to keep it fresh. Veal stock also freezes beautifully.

This recipe makes about two quarts of stock.

*Veal bones produce a lot of scum, which can ruin the stock. The method described in this recipe is the easiest way to get rid of this scum.

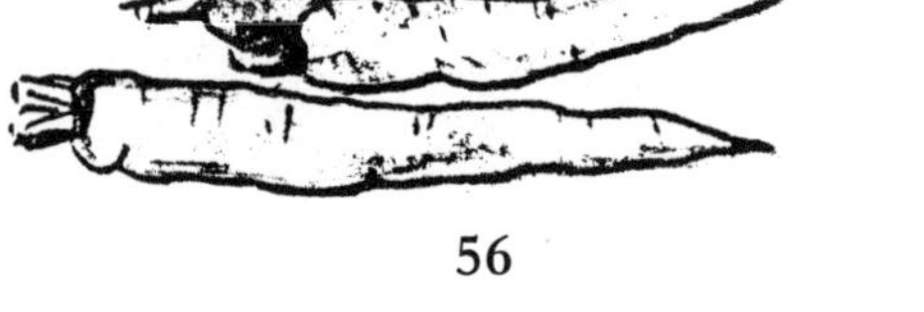

VEAL DEMI-GLACE

I like to make a large supply of veal demi-glace once or twice a year. Since demi-glace is such a time consuming job, I usually take two or even three days to make this sauce, as I do not like to let it cook unattended during the night.

Brown all the bones and vegetables one day and get the stockpot ready. Then simmer the sauce for as much time as you have.

Turn off the heat and cover the stock. Then finish cooking it the next morning. Strain, cool down and refrigerate. Once the sauce has chilled, either the same or the next day, remove any fat that has formed on the surface.

I then place the jellied demi-glace into a saucepan, heat it until it melts, and freeze the concentrated demi-glace in ice-cube trays. Once frozen, I remove and wrap the cubes individually in aluminum foil and return them to the freezer. This way I have a small measured amount of demi-glace handy at all times to add to sauces or to use for flavoring dishes.

The amount of demi-glace you make will depend on how large a stockpot you have available. The larger the pot, the more you can make at one time. It is a messy and time consuming job, but the resultant flavor that demi-glace imparts to sauces and foods makes it well worth the effort.

15 pounds veal bones, cut into pieces
3 large onions, chopped but not peeled
3 large carrots, chopped
3 stalks celery, chopped
water
2 or 3 tomatoes, chopped
3 cloves garlic, unpeeled
2 bay leaves
8 to 10 parsley sprigs
1 tsp. thyme

Place the veal bones in two or three roasting pans. Brown them in a 450 degree oven for one hour, turning them once.

Add the onions (with the skins), carrots and celery to the roasting pans. Continue to roast the bones and the vegetables for another hour.

Transfer all the bones and vegetables to one very large stockpot. Use a slotted spoon.

Pour off any fat from the roasting pans. Deglaze each pan by adding a cup of water to the pan. Heat, scraping the bottom of the pans well to loosen the brown residue that has formed during roasting. Add this liquid along with the residue to the stockpot. Repeat this process again, if necessary, to loosen all of the sediment.

Add the tomatoes, garlic, bay leaves, parsley and thyme to the stockpot. Do not add any salt to the demi-glace, it has been left out on purpose.

Fill the pot with enough water to cover all the bones and vegetables.

Bring the water to a boil and skim off any scum that rises to the surface of the liquid.

Simmer the demi-glace for about eight to ten hours. Skim the surface and add more water as needed to keep the bones covered.

Strain the sauce well. Let it cool and remove any fat that rises to the surface.

Place the sauce into a clean pan and reduce until it is well concentrated, at least by half.

I usually end up with about three cups of wonderfully concentrated sauce.

The demi-glace will keep for a few weeks in the refrigerator. I prefer to store it in the freezer as it keeps indefinitely there. See the method described at the beginning of the recipe.

Do not add salt to the demi-glace as it cooks. Since the sauce ends up in a very concentrated form, adding salt while it is cooking would make it taste too salty. Just add salt and pepper to taste when cooking with the demi-glace.

ASPIC

This is a very fast short-cut aspic recipe to be used as a glaze. It is not for serving as an iced soup or for eating separately. True aspic takes a lot of time to make and certainly is delicious. However, if you only need a glaze, this recipe works well and takes very little effort.

one 10½ ounce can consummé 2 tsp. gelatin

Chill the can of consummé before opening. This will allow the fat to harden on the surface of the soup. Open the can and remove the fat.

Place the consummé in a small saucepan and heat so that it will melt. Remove the pan from the heat.

Sprinkle the gelatin on the surface of the liquid and allow it to soften for a few minutes.

Return the pan to the heat and bring the liquid to a boil, stirring to disolve the gelatin.

Remove the pan from the heat and chill until the liquid becomes thick enough to use for a glaze.

If the aspic hardens too quickly, place the pan in some hot water or heat it again for a few seconds.

If the aspic is too soft, place the pan in a bowl of ice cubes, to set the gelatin.

Spoon the aspic over the food you would like to garnish or paint it on with a brush.

FISH STOCK

- 2 to 3 pounds fish bones and heads of non-oily fish
- 2 Tbsp. butter or oil
- 1 onion, chopped
- 1 large or 2 small carrots, chopped
- 1 stalk celery, chopped
- green tops of 1 leek, chopped
- salt
- white pepper
- 1 bay leaf
- ½ tsp. thyme
- ½ tsp. fennel seeds
- 6 to 8 parsley sprigs
- 1½ cups white wine
- 6 cups or more water

Wash the fish bones and heads well to remove any clotted blood. Remove the gills from the heads. I always use some fish heads, as they give a lot of flavor to the stock.

Heat the butter or oil in a large pan or stockpot. Add the chopped onion, carrots, celery and leeks. Cook, stirring, for a few minutes.

Add the fish bones and heads and continue to cook and stir for a few minutes.

Add the salt, pepper, bay leaf, thyme, fennel seeds and parsley.

Deglaze the pan with the white wine, scraping well. Add enough water to cover all of the bones and vegetables.

Bring the water to a boil, lower the heat to a simmer, and cook for thirty minutes. Skim off the white scum as it forms at the top of the pot.

Strain the stock.

If the fish stock is weak, it can be boiled down a little and concentrated after it has been strained. Do not boil for more than thirty minutes with the bones, as the stock will turn bitter.

Fish stock can be refrigerated for a few days or frozen for a few months.

This recipe will make about one quart to a quart and a half of stock.

FISH VELOUTÉ

A veloute is nothing more than a fish stock that has been thickened with a butter and flour roux and simmered for a while. This recipe is used as a base for many fish sauces.

2 Tbsp. butter
2 Tbsp. flour
2 cups fish stock, page 59

Melt the butter in a saucepan and add the flour. Cook and stir for a minute or two. Remove the pan from the heat and cool a little.

Heat the fish stock to the boiling point in a separate pot.

Add the hot stock to the cooled roux, stirring. Simmer the sauce for about twenty minutes until the floury taste is gone.

Use this Velouté as a base for fish sauces.

SAUCE BADANIA

Both the Fish Velouté and the vegetables can be prepared up to a day ahead of time and stored in the refrigerator until needed.

1 recipe Fish Velouté
¼ cup julienned carrots
¼ cup julienned celery
¼ cup white wine
1 egg yolk
¼ cup heavy cream
1 Tbsp. chopped dill
salt, white pepper

Prepare the Fish Velouté and reserve.

Cook the julienned carrots and celery in boiling salted water just until they are tender. This will only take a few minutes.

Refresh the vegetables under cold water, drain them well and set them aside until needed.

Add the wine to the Velouté and bring it to a boil.

Mix the egg yolk with the heavy cream (liason) and reserve.

Add the vegetables and the dill to the Velouté. When the sauce returns to a boil, remove it from the heat.

Stir in the liason, season to taste with salt and pepper and serve immediately.

Do not reheat the sauce once you have added the liason.

This recipe makes about two cups of sauce.

Serve Sauce Badania with poached or broiled fish or Fish Quenelles, page 17.

SAUCE DORIA

This is a last minute sauce. Do not put it together until you are ready to serve. However, you can have the Veloute prepared ahead, the cucumber diced and the liason mixed. It will only take you a few minutes to assemble the sauce.

1 recipe Fish Velouté	1 egg yolk
½ cucumber	¼ cup heavy cream
½ cup champagne	salt, white pepper

Prepare the Fish Velouté and reserve.

Peel, seed and dice the cucumber.

Heat the Velouté to the boiling point. Add the cucumber to the Velouté and cook for just a minute.

Add the champagne and continue to cook just until the sauce comes to a boil. Remove the sauce from the heat.

Mix together the egg yolk with the heavy cream.

Stir egg and cream mixture (liason) into the sauce, season to taste with salt and pepper and serve immediately.

Do not reheat the sauce once you have added the liason.

This recipe makes about two cups of sauce.

Serve Sauce Doria with poached or broiled fish.

SAUCE DUGLERE

1 recipe Fish Velouté	¼ cup heavy cream
2 tomatoes	1 to 2 Tbsp. butter
1 egg yolk	salt, white pepper

Prepare the Fish Velouté and reserve.

Peel, seed and dice the tomatoes.

Heat the Velouté to the boiling point.

Mix the egg yolk with the heavy cream (liason) and reserve.

Add the prepared tomatoes to the boiling sauce, then remove it from the heat.

Add the butter and swirl the pan until it is melted.

Add the liason to the sauce, stir, season to taste with salt and pepper and serve immediately.

Do not reheat the sauce once you have added the liason.

This recipe makes about two cups sauce.

Serve Sauce Duglère with poached or broiled fish.

COURT BOUILLON

Court Bouillon is a vegetable flavored stock used for poaching fish. Do not throw out Court Bouillon after using as it can be strained and re-used a few times. The stock will keep in the refrigerator for two or three days or it can be frozen. The Court Bouillon can be used as a base for soups or sauces, also.

1 carrot
1 stalk celery
1 small onion
pinch thyme
1 bay leaf
dash pepper
½ tsp. salt
2 cups water
½ cup white wine, optional

Coarsely chop the carrots, celery and onion and place the vegetables in a saucepan.

Add a pinch of thyme, the bay leaf, some pepper and the salt.

Add the water and the wine, if used, then bring the liquid to a boil. Lower the heat and simmer for twenty to thirty minutes.

You can poach fish in the liquid at this point. Or you can strain off the vegetables, return just the liquid to the pot and then poach the fish.

SAUCE MORNAY

3 Tbsp. butter
3 Tbsp. flour
1 cup milk
1 cup stock*
salt, pepper
dash nutmeg
1 cup grated Swiss or Gruyere cheese

Melt the butter in a saucepan. Stir in the flour. Cook for a minute and remove the pan from the heat. Do not allow this roux to turn brown.

Heat the milk and the stock together. When it comes to a boil, add this hot liquid to the cooled roux, mixing well with a wire whisk.

Add a dash of salt, pepper and nutmeg.

Simmer the sauce, stirring every few minutes, for about fifteen to twenty minutes.

Add the cheese and stir until it is melted. Taste and correct the seasonings. The sauce will be very thick.

You can substitute part Parmesan cheese for some of the Swiss cheese, but not more than half.

*Chicken, fish, veal or vegetable based stock can all be used to make a Sauce Mornay.

SAUCE SUPREME

2 Tbsp. chopped shallots
2 Tbsp. butter
½ cup white wine
1 cup chicken stock
salt, pepper
½ cup heavy cream
Optional liason: 2 egg yolks
½ cup heavy cream

Heat the butter in a saucepan. Add the chopped shallots and cook them for a minute or two in the butter.

Pour the white wine and the chicken stock into the pan. Season with salt and pepper and cook to reduce the sauce just a little.

Add the heavy cream and reduce the sauce until just a little more than half remains in the pan.

The sauce can be prepared to this point early in the day and refrigerated until serving time.

When ready to serve, heat the sauce.

If you would like your sauce to have an even richer taste, mix together the egg yolks and the heavy cream for the liason. Stir this liason into the hot sauce and serve immediately.

Do not reheat the sauce once the liason has been added.

This recipe makes about one cup of sauce.

Serve with the Poulet en Croûte or any chicken dish.

SAUCE BEURRE BLANC

Both the Sauce Beurre Blanc - or white butter sauce - and the White Wine Sauce which follows are very rich and are absolutely wonderful. Use either of them to dress up plain poached, sautéed or broiled fish.

3 Tbsp. chopped shallots
¼ cup white wine
¼ cup white wine vinegar
salt
1 cup butter

Combine the shallots, wine, vinegar and a pinch of salt in a small saucepan.

Bring the liquid to a boil and reduce until only a tablespoon or even less is left in the saucepan.

Remove the pan from the heat.

Add the butter slowly, whisking constantly. If the butter stops melting, and only then, place the saucepan back over very low heat for just a minute.

The sauce will form an emulsion when all of the butter is

incorporated. Work slowly and heat the pan as little as you can.

Keep the sauce warm over a pan of hot water until needed. Do not reheat as the sauce will break down and separate.

The sauce can be kept warm for about thirty minutes.

This recipe makes about one cup of sauce.

Serve the Sauce Beurre Blanc with the Seafood Timbales, page 15. This sauce is also wonderful with any plain poached or broiled fish.

WHITE WINE SAUCE

2 Tbsp. chopped shallots
½ cup white wine
salt
1 cup heavy cream
1 tsp. lemon juice
white pepper

Place the shallots and the white wine in a small saucepan. Add a pinch of salt.

Cook until the shallots are soft and the wine is reduced by half.

Add the heavy cream and continue to cook the sauce until it is reduced and is thick enough to coat the back of a spoon.

Add the lemon juice and salt and pepper to taste.

Serve hot. This recipe makes about one cup of sauce.

A White Wine Sauce is wonderful with fish. Serve with the Poisson en Croûte recipe, page 88. Also use this sauce with poached or sautéed scallops, filet of sole, trout or striped bass, etc.

MAYONNAISE

I sometimes like to use a combination of oils when I make mayonnaise. I find if I use all olive or peanut oil, the flavor is very strong. So use one or the other mixed with plain salad oil, or use just all plain salad oil.

1 whole egg plus 1 egg yolk
1 Tbsp. white wine vinegar
½ tsp. Dijon Mustard
salt
white pepper
1 cup salad oil or ½ cup salad oil and ½ cup peanut or olive oil

Food processors are great for making mayonnaise quickly and effortlessly.

Place the egg and the extra yolk in the processor which has been fitted with the steel blade.

Add the vinegar, mustard and a little salt and pepper. Turn the motor on for a few seconds.

Remove the plunger and pour the oil very slowly into the machine while it is running.

Taste and correct the seasonings.

The mayonnaise will keep fresh for up to two weeks if it is covered and stored in the refrigerator.

This recipe makes a little more than one cup of mayonnaise.

To make the mayonnaise in a blender, use two egg yolks instead of the one whole egg, plus one yolk. Follow the same recipe.

The same recipe and method used for a blender can be used to make mayonnaise in a mixer, or by hand. Use just egg yolks.

Herb Mayonnaise:
Mix three to four tablespoons of finely chopped fresh herbs into your mayonnaise. You can use fresh parsley, dill, chives, tarragon, basil or even watercress. I like a combination of equal parts of chopped parsley, watercress and tarragon mixed together. This is especially good with fish.

TOMATO COULIS

This is a wonderfully fresh tasting tomato sauce. Since the tomatoes have not been cooked, they have not lost any of their flavor. Naturally, the better the tomatoes, the better the sauce.

3 large tomatoes
1 small clove garlic
3 Tbsp. oil
2 Tbsp. chopped parsley
2 Tbsp. chopped fresh tarragon
salt, pepper

Peel, seed and coarsely chop the tomatoes. Place them in a blender or food processor with the garlic and then purée.

With the motor running, slowly add the oil and then the herbs.

Correct the seasoning to taste. Chill the sauce.

Serve cold with the Salmon Pâté, page 47.

This recipe makes about one and one-half cups of sauce.

CUMBERLAND SAUCE

2 oranges
1 lemon
Additional orange juice to make one cup
Additional lemon juice to make one-half cup
¼ cup dry mustard powder
1½ cups red wine
dash cayenne pepper
1½ cups currant jelly

Peel the rind from the two oranges and one lemon very thinly so as not to remove the white bitter pith along with the rind.

Cut the rind into fine julienne slices.

Place the rind in a small saucepan of cold water and bring the water to a boil. Drain and refresh the rind under cold water.

Cut and squeeze the oranges and the lemon, adding additional juice to make the amounts needed.

Place the mustard powder in a saucepan. Gradually stir in the wine. Add the juices, the blanched rind and a dash of cayenne pepper.

Bring the sauce to a boil and then simmer until the volume of the mixture is reduced by half.

Stir in the currant jelly and continue to simmer for another fifteen or twenty minutes.

Chill. Serve the Cumberland Sauce cold, with meat pâtés.

This recipe makes about two cups of sauce.

Cumberland sauce will keep for a few weeks, if covered and refrigerated.

Soups

Most soup recipes call for the addition of a stock - usually chicken or beef. As always, home-made is best, but it is perfectly acceptable in many cases to substitute a good brand of canned stock or even bouillon cubes in these recipes. Most soups contain so many ingredients that it is hard for all but the most discerning palate to tell if the stock used was home-made or not.

Canned soups and bouillon cubes tend to be much saltier than homemade stocks. So, be careful when using them not to add too much additional salt to your soup. Some canned soups are concentrated in a double strength form and will need to be diluted before using.

I would not suggest using anything but a home-made fish stock for the fish soup recipes in this chapter. It is easy to make and anything that you can buy cannot compare in taste.

CHICKEN BARLEY SOUP

The addition of the chicken meat and barley used in this version of a chicken-vegetable soup make it a hearty and nutritious first course. For an even richer soup, substitute chicken stock for the water called for in this recipe.

¼ cup pearl barley
1 onion, chopped
1 carrot, diced
1 stalk celery, diced
1 leek, diced
1 parsley root, diced
2 Tbsp. butter or margarine
salt, pepper
2 Tbsp. flour
6 cups water
1 small chicken, cut into quarters
½ tsp. thyme
1 bay leaf

Pre-cook the barley in boiling salted water for thirty minutes. Rinse well, drain, and reserve.

Heat the butter or margarine in a stockpot. Add the diced onion, carrot, celery, leek and parsley root to the pot.

Simmer the vegetables for about five minutes, until they soften a little. Season with salt and pepper.

Sprinkle the flour over the vegetables. Stir and cook for a few minutes. Add the water gradually, stirring and scraping the bottom of the pot.

Add the chicken and bring the soup to a boil. Skim the surface well to remove any scum that rises to the top.

Stir the thyme, bay leaf, salt, pepper and the partially cooked barley into the soup.

Simmer, covered, for about one hour or until the vegetables and chicken are tender.

Remove the chicken and let it cool until it can be handled easily. Dice the meat, discarding the skin, bones and gristle.

Degrease the soup by removing any visible fat from the surface with a spoon.

Add the meat back to the soup, heat and correct the seasonings.

Serve hot. This recipe serves six to eight.

This soup both reheats well and can be frozen. When reheating, you may have to add some extra water or chicken stock to your soup. The barley tends to absorb a lot of liquid, making the soup very thick.

CHICKEN, LEEK AND ASPARAGUS SOUP

This is a cream of chicken soup with the added flavor of leeks and a delicate touch of white asparagus. Fresh asparagus, white or otherwise, can be used as well.

4 Tbsp. butter
1 onion, chopped
3 leeks, white part only, chopped
2 stalks celery, chopped
salt, pepper
4 Tbsp. flour
6 cups chicken stock
1 bay leaf
1 cup heavy cream
1 to 2 cups diced cooked chicken
1 small can white asparagus, diced

Melt the butter in a large saucepan. Add the onion, leeks, celery, salt and pepper. Cook the vegetables for a few minutes.

Add the flour and stir well. Cook for one minute, then gradually stir in the chicken stock.

Add the bay leaf and continue to cook the soup over a low heat until all the vegetables are tender, about thirty to forty minutes.

Strain the soup, discarding the vegetables, and return the soup to the stockpot. Stir in the heavy cream.

The soup can be prepared to this point and refrigerated for a few days or frozen. Do not add the asparagus until serving time as it tends to fall apart if reheated.

When ready to serve, heat the soup. Add the diced chicken meat and the asparagus. When it is hot, serve.

This recipe serves six to eight.

POTAGE OF CELERIAC

Celeriac or celery root has a lovely flavor and is a much neglected vegetable in this country. When available, it makes a delightful cream soup.

1 cup diced potato (1 large)
2 cups diced celeriac (about 3 small)
3 cups chicken stock
salt, white pepper
½ cup heavy cream
2 Tbsp. butter, optional

Place the diced potatoes and celeriac into a large pot with the chicken stock and a pinch of salt.

Bring the liquid to a boil, then cover and simmer until the vegetables are tender, about forty-five minutes.

Remove the pot from the heat and let it cool a little.

Purée the soup in a blender or a food processor.

Return the soup to the pot and stir in the cream. Heat and and season to taste with salt and white pepper.

If you would like the soup a little richer, stir in the optional butter.

Serve hot. This recipe serves four to six.

This soup both reheats and freezes beautifully. Do not add the butter until serving time.

POTAGE de LEGUMES

This is a wonderfully rich tasting soup and is one of my favorites. Both the flavor and consistancy of this soup would make you think that it contains lots of heavy cream, when, in fact, it is mainly puréed vegetables.

½ cup butter
2 carrots, sliced
1 large white turnip or 2 small, sliced
2 leeks, white part only, sliced
2 stalks celery, sliced
1 large potato, peeled and sliced
salt
pinch sugar
3 cups water
To thin: ½ cup light cream or more water
white pepper
2 Tbsp. chopped parsley

Heat the butter in a large saucepan.

Add the carrots, turnips, leeks, celery and potatoes. Season with salt and a pinch of sugar.

Cover and simmer the vegetables for twenty minutes.

Add the water to the vegetables and bring it to a boil. Cover and simmer the soup for another twenty minutes.

Cool a little. Purée the soup in a food mill, food processor or blender.

Return the soup to the saucepan and thin with either a little water, the cream or a mixture of both.

Season to taste with lots of fresh white pepper and salt.

Serve the soup hot, garnished with the chopped parsley.

This recipe serves six.

This soup can be made completely ahead of time, except for the parsley garnish, of course. It freezes beautifully or it can be kept in the refrigerator for three or four days.

Margarine can be substituted for the butter in this recipe.

LEEK AND POTATO SOUP

An old-fashioned favorite with just a touch of cheese to make a difference.

2 medium leeks
2 Tbsp. butter or margarine
1 Tbsp. flour
2 cups chicken stock
2 cups water
2 potatoes, diced
salt, pepper
½ cup grated Swiss cheese

Wash the leeks well and slice them into quarter-inch pieces. Use the whites and all of the greens except the tough outer leaves.

Place the leeks in a saucepan with the butter or margarine. Simmer the leeks, covered, for about ten or fifteen minutes, or until they soften.

Stir the flour into the leeks and cook for a minute or two.

Gradually stir in the chicken stock and the water.

Add the diced potatoes and season with a little salt and pepper.

Bring the liquid to a boil, then cover the pot and simmer the soup until the potatoes and leeks are tender, about forty minutes.

Serve the soup hot, with the grated Swiss cheese sprinkled on the top. This soup is also good plain, without the cheese.

This recipe serves four to six.

Leek and Potato Soup will keep well in the refrigerator for a few days. It can also be frozen. Do not add the cheese until serving time.

CREAM OF LIMA BEAN SOUP

This is one of the quickest and easiest soups there is to make. Use frozen lima beans and a can of chicken stock and you can have a hot and delightful soup in less than a half hour from start to finish.

1 ten-ounce package frozen Fordhook lima beans
1 ten-ounce can chicken stock
1 small onion, diced
1 small clove garlic, sliced
salt, pepper
1 cup water, or more if needed
½ cup light cream

Place all the ingredients except the cream into a saucepan.

Bring the soup to a boil. Cover and lower the heat to a simmer.

Cook until the lima beans are tender, about twenty minutes. Stir the soup every now and then to make sure the lima beans are not sticking.

Purée the soup in a food mill. If you use a blender or food processor, strain afterwards to remove the lima bean skins. They are very unpleasant in the soup.

Put the soup back into the pot and stir in the cream. Add additional water if the soup is still too thick.

Bring to a boil, correct the seasonings, and serve hot.

This recipe serves three to four.

This soup reheats well and can be frozen.

MUSHROOM, LIMA BEAN AND BARLEY SOUP

This is a hearty and delightfully satisfying soup that has been a family favorite for years. It is rich in flavor from the combination of both fresh and dried mushrooms along with the lima beans and barley. When making this soup, I like to double the recipe. This way I can keep some handy in the freezer.

½ cup dried lima beans
5 or 6 dried mushrooms
7 cups water, or more as needed
¼ cup pearl barley
3 Tbsp. butter or margarine
1 small onion, diced
1 or 2 carrots, diced
1 stalk celery, diced
½ pound fresh mushrooms, sliced
salt, pepper
2 Tbsp. flour
4 cups chicken stock*
2 Tbsp. chopped dill or parsley

Place the lima beans in a pot of water. Bring the water to a boil, cover the pot and turn off the heat. Let the lima beans pre-soak for one to two hours, or soak them overnight as the package directs. Drain.

Soak the dried mushrooms in one cup of water for a half hour. Drain and chop the mushrooms. Save the liquid.

Pre-cook the barley for thirty minutes in a pot of boiling salted water. Rinse the barley well and drain.

Heat the butter or margarine in the pan you will use to cook your soup.

Add the onions, carrots, celery and fresh mushrooms and sauté them for a few minutes. Add a pinch of salt and pepper.

Sprinkle the flour over the vegetables and stir it in.

Add the stock gradually and stir well.

Add the lima beans, barley, dried mushrooms, the reserved mushroom liquid and six cups of water to the pot.

Bring the liquid to a boil. Skim off any scum or fat as it rises to the surface while cooking.

Partly cover the soup and simmer until all the vegetables are tender, about one and one-half to two hours. Stir and skim occasionally.

The vegetables will absorb a good bit of water and you may have to add more as the soup cooks. When the vegetables are tender, thin the soup with water to the desired consistency. Bring the soup back to a boil.

Add salt and pepper to taste. Sprinkle with the chopped parsley, and serve hot.

This recipe serves six to eight.

This soup reheats well. It also freezes beautifully. The soup will probably need to be thinned again with water or chicken stock when reheating.

*All water can be used for this soup instead of chicken stock.

CURRIED CREAM OF PEA SOUP

This soup is very quick to make. The curry powder gives it just the right amount of spice and flavor. Out of season, you can substitute frozen peas for the fresh.

2 cups peas
1 small onion, chopped
1 stalk celery, diced
1 small potato, diced
1 small clove garlic, diced
2 cups chicken stock
2 cups water
1 tsp. salt
1 tsp. Madras curry powder
¾ cup light cream

Place all of the ingredients except the curry powder and the cream into a saucepan.

Cover and bring to a boil.

Simmer the soup for thirty to thirty-five minutes, or until the peas are tender. Let the soup cool for a few minutes.

Purée the soup in a food mill, food processor or blender. If using a processor or blender, taste and strain the soup if the bits of skin from the peas are not to your liking.

Return the soup to the pot and stir in the curry powder and the cream.

Bring the soup to a boil. Taste and correct the seasonings.

Serve hot. This recipe serves four.

This soup reheats well and can also be frozen.

POTAGE ST. GERMAIN

This is one of my favorite company soups. Its bright green color comes from the addition of the spinach leaves, as peas alone usually turn an unsightly gray-green color if cooked this long. The recipe will work with either fresh or frozen peas - but, as usual, fresh is better.

1 cup shredded lettuce leaves
1 cup shredded spinach leaves
3 Tbsp. butter or margarine
1 cup sliced leeks
4 cups peas plus ½ cup for garnish
2 Tbsp. chopped parsley
1 Tbsp. sugar
salt, pepper
5 cups chicken stock
Optional: ¼ cup heavy cream

Wash and shred the lettuce and the spinach.

Place into a large pot the butter, leeks, lettuce, spinach, peas, parsley, sugar and a little salt and pepper.

Add two cups of the chicken stock and bring the soup to a boil. Cover and simmer for thirty minutes, or until the vegetables are tender.

Let the soup cool a little. Purée in a food mill, food processor or blender. For this soup, I like the texture that the food mill produces best, but any way will work.

Return the soup to the saucepan and add the rest of the stock.

This soup can be completed to this point and refrigerated for a few days or frozen.

Bring the soup to a boil. Taste and correct the seasonings.

Cook the peas to be used for the garnish separately in boiling water with a pinch of salt and sugar added. Cook only until just tender, as you want the peas to remain bright green in color. Refresh under cold water and drain.

When ready to serve, add the peas to the soup and, if you like, a little heavy cream.

Serve the soup hot with croutons on the side. This recipe serves six to eight.

CREAM OF TOMATO SOUP

Naturally, the better the tomatoes, the better the soup they will make. All tomatoes, once cooked, do change in flavor and lose their fresh taste. Therefore, I like to add one or two peeled, seeded and diced tomatoes to this soup at the last minute. This late addition will give your soup a much fresher flavor.

4 large tomatoes
3 Tbsp. butter
1 large onion
3 Tbsp. tomato paste
salt, pepper
½ tsp. thyme
1 clove garlic, crushed
1 tsp. sugar
3 Tbsp. flour
2½ cups chicken stock
2 cups water
1 cup heavy cream

Cut the tomatoes into eighths, do not peel or seed them.

Heat the butter in a deep saucepan. Add the onions and cook them until they are soft.

Add the cut tomatoes, the tomato paste and salt and pepper. Cook and stir for a few minutes.

Add the thyme, the garlic and the sugar. Stir in the flour and cook for one minute longer.

Add the chicken stock and the water. Stir well and simmer for thirty minutes.

Put the soup through a food mill. Or you can purée it in a blender or food processor and then pass it through a sieve. You want to remove the bits of tomato skin and seeds. If you removed them before cooking, the soup would not have as much flavor.

Return the soup to a clean saucepan and add the cream.

Correct the seasonings and serve hot.

This recipe serves six to eight.

Cream of Tomato Soup can be both reheated and frozen. If using the fresh tomato garnish suggested, do not add until serving time.

POTAGE NIVERNAISE

This is a wonderful creamy soup. Try to use baby white turnips if you can get them. They are very sweet and work just perfectly here. I tasted a soup like this in Paris and was intrigued by its unusual and delightful flavor.

6 Tbsp. butter
1 pound white turnips, sliced thin
2 large potatoes, sliced
salt, pepper
4 cups chicken stock
1 cup heavy cream
Croutons

Melt three tablespoons of butter in a saucepan.

Add the turnips and the potatoes, salt and pepper. Stir and cover with a lid.

Simmer for ten to fifteen minutes, stirring occasionally, until the vegetables begin to soften.

Add the chicken stock to the vegetables. Bring the soup to a boil and cover. Simmer, stirring every now and then, until the vegetables are tender, about thirty minutes.

Let the soup cool a little then purée it in a food mill, food processor or blender.

Return the soup to the saucepan and stir in the cream.

Heat the soup and taste to correct the seasonings.

If the soup is too thick, you can thin it with the addition of a little more stock or some milk.

The soup can be prepared to this point ahead of time. It can be frozen or refrigerated.

When ready to serve, bring the soup to a boil. Stir in the remaining three tablespoons of butter.

Serve hot with croutons on the side.

This recipe serves six.

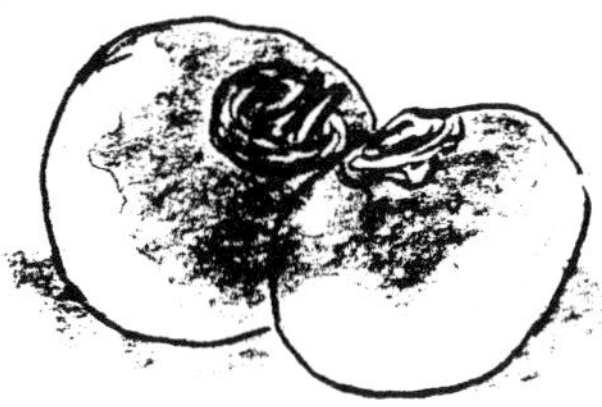

THANKSGIVING BISQUE

This soup is named Thanksgiving Bisque because it was first taught in our holiday dinner class. But you certainly do not have to wait for Thanksgiving to make this soup. Rich and deliciously flavored with apples and squash, it is good anytime.

1 small butternut squash
4 Tbsp. butter
1 onion, chopped
2 apples, peeled, cored and chopped
4 Tbsp. flour
6 cups chicken stock
salt, pepper
dash marjoram
2 egg yolks
½ cup heavy cream
Croutons - optional

Peel, seed and cut the squash into pieces.

Melt the butter in a large saucepan and add the onions, apples and the squash. Cook and stir for a few minutes.

Stir in the flour and cook for one more minute. Gradually stir in the chicken stock.

Season the soup with a little salt and pepper. Add the marjoram and simmer for about forty-five minutes, or until the squash is tender.

Cool the soup a little then purée it in a blender or food processor.

The soup can be prepared to this point ahead of time and refrigerated for a few days or frozen.

Return the soup to the pot and heat. Mix together the egg yolks and heavy cream. Stir this mixture into the hot soup and serve immediately.

This recipe serves six to eight.

Do not reheat the soup once you have added the egg and cream liason.

SPLIT PEA SOUP

This is a wonderfully satisfying cold weather soup with a rich and hearty flavor. It is my niece, Robin, and nephew, Lee's favorite way to begin a Sunday night supper.

2 cups split peas (1 pound bag)
2 quarts water
1 smoked ham hock
1 large onion, diced
2 carrots, diced
2 stalks celery, diced
1 parsley root, diced
1 bay leaf
½ tsp. thyme
salt, pepper
Croutons or diced frankfurters

Wash and sort over the split peas. Put them in a large stockpot with the two quarts of water.

Bring the water to a boil, cover and let sit for one hour to soften the peas.

Add the ham hock, diced vegetables, bay leaf and thyme to the pot. Cover and simmer for two hours.

Remove the ham hock from the soup. Dice the meat and reserve. Discard the bone.

Purée the soup through a food mill, a food processor or a blender.

Return the soup to the pot. Add the diced meat and lots of pepper and salt to taste. Sometimes the smoked meat is very salty, so do not add extra salt to your soup until this point, and only if needed.

The soup will be very thick. We like it that way but you can thin it with a little water or chicken stock if you prefer.

Serve the soup with croutons on the side. Or slice and sauté one or two frankfurters in a spoonful of oil. Drain the frankfurters and add them to the soup.

This recipe serves eight to ten.

When refrigerated or frozen, this soup tends to thicken. Dilute with a little water before heating.

CREAM OF CORN SOUP

This is another quick soup recipe - it should take about twenty minutes to prepare from start to finish. Children love this soup, but so do most adults, as well.

2 Tbsp. butter
2 Tbsp. flour
2 cups canned creamed corn
2 cups milk
1 cup chicken stock
2 tsp. sugar
pinch salt

Melt the butter in a saucepan. Add the flour. Stir and cook for a minute or two to make a roux.

Mix the creamed corn into the roux. Then stir in the milk and the chicken stock.

Add the sugar and salt and bring the soup to a boil, stirring often.

Simmer the soup for fifteen minutes, stirring occasionally to keep the corn from sticking.

Correct the seasonings and serve hot.

This recipe will serve six.

Water or milk can be substituted for the chicken stock in this recipe if you want to make a completely meatless version.

This soup can be reheated or frozen if necessary. It is best fresh.

DAIRY NOODLE SOUP

This is one of the most economical and nutritious soups you can make. It is fast, easy and good, too.

1 Tbsp. butter
1 Tbsp. flour
3 cups boiling water
1 medium onion, diced
1 small carrot, diced
1 stalk celery, diced
1 parsley root, diced
½ green pepper, diced
1½ to 2 tsp. salt
white pepper
½ cup small noodles
1 Tbsp. chopped parsley
¼ cup grated Swiss cheese

Melt the butter in a saucepan. Add the flour and stir and cook until the flour is lightly browned.

Remove the roux from the heat and let cool a little.

Add the boiling water to the cooled roux, stirring.

Add the diced onion, carrot, celery, parsley root, green pepper, salt and pepper to the pot.

Bring the soup to a boil, cover and simmer for twenty minutes.

Add the noodles and cook until they are just tender, about twelve to fifteen minutes. Leave the lid slightly ajar when cooking the noodles.

Check the seasonings, stir in the chopped parsley and the cheese and serve immediately.

This recipe serves four.

This soup will thicken if it is allowed to sit for awhile. Thin with water if reheating the soup.

It can be frozen, but the vegetables will lose their crispness and the noodles will become mushy. Best when fresh.

BEEF AND BEAN SOUP

This soup is an adaptation of a recipe given to me by my brother, Hal. He likes the taste of soy sauce and adds some to the soup. I do not, so I skip it and just use salt and pepper.

Do not be afraid to substitute ingredients for whatever you have in the house. If you do not have spinach, use lettuce. Red cabbage would work as well as white and celery leaves are excellent chopped up in the soup. Cannoli beans would work as well as the great northern beans.

This is a wonderful tasting and nourishing soup. Do not be put off by the long list of ingredients - it is easy to make.

½ pound beef chuck, diced
2 Tbsp. oil
salt, about 1 Tbsp.
pepper to taste
1 onion, chopped
1 medium carrot, diced
1 stalk celery, diced
1 parsley root, diced
½ green pepper, diced
1½ cups shredded cabbage
1 clove garlic, crushed

1 small potato, peeled and diced
1 ten-ounce can beef bouillon
4 cups water
1 tsp. tomato paste
½ tsp. each thyme and marjoram
1 fifteen-ounce can great northern beans
¼ cup rice
½ cup shredded spinach
1 fifteen-ounce can chick peas
1 tsp. Worcestershire sauce

Trim the beef and dice it into small cubes. Season with a little of the salt and pepper.

Heat the oil in a stockpot. Add the beef and sauté over high heat, stirring, until the beef is browned.

Add the diced onion, carrot, celery, parsley root, green pepper, cabbage, garlic and potato to the pot.

Sauté the vegetables along with the beef for a few minutes. Add the beef stock and the water to the pot and bring the soup to a boil. Remove any scum that rises to the surface of the soup.

Stir in the tomato paste, thyme and marjoram and the rest of the salt and pepper.

Cover the soup and simmer for thirty minutes. Remove the lid and again remove any scum that has formed on the surface.

Add the great northern beans, the rice and the shredded spinach to the soup. Drain the canned chick peas and add them also.

Cover the soup and continue to simmer until the meat and vegetables are tender, about thirty minutes more.

Stir in the Worcestershire sauce and taste to correct the seasonings. Serve hot.

This recipe will serve ten.

The Beef and Bean Soup both reheats and freezes well.

HUNGARIAN GOULASH SOUP

To make a Hungarian Goulash Soup, I like to use a combination of paprika and cayenne pepper, as most paprika available in the United States is very mild in flavor. True Hungarian paprika tends to be much hotter in taste. This is a hearty and satisfying soup reminiscent of several that I tasted in Hungary.

1 slice doubled smoked bacon, diced*
1 large onion, chopped
salt, pepper
1 pound beef chuck, diced
1 clove garlic, chopped
1½ tsp. paprika
¼ tsp. cayenne pepper
¼ tsp. caraway seeds
5 cups water
1 tomato, peeled, seeded and diced
½ tsp. tomato paste
1 green pepper, preferably long sweet, diced
1 large potato, diced
½ cup fine egg noodles

Heat the bacon in a large pot. Add the onions and cook until they are golden.

Salt and pepper the diced beef. Add the beef to the pot containing the onions and brown the meat well on all sides.

Add the garlic, paprika, cayenne pepper, caraway seeds and salt to the pot. Stir the mixture for a minute or two.

Then add the water to the pot and bring it to a boil. Cover and simmer the soup for one hour.

Add the tomatoes, tomato paste and the green pepper to the soup. Stir, cover and continue to simmer for another thirty minutes.

Add the diced potatoes and simmer, covered, for another fifteen to twenty minutes.

Add the noodles and cook the soup for an additional ten minutes, or until the noodles and the potatoes are done.

Taste and correct the seasonings. This soup seems to need a lot of salt. Add more cayenne pepper if you like your soup very spicy.

Serve hot with lots of crusty bread.

This recipe will serve six as a soup course, or four as a main course.

Hungarian Goulash Soup can be reheated and freezes well.

Alternates: You can add one-half cup of barley to the soup instead of the noodles. Pre-cook the barley for thirty minutes in boiling salted water. Rinse well, drain and add the barley after the soup has cooked for a half-hour.

One cup of cooked white beans, either dried or canned, can also be added to the soup. Use the beans instead of noodles, or use both beans and noodles.

*Regular bacon or even just a tablespoon or two of oil can be used in place of the double smoked bacon. The double smoked bacon will give the soup a richer flavor.

VEGETABLE SOUP

Hearty, filling and nourishing, this has always been one of my favorite cold weather soups. My mother deserves and gets the credit for this recipe. I have very fond memories of fighting over the marrow bones as a child and still love the taste of the warm marrow spread on a piece of fresh rye bread.

- 1 or 2 large beef marrow bones
- 1½ pounds top rib of beef
- 4 quarts water
- 1 large onion, diced
- 4 carrots, diced
- 2 stalks celery, diced
- 1 small leek, chopped
- 1 large parsley root, diced
- 1 medium white turnip, diced
- 2 large tomatoes, peeled, seeded and diced
- 2 tsp. salt
- pepper to taste
- ¼ cup barley
- 1 cup diced string beans
- 1 cup peas
- 1 cup lima beans
- 1 cup corn
- 2 medium potatoes, diced
- 1 cup mushrooms, sliced
- 2 tsp. tomato paste

Have your butcher cut the marrow bones into sections. Place the meat and bones in a large stockpot and cover with half the water.

Bring the water to a boil and skim the scum off as it rises to the surface.

Boil for ten minutes and skim again. The bones contain a lot of coagulated protein that will cloud your soup, so this is a very necessary step.

Add the onion, carrots, celery, leek, parsley root, turnip and tomatoes to the pot along with the salt, pepper and the rest of the water. Bring the soup to a boil and then lower the heat to a simmer.

Meanwhile, pre-cook the barley in a separate pot of salted boiling water for thirty minutes. Drain and rinse well.

After your soup has been simmering for forty minutes, add the pre-cooked barley, string beans, peas, lima beans, corn, potatoes, mushrooms and the tomato paste.

Continue to cook the soup for another hour and fifteen

minutes. The barley and the vegetables should be tender. The total cooking time of the vegetable soup is about two hours and fifteen minutes.

At this point, the soup will be very thick and have a layer of fat on the top.

Lift the meat and bones out ot the soup. Discard the bones and reserve the meat.

Remove as much fat as possible from the soup by skimming the surface with a spoon or ladle.

Add two cups of cold water, stir, and skim again.

The soup can be reheated and served now or refrigerated. At this point, I prefer to refrigerate this soup overnight. The flavor improves and any fat you may have missed will have formed a hard layer on the surface. Lift off this layer before reheating.

Serve hot. This recipe serves ten to twelve as a soup course.

This soup keeps well in the refrigerator for five or six days. It also freezes beautifully. Thin with a little water when reheating.

Serve the reserved meat after the soup with horseradish and/or applesauce and rye bread. Or save the meat for another meal. If you are in a real hurry, you can substitute a package or two of frozen mixed vegetables for some of those used in the soup. Fresh, as always, will taste better.

CLEAR FISH SOUP

A marvelous fish soup, reminiscent of those I have eaten in the south of France. I served this soup for a private dinner that I cooked for The Confrerie du Bontemps de Sauternes et Barsac. It is one of the few soups that will go well with a Sauternes.

For a more economical soup, and one that is every bit as good, use about six pounds of fish heads and bones only. Most fish stores will be glad to give them away. I always use just the heads and bones myself, but you have the option of using just bones or whole fish when making this soup.

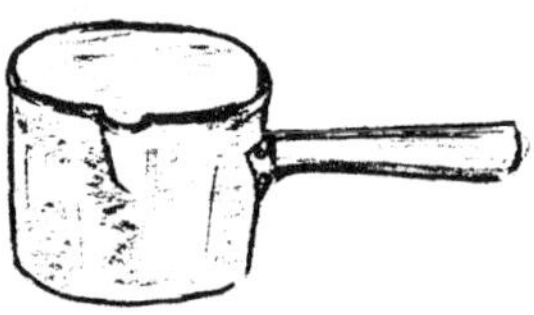

3 pounds assorted firm fleshed white fish, or 6 pounds of fish heads and bones
4 to 6 Tbsp. olive oil
2 leeks, chopped
1 onion, chopped
2 stalks celery, chopped
2 stalks fennel, chopped
2 cloves garlic, chopped
1 small can plum tomatoes (1 cup)
½ tsp. fennel seeds
1 bay leaf
1 tsp. thyme
1 tsp. oregano
salt, pepper
boiling water to cover
piece dried orange peel
pinch saffron
pinch cayenne pepper

Wash the fish heads well and remove the gills. Chop the bones. If you are using whole fish, buy cheap ones such as porgies or whitings. Chop them into pieces. Wipe the fish dry.

Use a very large skillet to start the soup. Heat the olive oil and add the leeks, onion, celery and fennel stalks to the pan. Sauté for a few minutes.
Add the fish and/or fish bones and heads. Stir and cook over high heat until the fish just begins to turn color.

Add the garlic, tomatoes, fennel seeds, bay leaf, thyme, oregano, salt and pepper to the pot.

Now what you do depends on the pots you have. If your original pot is very large, just continue right along. If not, transfer the entire contents of the skillet to a stockpot.

Pour in enough boiling water to cover the fish and vegetables. Add the orange peel and simmer for thirty to forty minutes.
Dry the saffron threads. Place them on a heat-proof plate over a small pot of boiling water for five minutes. Then crush and reserve.

Strain the fish soup through a sieve, pressing well to get out all of the juices. Discard all the bones and the solids.

Place the soup back into a clean pot. Add the saffron powder, a dash of cayenne pepper and salt to taste. Simmer for a few minutes and remove any fat that rises to the surface of the soup.

The soup can be served plain, with croutons or even with some cooked pasta. This recipe serves six to eight.

The Clear Fish Soup can be refrigerated for a few days. Lift off any fat layer that forms on the surface before reheating. It also freezes very well.

CHIOPINO

This soup is really a meal in itself. Serve with lots of crusty french bread or garlic bread and a hearty red wine. Follow with cheese and fruit or just a substantial dessert for a lovely meal.

Soup Base:

3 Tbsp. olive oil
1 onion, chopped
1 large can Italian plum tomatoes
1 stalk celery, diced
½ green pepper, diced
2 cloves garlic, chopped
1 cup tomato purée
1 cup red wine
1 tsp. basil
1 tsp. oregano
1 Tbsp. chopped parsley
salt, pepper

Fish:

2 pounds of a mixture of any of the following firm fleshed white fish: Halibut, red snapper, fluke, bass, etc.
1 lobster tail, optional
½ pound shrimp
1 dozen clams, in their shells
½ pound sea scallops

First make the soup base. Heat the oil in a large pot. Add the onion and sauté for a few minutes.

Chop the plum tomatoes a little, reserving the liquid.

Add the celery, green pepper, garlic, tomatoes (and their liquid), tomato purée, wine, basil, oregano, parsley, salt and pepper to the pot containing the onions.

Bring this soup base to a boil, cover and simmer for one hour. Taste and correct the seasonings.

The soup base can be prepared to this point ahead of time and refrigerated.

Cut the fish into serving sized pieces. If you are using a lobster tail, cut it into chunks. Scrub the clams well.

Leave the shells on the shrimp if you do not mind the mess of eating them that way. If you do, peel them.

Wait until fifteen minutes before serving time and bring the soup base to a boil.

Add the cut-up fish to the boiling base. Cover and simmer for five minutes.

Add the shellfish, cover again and simmer until done. This will take from five to ten minutes at the most.

Serve the Chiopino immediately with lots of hot crusty bread.

This recipe will serve four to six as a main course.

FISH CHOWDER

This is another of those wonderful one-dish dinners. The ingredients can be varied as to your taste and wallet. The shellfish can even be eliminated and just fish fillets used. If you do so, double the amount called for in the recipe.

Any firm fleshed fish that is one inch or more thick can be used for the chowder. Try halibut, tilefish, scrod or even fluke.

12 shrimps, in the shells
Optional: fresh mussels and/or clams
3 Tbsp. butter
1 onion, chopped
1 leek, white part only, chopped
1 stalk celery, diced
1 green bell or 2 long sweet peppers, diced
2 or 3 cloves of garlic, crushed
salt, pepper
½ tsp. thyme
4 large tomatoes, seeded and diced
½ cup white wine
3 cups Fish Stock, page 59
1 Tbsp. tomato paste
1½ pounds fish fillets
¾ pound sea scallops
½ cup thin soup noodles, cooked
2 Tbsp. chopped parsley

Slit the shrimp down the back with a scissors. Remove the veins but leave the shells on. Wash the shrimp and set them aside.

If you are using mussels, scrub them well and remove the beards. Scrub the clams well, also. Discard any shellfish that are not closed. Soak them in cold water for an hour or two to remove the sand. Sometimes I add a teaspoon of cornmeal to the water while they are soaking. It helps the shell fish to plump up and rid themselves of sand.

Heat the butter in a large pot. Add the onions and the leeks. Sauté them for five minutes or until they are fairly tender.

Add the celery, green pepper, garlic, salt, pepper and thyme to the pot. Continue to cook for three more minutes.

Add the chopped tomatoes and cook for another minute.

Add the white wine, fish stock and the tomato paste to the pot. Stir and bring the soup to a boil.

Salt and pepper the fish steaks. Cut them into two-inch portions. Add the cut fish and the shrimp to the pot, cover and cook for three to four minutes.

Add the scallops and the mussels and clams, if using, plus the cooked noodles to the pot. Cover and simmer for an additional five to six minutes.

Cook the soup only until the fish fillets are done. Be careful not to overcook the fish as it should still be firm, not falling apart. The vegetables should still be crunchy at this point, also. Add the chopped parsley to the soup and serve immediately. This recipe serves four to six as a main course.

LOBSTER BISQUE

Delicate, yet rich in flavor and expensively delicious for those times when you can afford to be a little extravagant.

6 Tbsp. butter
1 stalk celery, diced
1 carrot, diced
1 small onion, chopped
salt, pepper
1 clove garlic, chopped
2 lobster tails
2 Tbsp. flour
½ cup white wine
3 cups Fish Stock, page 59
1 Tbsp. tomato paste
1 tsp. paprika
1 tsp. lemon juice
1 Tbsp. brandy
½ cup heavy cream

Heat four tablespoons of the butter in a large pot.

Add the chopped celery, carrot and onion to the pot and cook for about five minutes. Season with salt and pepper.

Add the garlic and the lobster tails to the pot and cook for a few minutes. Stir in the flour.

Deglaze the pot with the white wine, scraping the bottom well. Then add the fish stock, the tomato paste and the paprika.

Bring the liquid to a boil and stir. Cover and simmer the soup for thirty minutes.

After thirty minutes, remove the lobster tails from the soup and let them cool a little. Remove the meat from the lobster shells and reserve. Discard the shells.

Purée the soup and the lobster meat using a food processor or a blender. Add the soup back to the pot. Stir in the lemon juice, brandy and cream.

The soup can be completed to this point and refrigerated or frozen until serving time.

Heat the soup and boil for just a minute or two. Taste and correct the seasonings.

Add the remaining two tablespoons of butter to the Lobster Bisque and swirl until the butter is melted.

Serve hot. This recipe serves six small portions. The bisque is very rich.

Fish

I have used the term "skin side up" in some of the fish recipes. This does not mean that you should use fish fillets with the skin on them. The skin should always be removed when you are rolling a fillet.

The term merely means that the side of the fish that had the skin on it, or the darker side, should be facing up. Because of the tissue structure of the fish, it will roll easier this way. It will also look better with the whiter side of the fillet showing.

FISH WITH AN ASPARAGUS SAUCE

This is an elegant and delightful combination. The pale green of the asparagus sauce against the white of the fish pleases the eye as well as the palate.

3 Tbsp. butter
3 Tbsp. flour
1 cup Fish Stock, recipe page 59
1 cup light cream
8 small fish fillets, flounder, bass, etc.
salt, pepper
2 Tbsp. shallots, chopped
1 cup white wine
12 cooked asparagus spears

Melt the butter in a saucepan. Add the flour, stir and cook for a minute.

Mix the fish stock and the cream together. Stir this liquid gradually into the roux. Bring to a boil and cook slowly, stirring occasionally for fifteen minutes. Set the sauce aside.

Sprinkle the fish fillets with salt and pepper. Roll them, skin side in, into paupiettes, or little rolls.

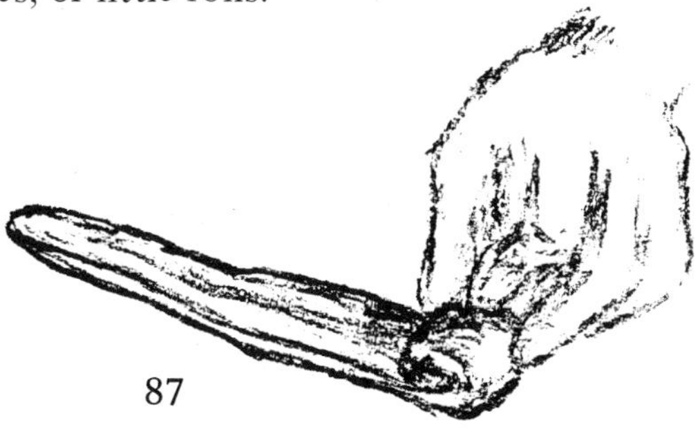

Butter a small baking pan. Sprinkle the chopped shallots over the bottom of the pan.

Place the rolled fish fillets into the pan. Pour in the white wine.

Cover the pan with buttered parchment or waxed paper. Place into a 375 degree oven and bake until the fillets are cooked. This will take about ten minutes, depending on the thickness of the fillets.

Remove the fish with a slotted spoon to a serving platter and keep warm.

Reduce the liquid in the fish pan until just one-half cup remains.

Place the reserved white sauce and the reduced liquid from the fish into a food processor or blender.

Cut the tips off the cooked asparagus spears and reserve them for the garnish.

Coarsely chop the rest of the asparagus spears and add them to the food processor. Do not use the woody bottom part of the stalks.

Blend the sauce until it is very smooth. Taste and correct the seasonings.

Pour the sauce back into the pan, return it to the stove and heat. When hot, stir in the reserved asparagus tips. Pour the sauce over the fish fillets and serve.

This recipe serves four as a main course or eight as an appetizer.

You can garnish the platter with additional asparagus spears if you like.

If you prefer an even richer sauce, you can add one-quarter cup of heavy cream mixed with two egg yolks, at the last minute.

Do not boil the sauce once this liason has been added.

POISSON en CROUTE

This is an elegant do ahead party dinner dish. The presentation is spectacular and well worth the effort.

4 small fillets of striped bass or red snapper
½ pound flounder or fluke
1 egg white
salt, pepper
1 cup heavy cream
2 packages frozen puff pastry, thawed
flour
egg wash
White Wine Sauce, page 64

Skin the red snapper or striped bass fillets and set aside.

Grind the flounder in a blender or a food processor. Add the egg white, salt and pepper and process again.

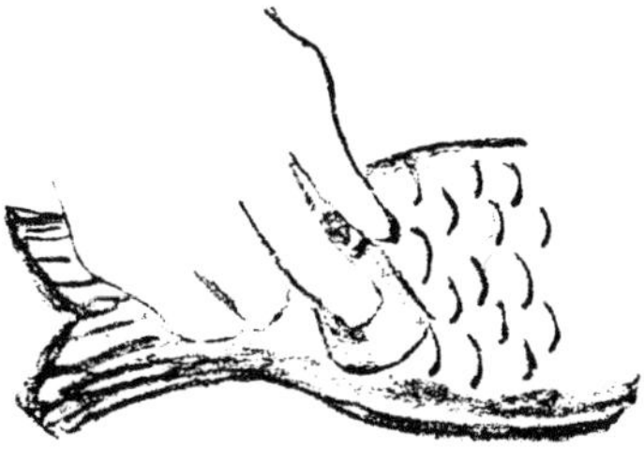

Remove the fish purée from the machine and refrigerate until it is well chilled.

Stir half the heavy cream into the chilled fish purée, a little at a time, until a thick paste is formed. Softly whip the rest of the cream and fold it into the fish mixture.

Correct the seasonings. Keep the fish mousse chilled until ready to use.

Roll out one package of the puff pastry sheets just a little. Cut four fish shapes that are larger than the fillets.

Place the pastry fish shapes onto a lightly floured baking sheet.

Dry the fish fillets well and sprinkle them with salt and pepper. Divide the fish mousse between the four fillets and spread it evenly over the top of the fillets.

Place the fillets, mousse side up, on top of the cut out puff pastry.

Roll out the second package of puff pastry a little thinner than the first.

Cut out another set of fish shapes a little larger than the first ones.

Paint around the edges of the bottom crust with the egg wash using a pastry brush.

Place the top crust over the fish. With your fingers, pinch to seal the two edges together well.

Using the tines of a fork dipped in flour, mark the tail of the fish.

Cut scale shapes on the top crust by snipping the very top of the crust lightly with a scissors. An alternate way to make scale shapes is to use the large rounded edge of a pastry-tube tip to mark the scales.

Paint the whole top of the fish with the egg wash.

Using a small strip of leftover pastry, place a dot for the eye and a line to mark the head of the fish. Paint the decorations with the egg wash.

Bake the fish in a 400 degree oven until well browned, about thirty minutes. Serve the White Wine Sauce separately. This recipe serves four.

This fish can be completely prepared early in the day and kept in the refrigerator until time to bake.

Alternate: Buy one large fillet of fish and assemble just one giant pastry fish. Cut into four pieces to serve.

RED SNAPPER WITH A SOUR CREAM TOPPING

This is a fast and easy dish. The onion and garlic blend with the sour cream and cheese to give the fillets a marvelous taste. Even fish haters like this preparation.

1 large onion, chopped
2 Tbsp. butter
2 cloves garlic, crushed
salt, pepper

4 red snapper fillets
1 cup sour cream
¼ cup grated Swiss cheese

In a frying pan, sauté the onion in the butter until it is tender and begins to brown.

Add the garlic, salt and pepper and continue to sauté for another minute or two. Remove the pan from the heat and let the onions cool a little.

Butter a casserole that is large enough to hold the four fish fillets without having them overlap.

Wash and dry the fillets and place them in the casserole, skin side down. The skin can be removed from the fillets, if you prefer.

Salt and pepper the fish.

Divide the cooked onion mixture and spread it evenly over the four fillets.

Spread a quarter cup of sour cream evenly on each fillet, over the onions.

Sprinkle the sour cream topping with the grated cheese.

The fish can be cooked now or placed in the refrigerator until baking time.

Place the casserole in a 375 degree oven for thirty minutes. The fish should be cooked through and the topping lightly browned.

Serve immediately. This recipe serves four.

Different fish can be used for this recipe other than red snapper. Any firm-fleshed white fish fillet of about a half-inch thickness will work. If you use fillets that are much thinner, you will have to shorten your baking time. Striped bass or fluke or sea trout work beautifully, as does the snapper.

SALMON WITH HERB BUTTER

This herb butter is equally good on other fish as well as the salmon. Try it over red snapper or striped bass or even swordfish. Fast, easy and good.

4 salmon steaks, one-inch thick
salt, pepper
juice ½ lemon
1 Tbsp. butter

Herb Butter:
- 2 Tbsp. chopped shallots
- 2 cloves garlic, crushed
- 6 Tbsp. butter
- ½ cup white wine
- salt, pepper
- 2 tsp. lemon juice
- 2 Tbsp. chopped dill
- 2 Tbsp. chopped parsley

Sauté the shallots and the garlic in two tablespoons of the butter.

When they just begin to brown, pour in the white wine. Add salt, pepper and the lemon juice. Set the sauce aside.

You can prepare part of the sauce ahead of time to this point.

Place the salmon steaks in a broiler-proof pan.

Sprinkle the steaks with salt and pepper. Squeeze a little lemon juice on top and dot them with the butter.

Broil the salmon under medium heat for about five to seven minutes on each side, or until done.

When the fish is cooked and ready to serve, bring the herb butter to a boil.

Remove the pan from the heat. Add the chopped dill and parsley and the remaining butter.

Swirl the pan until the butter has been absorbed. The sauce will thicken a little by the addition of the butter in this manner.

Place the salmon steaks on a serving plate, pour the herb butter over the fish and serve.

This recipe serves four.

BROILED SHAD

2 chopped shallots
½ cup butter
2 Tbsp. lemon juice
salt, pepper
pinch thyme
2 large boned shad fillets
1 Tbsp. chopped parsley

Mix the shallots, butter, lemon juice, salt, pepper and thyme in a small saucepan.

Heat and simmer for a minute or two.

Place the shad, skin side down, into a buttered oven-proof pan. Spoon the sauce generously over the top of the shad.

Cook the fish under a broiler, turned to a low setting, for about twenty minutes. The shad should be tender and the topping browned.

Do not turn the fish, broil the tops of the fillets only.

Sprinkle with the chopped parsley and serve immediately.

This recipe serves four.

SHAD ROE

In our house, we like some of each - one piece of shad roe served along with a slice of shad. It is easy to do both together as they are cooked in the same sauce.

Make the sauce for both in a frying pan, then remove enough for the shad fillets. Cook your roe in the sauce remaining in the pan. Simple and delightful.

Or cook the shad roe alone, as in the recipe.

1 chopped shallot
¼ cup butter
1 Tbsp. lemon juice
salt, pepper
pinch thyme
2 pairs shad roe
1 Tbsp. chopped parsley

Mix the shallots, butter, lemon juice, salt, pepper and thyme in a shallow frying pan just large enough to hold the roe.

Wash and dry the shad roe.

Place the roe into the sauce. Cover with a lid and simmer on a very low heat for four to five minutes.

Turn very carefully so as not to break the membrane covering the roe. Cover again and simmer for another three or four minutes.

Sprinkle the roe with the chopped parsley and serve immediately with a wedge of lemon on the side.

This recipe serves two portions alone, or four portions along with the shad.

STRIPED BASS IN A CURRIED CREAM SAUCE

This dish can be cooked in either of two ways. Both work very well. You can start with a Court Bouillon, poach your fish in this, then make the sauce out of the resulting liquid.

Or you can make your sauce separately using a Fish Stock and cook the fillets any way you like - poached, grilled, sautéed. The sauce is superb either way.

The fish is good served with a rice pilaf. Or place the fish on a bed of cooked spinach, then pour the sauce over both and serve.

Other fish fillets can be used besides striped bass. Try red snapper, trout or fluke. Even rolled fillets of sole or flounder will work well.

1 recipe Court Bouillon, page 62, or 2/3 cup rich Fish Stock, page 59
white wine
1 tsp. lemon juice
1 Tbsp. butter
4 striped bass fillets
1 1/3 cups heavy cream
¼ tsp. curry powder
salt, pepper

1. Using the Court Bouillon:

Make the Court Bouillon, adding one cup of white wine to the basic stock.

After the Court Bouillon has been cooked and strained, add the lemon juice and the butter.

If you already have some Court Bouillon made, heat a cup or two with the wine, lemon juice and the butter.

Poach the fish fillets in the Court Bouillon until they are cooked, about five to seven minutes, depending on the thickness of the fillets.

Remove the fillets and place them on an oven-proof serving platter. Cover the fish with a piece of aluminum foil and put the platter into a very low oven to keep warm while you are preparing the sauce.

Strain the Court Bouillon again and measure the liquid. You will need two-thirds of a cup. If there is more, boil it down until you reach that amount. If less, add white wine to make up the difference.

Place the heavy cream and the reduced Court Bouillon into a large saucepan (the liquid will boil up and spill over the sides if your pan is small).

Boil hard and reduce until you have one cup of liquid left. Stir in the curry powder and season to taste with salt and pepper.

Remove the fish fillets from the oven, pour the sauce over them and serve. This recipe serves four.

2. Using Fish Stock:

If you are making your sauce separately, nothing could be simpler.

Start with a well flavored Fish Stock. If it is thin tasting, boil it down until you have two-thirds of a cup of rich stock.

Then just add the cream and boil it down until one cup of liquid remains. Add the curry, season with salt and pepper and serve over your cooked fish fillets.

BAKED TILEFISH WITH A TOMATO AND MUSHROOM SAUCE

The tomato and mushroom sauce is delightful over almost any thick fish fillet you would like to bake, such as sea trout, striped bass, red snapper, halibut, etc.

1 large fillet of tilefish
butter for the pan
salt, pepper
1 tsp. lemon juice

Sauce:
- 1 Tbsp. chopped shallots
- 1 Tbsp. butter
- 4 large mushrooms, sliced
- 1 tomato, seeded and chopped
- salt, pepper
- 2 tsp. flour
- 1 ounce white wine
- ¼ cup light cream
- ¼ cup heavy cream
- 2 Tbsp. chopped parsley

First, prepare the sauce.

Sauté the shallots in the butter for one minute in a small saucepan.

Add the mushrooms and the tomato and cook for an additional minute. Season with salt and pepper.

Stir the flour into the mushroom-tomato mixture. Add the wine and the two kinds of cream.

Simmer the sauce for about thirty minutes over a low heat. Stir occasionally to keep the sauce from sticking. The sauce should thicken nicely.

The sauce can be prepared to this point up to a day ahead of time and refrigerated.

Place the tilefish, skin removed, into a buttered flat casserole. Season the fish with salt and pepper and sprinkle with the lemon juice.

Spread the cooked sauce evenly over the top of the fish. Warm the sauce a little first if it has been refrigerated.

The fish can be prepared to this point a few hours ahead of time and refrigerated.

Bake the casserole in a 375 degree oven for twenty to thirty minutes, or until the fish tests done.

Cooking time will depend on the thickness of the fish - just be careful not to overcook the fillets.

Sprinkle the top of the sauce with the chopped parsley and serve directly from the casserole.

This recipe serves four.

SAUTEED CRABMEAT

This makes an extravagant but absolutely delicious dish. Serve for lunch, dinner or as an appetizer - good all ways.

2 cups crabmeat (8 ounces)
2 Tbsp. chopped shallots
2 Tbsp. butter
1 ounce white wine
¾ cup heavy cream
1 Tbsp. lemon juice
salt, pepper

Pick over the crabmeat and remove and discard any shells.

Place the shallots and the butter into a frying pan and sauté them for one minute.

Add the crabmeat to the shallots and continue to sauté for for another minute.

Add the white wine and the cream to the pan. Cook slowly until most of the liquid is absorbed by the crab. This should take between six and eight minutes.

Add the lemon juice to the crabmeat. Season to taste with salt and pepper.

Serve immediately. This recipe serves four.

BOILED SHRIMP

1 pound raw shrimp, in the shells
1 recipe Court Bouillon, page 62

Follow the recipe for Court Bouillon, leaving the vegetables in the liquid.

Add the shrimp to the Court Bouillon and simmer them for just a few minutes.

The color of the shrimp meat will change from gray to white and the shells will turn pink. Do not overcook the shrimp as they will become tough.

Pour the entire contents of the pot through a strainer. Let the shrimp cool a little, then peel and clean them.

Save the strained Court Bouillon for another use. The shrimp shells give it a lovely flavor.

The shrimp can be served cold as an appetizer. Try them with an Herb Mayonnaise instead of the usual cocktail sauce.

One pound of cooked shrimp will serve five or six as an appetizer.

Use the cooked shrimp for the Shrimp Quiche recipe, or the Salmon Pâté with Foie Gras, etc.

Cooked shrimp can be kept refrigerated for a few days.

SCAMPI

This recipe is a fast and delicious way to cook shrimp - it is my son's favorite, as a matter of fact. Serve with a rice pilaf.

5 to 6 Tbsp. butter
1 pound raw shrimp, peeled
salt, pepper
2 cloves garlic, crushed
½ cup dry Vermouth
2 Tbsp. chopped parsley

Melt four tablespoons of the butter in a frying pan.

Add the raw shrimp to the pan. Sprinkle the shrimp with salt and pepper and sauté them over high heat for one minute on each side. Cook just until the shrimp lose their opaqueness and turn white.

Stir the chopped garlic into the shrimp. Add the Vermouth and cook over a very high flame for another two minutes.

Add the chopped parsley and the remaining butter.

Mix well and serve immediately.

This recipe serves three to four as an entrée. It also makes a wonderful first course.

SHRIMP CREOLE

A tomato and green pepper sauce with just the right amount of spices and herbs. The perfect complement for shrimp - serve with a rice pilaf.

1½ pounds raw shrimp, peeled
2 cups canned plum tomatoes
1 medium onion, chopped
2 Tbsp. oil
salt, pepper
1 carrot, diced
1 stalk celery, diced
1 green pepper, diced
2 small cloves garlic, crushed
¼ cup tomato paste (4 Tbsp.)
½ tsp. oregano
½ tsp. thyme
1 tsp. basil
¼ cup white wine
¼ cup water
Garnish: 1 Tbsp. chopped parsley

Peel and clean the shrimp. Reserve them.

Drain and chop the tomatoes. Save the drained liquid.

In a frying pan, sauté the onion in the oil until it is soft. Season with salt and pepper.

Add the chopped carrot, celery and green peppers to the pan. Cook and stir for a few minutes.

Add the garlic, tomatoes, tomato paste and the herbs. Cook and stir for another minute.

Add the drained liquid from the tomatoes, the wine and the water. Scrape the bottom of the pan well after you have added the liquids.

Cover the pan and simmer the sauce for thirty minutes, stirring occasionally.

Taste the sauce and correct the seasonings.

The sauce can be prepared ahead of time to this point. Reheat before continuing with the recipe.

Add the raw shrimp to the sauce and stir. Cover and then simmer for five to six minutes.

Sprinkle the Shrimp Creole with the parsley and serve hot.

This recipe serves four to five.

The shells can be left on the shrimp for this dish, if you prefer. Slit the back of the shell and remove the veins. Add the shrimp to the sauce and increase the cooking time by a few minutes. The shrimp cooked with the shells will be very juicy and succulent but very messy to eat.

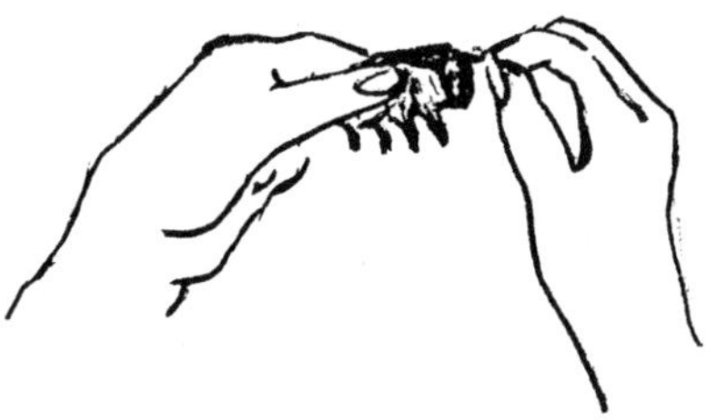

SHRIMP and SCALLOPS au GRATIN

1 recipe Court Bouillon, page 62
1 pound shrimp, in the shells
½ pound bay scallops
4 Tbsp. butter
2 Tbsp. shallots, chopped
2 Tbsp. flour
1 cup half and half
¼ cup heavy cream
¼ cup bread crumbs

Prepare the Court Bouillon according to the recipe, adding the optional one-half cup of white wine. Bring the liquid to a boil and simmer for twenty minutes, as instructed.

Add the shrimp to the Court Bouillon and cook for only a few minutes - just until the shrimp are done. The shells will turn pink and the shrimp meat will change from an opaque color to white.

Strain the Court Bouillon and return the strained liquid to the pot. Set the shrimp aside to cool.

Add the scallops to the Court Bouillon and poach for just a minute or two, only until they turn white.

Remove the scallops with a slotted spoon and set aside.

Reduce the Court Bouillon until one cup of liquid remains. While the liquid is reducing, heat two tablespoons of the butter in a small pan. Add the shallots to the butter and sauté them for a minute.

Add the flour to the pan with the shallots and cook and stir for another minute to make a roux. Remove the pan from the heat and set aside.

When the Court Bouillon has reduced so that just one cup is left, add the half and half. Return the liquid to the boiling point.

Add this hot liquid to the cooled roux, stirring. Simmer over low heat for fifteen minutes. Add the heavy cream and stir.

Meanwhile, peel and clean the shrimp. Cut them into dice the same size as the scallops.

Place the shell-fish into a buttered casserole. Pour the sauce over the fish.

Top with the bread crumbs and dot with the remaining butter.

The dish can be prepared to this point early in the day, covered and refrigerated. Return to room temperature before proceeding with the recipe.

Heat the casserole in a 400 degree oven for ten to fifteen minutes or until the sauce is hot and the topping is browned.

Serve immediately. Serves four.

The shrimp and scallop mixture can also be spooned into individual ramekins and served as an appetizer. This recipe will serve up to eight portions if used as an appetizer.

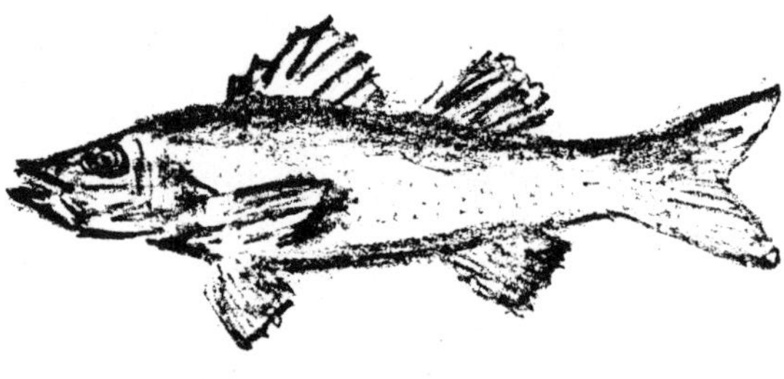

Poultry

CHICKEN WITH ARTICHOKES, CARROTS AND MUSHROOMS

The chicken is cooked with double smoked rather than regular bacon. The flavor of double smoked bacon is strong and gives this dish character. If you have to substitute regular bacon, do not blanch it first in water.

By mixing the chicken and beef stock the sauce will have a very rich taste. One or the other could be used alone, but do try it with both if you can. The demi-glace is used to enrich the sauce even further. If you have some, it is a nice addition but it can be eliminated without any harm to your sauce.

4 slices double smoked bacon
2 Tbsp. oil
24 pearl onions, peeled
1 chicken, cut into 8 pieces
salt, pepper
flour for dredging
1 large clove garlic, crushed
½ cup white wine
¾ cup chicken stock
¾ cup beef stock
3 or 4 carrots, cut into sticks
24 small mushrooms
1 bay leaf
1 tsp. thyme
1 tsp. tomato paste
1 Tbsp. Demi-Glace, page 57 (optional)
1 package frozen artichoke hearts, thawed*
1 or 2 Tbsp. chopped parsley

Dice the double smoked bacon. Place the bacon into a small saucepan of cold water. Bring the water to a boil, cook for one minute and drain well.

Heat the oil in a frying pan. Add the bacon and the pearl onions and cook for a few minutes.

Salt and pepper the chicken pieces. Dredge them lightly in flour. Add the chicken to the pan and brown it lightly, turning.

When browned, remove the chicken and the pearl onions and reserve. The bacon can remain in the pan.

Pour off any extra oil that remains in the pan.

Place the pan back on the heat, add the garlic and cook for just a few seconds.

Pour in the wine and the chicken and beef stocks. Scrape the bottom of the pan well.

Add the carrots, mushrooms, bay leaf, thyme, tomato paste and the Demi-Glace. Sprinkle with salt and pepper.

Return the chicken and the pearl onions to the pan. Bring the sauce to a boil, then cover and simmer for ten minutes.

Defrost and drain the artichoke hearts. Add them to the pan, cover again and continue to simmer for an additional ten to fifteen minutes, or until the chicken and vegetables are tender.

If there is a lot of liquid left in the pan, remove the cover and reduce the sauce over high heat until about three-quarters of a cup remains.

Sprinkle the chicken and the vegetables with the chopped parsley and serve immediately.

This recipe serves four.

*If you do not like artichoke hearts, you can substitute sliced potatoes, adding them along with the carrots. Or just use carrots, onions and mushrooms.

This dish is best when fresh. Reheat only if absolutely necessary.

CHICKEN WITH WHOLE SHALLOTS

Whole shallots cooked this way are sweet and delicious and not at all strong in flavor. Try this dish once for a delightful surprise.

24 whole shallots
2 Tbsp. oil
2 Tbsp. butter
1 chicken, cut into 8 pieces
salt, pepper
flour for dredging

½ pound mushrooms, sliced
1 cup white wine
1 cup chicken stock
1 Tbsp. fresh tarragon, chopped
3 Tbsp. chopped parsley

Clean and peel the shallots, but leave them whole.

Heat the butter and the oil in a large frying pan.

Salt and pepper the chicken and dredge the pieces lightly in flour.

Add the chicken to the frying pan and brown well on both sides. Remove the chicken and reserve.

Pour the extra fat out of the pan so that only about one tablespoon remains.

Add the whole shallots to the pan and sauté them for a minute or two.

Add the mushrooms to the pan. Sprinkle them with a little salt and pepper. Continue to cook and stir until the mushrooms are fairly dry.

Pour the white wine and the chicken stock into the pan, scraping the bottom of the pan well.

Return the chicken, cover and simmer for about twenty minutes, or until the chicken feels tender.

If the sauce becomes very reduced while the chicken is cooking, do not be afraid to add a little water to the pan.

Add the fresh tarragon and the parsley to the chicken and stir in these herbs. Taste to correct the seasonings and serve immediately.

This recipe serves four.

Margarine can be substituted for the butter in this recipe or all oil can be used.

Just chicken breasts can be used instead of a whole chicken. Reduce the cooking time by half.

CHICKEN WITH MUSHROOMS AND TOMATOES

This dish is similar to one that I tasted in the south of France. No cream and very little butter - just chicken and vegetables in a delectable sauce.

1 chicken, cut into 8 pieces
salt, pepper
flour for dredging
2 Tbsp. oil
2 Tbsp. butter
3 Tbsp. chopped shallots
½ pound mushrooms, sliced
1 clove garlic, crushed
2 tomatoes, peeled, seeded and diced
¼ cup Cognac or brandy
½ cup white wine
1 cup chicken stock
pinch cayenne pepper
2 Tbsp. chopped parsley

Sprinkle the chicken with salt and pepper and dredge the pieces lightly in flour.

Heat the oil in a frying pan.

Add the chicken pieces to the pan and brown them on all sides. Remove the chicken and pour the extra fat out of the pan.

Add the fresh butter to the pan. When melted, add the shallots and sauté them for a minute. Add the mushrooms to the pan and cook for a few minutes longer.

Stir in the garlic and the tomatoes and sauté the vegetables for another minute or two.

Deglaze the pan with the Cognac, white wine and the chicken stock, scraping well. Season the sauce with a little salt, pepper and the cayenne pepper.

Add the chicken back to the pan and simmer until tender, about twenty to thirty minutes.

Remove the chicken to a serving plate and keep warm.

Remove any grease you see on the top of the sauce with a spoon or ladle. Raise the heat and reduce the volume of the sauce a little.

Add the parsley and stir. Pour the sauce over the chicken and serve immediately. This recipe serves four.

This dish is best when freshly cooked. Reheat only if absolutely necessary.

Margarine can be substituted for the butter used in this dish.

CHICKEN PAPRIKASH WITH RICE

Paprikash is a hearty and filling meal, especially when made with rice. The sour cream can be left out if you prefer but it does give the dish a rich and lovely flavor.

2 Tbsp. butter or margarine
1 chicken, cut into 8 pieces
salt, pepper
flour for dredging plus ½ tsp.
1 large or 2 medium onions, diced
1 small clove garlic, crushed
1 tsp. paprika
¼ cup water, or more
¼ cup sour cream
2 cups boiled rice

Heat the butter or margarine in a frying pan.

Sprinkle the chicken pieces with salt and pepper and dredge them lightly in flour.

Sauté the chicken in the butter or margarine, turning, until lightly browned. Remove the chicken.

Pour off all but two tablespoons of fat from the pan.

Add the onions to the pan, sprinkle them with salt and pepper and cook slowly until they turn golden.

Add the garlic and the paprika to the pan. Stir in the quarter cup of water, scraping the bottom of the pan well.

Return the chicken to the pan, cover and simmer for about twenty minutes or until the chicken is almost tender.

Add more water if needed, to keep the chicken from sticking as it cooks.

Stir the half teaspoon of flour into the sour cream and add this mixture to the chicken. Mix well and cook for a minute or two.

Stir the cooked rice into the chicken. Cover and simmer for three or four minutes. Taste to correct the seasonings and serve.

This recipe serves four.

This dish can be reheated, but is best when fresh. I do not recommend freezing as the rice will be soggy when thawed.

CHICKEN PAPRIKASH WITH POTATOES

This recipe is really more of a "Pörkölt" than a "Paprikàs" in that cream is not added to the sauce.

The potatoes take on a delightful flavor from being cooked with the paprika and the onions.

1 small chicken, cut into 8 pieces
salt, pepper
2 Tbsp. butter or margarine
1 large or 2 medium onions, chopped
1 small clove garlic, crushed
1 tsp. paprika
½ cup or more water
3 medium sized potatoes, sliced

Sprinkle the chicken with salt and pepper.

Heat the butter or margarine in a frying pan and add the chicken. Sauté, turning, until the chicken is browned on all sides.

Remove the chicken and pour off all but two tablespoons of fat from the pan.

Add the onions to the pan, sprinkle them with salt and pepper and cook them slowly until they are golden.

Stir the garlic and the paprika into the onions.

Pour the half cup of water into the pan and stir and scrape the bottom of the pan well.

Return the chicken to the pan and add the sliced potatoes.

Cover and simmer for twenty to twenty-five minutes, until the chicken and the potatoes are tender. Taste to correct the seasonings.

Add more water, if needed, to keep the potatoes from sticking as they cook.

Serve immediately. This recipe serves four.

This dish is best fresh as the potatoes tend to fall apart if reheated.

CHICKEN PRIMAVERA

This is a marvelous combination of chicken and vegetables in a light cheese sauce. I first tasted chicken prepared this way in a restaurant in New York City and liked it so much that I came home and invented my own version of the recipe. Other vegetables can be substituted for the ones suggested if you prefer. Just remember to vary their color, flavor and textures.

4 Tbsp. butter
2 Tbsp. flour
1 cup chicken stock
1 cup half and half
1 chicken, about 3 pounds
salt, pepper
flour for dredging
3 to 4 Tbsp. oil
1 cup diced zucchini
1 cup diced carrots
1 cup peas
1 cup diced mushrooms
½ cup diced red pepper
½ cup sliced snow pea pods
½ cup water
¾ cup white wine
½ cup grated Swiss cheese

First prepare the cheese sauce. Melt two tablespoons of the butter in a small saucepan. Add the flour and cook for a minute or two.
Remove the pan from the heat and gradually stir in the stock and the half and half. Return the sauce to the heat and simmer for fifteen minutes, stirring occasionally.

While the sauce is cooking, prepare the chicken. Cut off the wings. Reserve the wings and the giblets for making stock.

Cut the chicken in half and then into quarters. Separate the drumsticks from the thighs. Cut each breast into half. You should end up with eight pieces of chicken, four white meat and four dark.

Heat the oil in a frying pan.

Sprinkle the chicken pieces with salt and pepper and dredge them lightly in the flour.

Place the chicken into the hot oil and sauté until well browned on both sides. This should take about ten to twelve minutes.

While the chicken is browning, cook the vegetables.

Heat the remaining two tablespoons of butter in a large frying pan. Add all of the cut vegetables to the pan and sprinkle them with a little salt and pepper. Stir and fry for a minute or two.

Pour the half cup of water over the vegetables and immediately cover the pan with a lid. Steam the vegetables for three or four minutes. You want them to be barely tender as they will cook again a little.

Once the chicken is well browned, remove and add the pieces to the pan containing the cooked vegetables.

Pour the oil out from the pan in which you browned the chicken and deglaze the pan with the white wine, scraping well.

Cook for a few minutes, then pour this wine into the pan containing the chicken and the vegetables.

Stir the grated cheese into the cooked cream sauce and add this sauce to the pan also.

Cook everything together, stirring often, for about five minutes.

Taste to correct the seasonings and serve hot.

This recipe will serve four.

This dish is best when served fresh. The chicken and vegetables both tend to lose their crispness if reheated.

All chicken breasts can be used to prepare this dish. Cut them in half as the recipe instructs and sauté them for eight to ten minutes only. Partially cooked string beans can be used in place of the snow pea pods, if they are unavailable.

COQ au VIN

Most Coq au Vin dishes call for cooking the chicken in red wine, but I prefer the taste of the chicken cooked in white wine. The Coq au Vin is milder and, I think, more flavorful.

1 chicken, cut into quarters
salt, pepper
3 Tbsp. butter or margarine
1 onion, chopped
2 medium carrots, cut into eighths
1 small clove garlic, crushed
½ pound whole small mushrooms
2 Tbsp. flour
1 cup white wine
1 cup chicken stock
1 tsp. tomato paste
1 bay leaf
1 tsp. thyme
1 Tbsp. chopped parsley

Season the chicken pieces with salt and pepper.

Heat the butter or margarine in an oven-proof pot. Add and sauté the chicken until it is lightly browned on all sides. Remove the chicken and reserve.

Add the onion and the carrots to the pan and sauté them for a few minutes. Then add the garlic and the mushrooms.

Sprinkle the flour over the vegetables and mix it in.

Deglaze the pan with the white wine and the stock, stirring well.

Add the tomato paste, bay leaf, thyme, salt and pepper.

Return the chicken to the pot, bring the liquid to a boil and cover.

Place the chicken into a 375 degree oven and cook for forty-five minutes to one hour or until the chicken is tender.

Stir in the parsley and serve the Coq au Vin with buttered noodles.

This recipe serves four.

The Coq au Vin can be reheated, but it tastes best when fresh. It can also be frozen if necessary.

CHICKEN IN A POT WITH CORN BREAD STUFFING

This stuffing is so good, it is worth making the corn bread just to use for this recipe. Plain bread stuffing will never taste the same.

1 whole fryer, about 3½ pounds
salt, pepper
1 Tbsp. oil
12 pearl onions
½ cup white wine
½ cup chicken stock
½ tsp. tomato paste
½ bay leaf
pinch thyme
12 new potatoes
2 carrots, cut into chunks

Stuffing:

2 slices bacon, diced
1 small onion, chopped
1 Tbsp. butter or margarine
½ cup diced celery
2½ cups Corn Bread with Parsley, page 185
1 Tbsp. chopped parsley
pinch sage
1 egg
salt, pepper

First make the stuffing. In a frying pan, sauté the diced bacon with the onion until the onion turns golden and the bacon just begins to crisp.

Add the butter or margarine and the celery and continue to cook, stirring occasionally, until the celery is tender. Let the vegetables cool for a few minutes.

Crumble the corn bread into a bowl. Add the bacon and vegetable mixture, the chopped parsley, sage, egg and salt and pepper to taste. Mix well.

The stuffing can be prepared ahead of time and refrigerated, separately from the chicken, until needed.

Wash and dry the chicken. Sprinkle the cavity with salt and pepper.

Pack the stuffing into the chicken and either sew up the opening or close with a toothpick or a small metal skewer.

Turn back the wing tips and truss the chicken so that it will keep its shape while cooking.

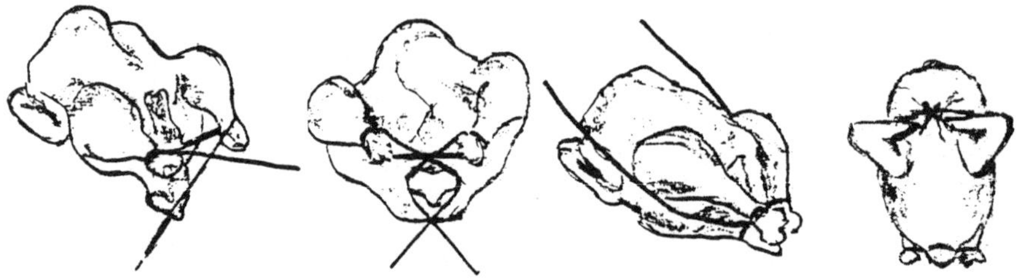

Heat the oil in an oven-proof roasting pan. Sprinkle the chicken with salt and pepper and brown it a little on all sides in the pan.

Remove the chicken from the pan and add the pearl onions. Brown them a little also, then remove the onions.

Pour off any extra fat that remains in the bottom of the pan.

Pour in the wine and the chicken stock. Add the tomato paste, bay leaf and thyme. Season with salt and pepper. Bring the sauce to a boil.

Add the chicken and the onions back to the pot. Add the potatoes and the carrots.

Cover the pot with a lid and place it into a 375 degree oven for forty minutes.

Remove the lid and continue to cook, basting the chicken occasionally, for another twenty minutes or until the chicken tests done.

When the chicken is done, the drumsticks should move freely. If pierced with a fork, the juices should run clear and the stuffing should feel hot all the way through.

Remove the chicken and let it rest for ten minutes before carving.

If there is a lot of liquid in the pan, simply boil it down over high heat until it thickens into a sauce. You want about one cup of liquid left.

Remove the strings and carve the chicken. Serve it surrounded by the vegetables and the stuffing. Serve the sauce on the side.

This recipe serves four.

If you use frozen pearl onions instead of fresh ones, they will need less cooking time. Do not brown them, just add them in with the rest of the vegetables while they are still frozen.

If you do not have the Corn Bread with Parsley, use a plain corn bread for the stuffing and add a little extra fresh parsley.

POULET à la CREME

This is a wonderful way to use up cooked chicken. Rich, creamy and delicious, you would never believe that it was made from leftovers.

4 ounces medium egg noodles
2 Tbsp. chopped shallots
4 Tbsp. butter
1 cup sliced mushrooms
salt, pepper
3 cups cooked chicken, cut into large dice
½ cup leftover chicken gravy or stock
1 cup heavy cream
1 tsp. flour
½ cup sour cream
3 Tbsp. chopped parsley
¼ cup grated Swiss cheese
¼ cup bread crumbs

Cook the noodles in boiling salted water so that they are still firm. They will cook again. Drain well.

In a large frying pan, sauté the shallots in two tablespoons of the butter for a minute or two.

Add the mushrooms, salt and pepper and continue to cook for about five minutes, stirring often.

Add the chicken to the pan and cook until it is hot. Then stir in the leftover gravy or chicken stock.

Mix in the cooked noodles stirring well to separate them.

Add the heavy cream and cook for another minute or two.

Mix the flour into the sour cream and stir this mixture into the chicken and noodles. Cook for a minute. Add the chopped parsley, taste and correct the seasonings.*

Pour the chicken and noodles into a buttered casserole. Sprinkle the top with the grated cheese and the bread crumbs. Dot with the remaining two tablespoons of butter.

This casserole can be completely prepared ahead of time and refrigerated until ready to bake.

Bake the casserole in a 400 degree oven for ten to fifteen minutes, or until hot and browned.

Serve hot. This recipe serves four.

*The cheese and bread crumb topping can be eliminated and the chicken and noodles served once they are hot, at this point.

ROASTED SPLIT CHICKEN WITH HERBS

Chicken cooked with a thin layer of stuffing between the skin and the meat has an extraordinary flavor. The skin becomes crisp and browned, while the meat is kept moist and tender by the stuffing layer.

There are two ways to cook a chicken stuffed under the skin. The first recipe calls for a sauce made from the pan drippings. In the second, the chicken is first marinated in herbs and then roasted with no sauce. We like both - try it once each way.

1 small whole chicken, 3 pounds
4 mushrooms, finely chopped
2 shallots, finely chopped
5 Tbsp. chopped parsley
1 Tbsp. chives, minced
1 tsp. tarragon
2 Tbsp. cream cheese
salt, pepper
2 Tbsp. oil
1 clove garlic, crushed
1 cup chicken stock

Split the chicken down the back and cut out the backbone. Lay the chicken flat, skin side up, with the neck toward you.

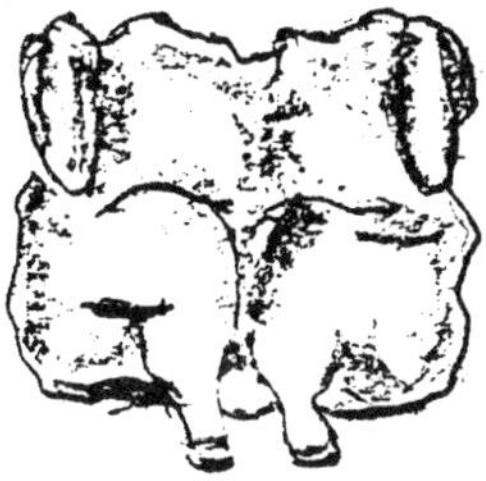

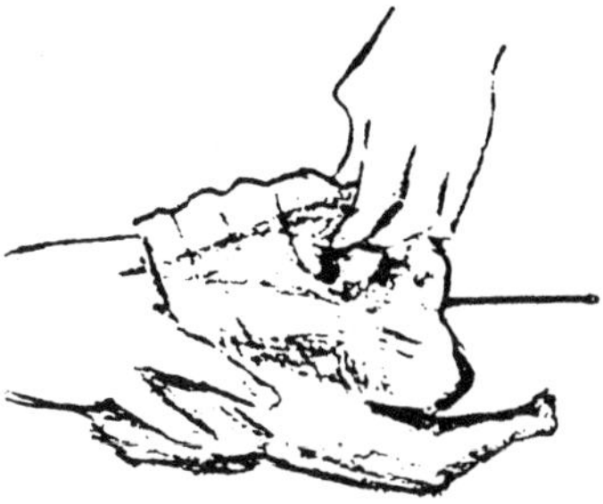

With your fingers, start at the neck and gently separate the skin from the body of the chicken, leaving it attached at the sides. Loosen the skin around the drumstick area also.

Put the chopped mushrooms, the shallots, four tablespoons of the parsley, the chives, tarragon, cream cheese and some salt and pepper into a small bowl. Work together until well mixed.

Gently place the stuffing between the skin and the meat of the chicken, smoothing it as evenly as possible with your fingers. Try to cover the drumstick area with some of the filling.

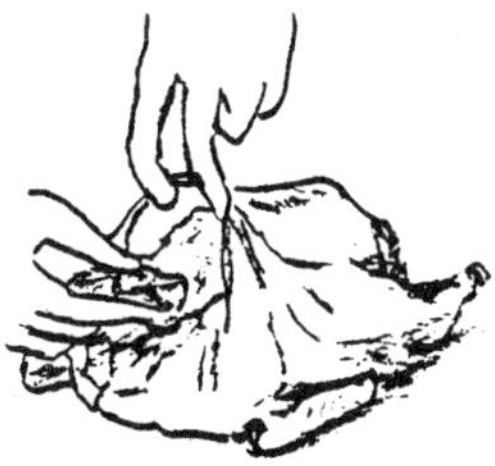

Season both sides of the chicken with salt and pepper. Rub the skin of the bird with a little of the oil.

Brush the rest of the oil over the bottom of a roasting pan with very low sides. Place the chicken in the pan, skin side up.

The chicken can be prepared to this point a few hours ahead of time and refrigerated. Bring to room temperature before cooking.

Roast in a 425 degree oven for about thirty-five minutes or until the chicken tests done. This is enough time for a small chicken to cook. If you are using a large one, increase the time proportionately.

Remove the chicken to a serving platter and keep warm.

Pour off any extra fat from the roasting pan, then place the pan on the stove.

Heat the pan and add the garlic, the chicken stock and the remaining tablespoon of parsley. Scrape well to free the glaze from the bottom of the pan.

Cook to reduce the sauce by about one-third of its volume. Taste the sauce to correct the seasonings. Strain the sauce.

Carve the chicken into quarters and serve with the sauce on the side.

This recipe serves four.

Alternates:

Instead of using cream cheese in the stuffing, you can substitute butter or margarine.

For a richer sauce, add two tablespoons of butter to the sauce before straining.

ROASTED SPLIT CHICKEN WITH LIVER AND MUSHROOMS

1 small whole chicken
1½ tsp. thyme
1½ tsp. marjoram
1 tsp. oregano
2 Tbsp. oil - olive or regular
salt, pepper
1 chicken liver
4 Tbsp. butter
2 shallots, chopped
6 mushrooms, finely chopped
½ cup bread crumbs
1 Tbsp. chopped parsley
juice ½ lemon

A few hours before serving time, cut the chicken in half down the back, removing the backbone.

Separate the skin from the meat as described in the previous recipe.

Mix together one teaspoon each of the thyme, marjoram and oregano with the oil.

Rub this mixture onto the outside of the chicken. Do not place any of the marinade in the separation you have made between the skin and the meat.

Let the chicken sit for a few hours in this herb marinade.

Sprinkle the chicken liver with salt and pepper and sauté it in one tablespoon of the butter for a few minutes. Cook only until it is just browned on the outside and still pink on the inside. Remove the liver and reserve.

Add another tablespoon of butter to the pan and sauté the shallots for one minute.

Add the chopped mushrooms and some salt and pepper. Continue to cook until the mushrooms are dry. Cool a little.

Mash the reserved liver with a fork.

Place the liver, mushrooms, bread crumbs, the remaining one-half teaspoon each of the thyme and marjoram, the parsley, lemon juice, the remaining two tablespoons butter and salt and pepper into a bowl. Mix together well.

Spread this stuffing between the skin and the meat of the chicken, as evenly as possible.

Sprinkle the outside of the chicken with salt and pepper and place in a shallow oiled roasting pan.*

The chicken can be prepared to this point an hour or two ahead of time and refrigerated. Return to room temperature before cooking.

Roast in a 425 degree oven for thirty-five minutes, or until the chicken tests done.

Remove the chicken from the pan, cut into quarters and serve.

This recipe serves four.

Margarine can be substituted for the butter in this recipe.

*The herbs from the marinade have a tendency to char on the skin of the chicken. Some people like the flavor and some do not. If you do not, simply wipe the chicken with a paper towel to remove the marinade before roasting. Then sprinkle with salt and pepper, add a little oil to the bottom of the pan to keep the chicken from sticking, and proceed with the recipe.

PAELLA

This is a wonderful one-dish company meal. The combined flavors of the chicken, sausage, shellfish and the rice are absolutely delicious. You can assemble all of the ingredients ahead of time and just pop everything into the oven at the last minute.

12 mussels, in the shells
12 clams, in the shells
12 shrimp, unpeeled
2 onions, chopped
4 Tbsp. oil
½ pound sweet sausage, sliced
½ pound pork loin, cut into small dice
1 small chicken, cut into eighths
salt, pepper
2 cloves garlic, crushed
2 cups rice
4 cups chicken stock
pinch saffron
1 Tbsp. tomato paste
1 bay leaf
1 cup peas
1 green pepper, diced
¼ cup diced pimento
2 Tbsp. chopped parsley

Scrub the mussels and the clams well. Remove the veins from the shrimp, leaving the shells on.

In a large frying or paella pan, sauté the onions in the oil until they are golden.

Add the sausage and cook for a few minutes, turning to brown the meat.

Season the pork and the chicken with salt and pepper, add them to the pan and brown them well, also.

Add the garlic and the rice to the pan, stirring to coat all the grains of rice with the oil.

The paella can be prepared to this point and allowed to sit for an hour or two. Finish a half hour before serving time.

Add the chicken stock, saffron, tomato paste and the bay leaf to the pan and stir well. If you are using fresh peas, add them now. If the peas are frozen, defrost and add them later.

Bring the stock to a boil, cover and place the pan in a 375 degree oven for fifteen minutes.

Remove the pan from the oven and add the green pepper, pimento, all the shellfish and, if frozen, the peas. Stir well. Cover the pan again and place it back in the oven for another ten minutes.

Remove the lid and cook for five more minutes.

Garnish the paella with the chopped parsley and serve immediately.

This recipe will serve eight to ten.

CHICKEN BREASTS WITH BACON AND CHEESE

Fast and easy, this is a favorite with both children and adults.

My son, Mike, and his friends all love this combination. Count on two portions apiece for teenagers.

3 double chicken breasts
6 slices of Canadian bacon
5 Tbsp. oil
6 pieces of Swiss cheese
salt and pepper
flour for dredging

Remove the center breastbone and cut each chicken breast in half.

Skin and bone the chicken. Cut a pocket into the thick side of each breast, being careful not to cut a hole, if possible.

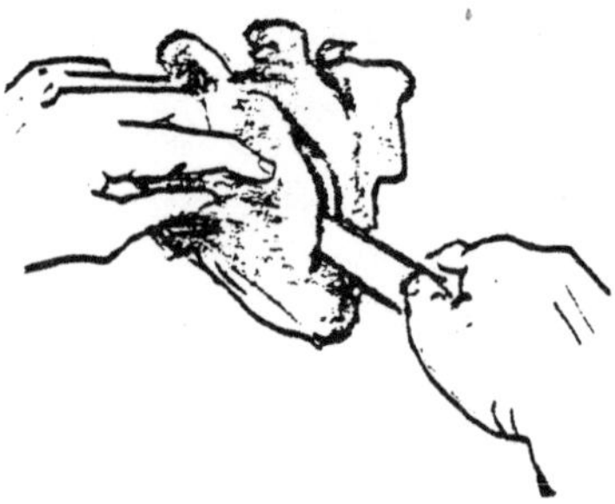

Sauté the Canadian bacon for a minute or two on each side in one tablespoon of the oil. Remove and let cool.

Cut the cheese into rectangular slices of one by three inches, about one-half inch thick.

Fold the bacon around the cheese and insert one piece of bacon-wrapped cheese into each pocket. This way, if you have a hole in the chicken, it will be covered by the bacon and not the cheese.

Salt and pepper the chicken breasts.

The chicken can be prepared ahead and refrigerated at this point.

When ready to cook, heat the remaining oil in a large frying pan.

Dredge the chicken breasts lightly in the flour, patting them well to seal the pocket.

Place the chicken breasts into the hot oil. Sauté for five minutes on each side. The chicken will be nice and crusty on outside and tender and juicy on the inside.

Serve immediately. This recipe serves three to six, depending on appetites.

If you do not have Canadian bacon, you can substitute regular bacon. Cook it without additional oil until it just begins to brown. Drain well and fold around the cheese.

The chicken will get a little dry if it has to be reheated, but it is edible. If you have any leftovers, the stuffed chicken breasts make a wonderful cold lunch.

CHICKEN AND NOODLE CASSEROLE

This dish can be completely assembled ahead of time and refrigerated or even frozen until needed. It can be served in either individual portions or as one large casserole.

If you are planning a buffet and want to serve something that will not need cutting, the chicken can be cut into bite-sized portions after it has been sautéed.

The recipe can be multiplied easily to feed a crowd. I usually find that one chicken breast is enough per person, since the noodles are filling.

The whole secret of having this dish taste good is to undercook everything the first time. It all has to be reheated and will finish cooking in the oven. If you pre-cook your chicken completely, it will be very dried out by the time it is served. The same with the noodles, they will be mushy. The cooking times in this recipe are correct. The only thing that is fully cooked the first time is the sauce.

2 double chicken breasts
salt, pepper
5 Tbsp. butter
flour for dredging plus 2 Tbsp.
1½ cups chicken stock
1 cup light cream
1 Tbsp. chopped shallots
½ pound mushrooms, sliced
2 Tbsp. oil
½ cup white wine
1 eight ounce package broad noodles
¼ cup grated cheese
1 cup fresh white bread crumbs

Skin and bone the chicken breasts and split them in half. Salt and pepper the chicken and set it aside.

In a saucepan, heat two tablespoons of the butter. Add two tablespoons of flour and cook for a minute or two. Gradually stir the chicken stock and then the cream into the roux.

Bring the sauce to a boil, season it with salt and pepper and simmer for about twenty minutes.

Melt two tablespoons of butter in a frying pan and add the shallots. Cook for one minute and add the mushrooms, salt and pepper. Cook for two minutes only, stirring. Remove the mushrooms and shallots from the pan and set them aside. Dredge the chicken breasts lightly in flour.

Wipe out your pan and add the oil. When it is hot, sauté the chicken breasts, turning, for two minutes on each side - just until they are browned but not cooked through.

Remove the chicken from the pan and reserve. Pour any excess oil out of the pan.

Deglaze the pan with the white wine, scraping well. Simmer for a few minutes and add the wine to your cooked sauce. Strain the resulting sauce to remove any sediment or lumps present. Taste the sauce and correct the seasoning.

Cook the broad noodles in boiling salted water, using about half the time suggested on the package. If it says seven minutes, three and one-half minutes is enough. Drain well.

Mix about a quarter of the sauce into the hot drained noodles. This will keep them from sticking together.

Now you are ready to assemble your dish. Butter the bottom and sides of one large or four small casseroles.

Place the layer of noodles in the casserole first. Then add the mushrooms and shallots. Place the chicken on top of the mushrooms. Pour the remaining sauce over the chicken.

Let the casserole cool for a few minutes.

Sprinkle the top of the casserole first with the grated cheese. Then cover with a thick layer of fresh bread crumbs. Dot with butter.

The casserole can be covered and refrigerated at this point or it can even be frozen.

Remove the casserole from the refrigerator a half hour before cooking time and uncover.

Place the casserole into a 375 degree oven for thirty minutes (or longer if frozen).

The sauce should be bubbling and the cheese and bread crumb crust browned. If the crust is not dark enough, place the casserole under a broiler for a few seconds.

Serve hot. This recipe serves four.

POULET en CROUTE

This was one of the most popular company dishes we ever taught. It was part of a do-ahead party dinner class, as the chicken can be assembled completely ahead of time. Poulet en Croûte is a no-fail and elegant main course.

This dish is perfectly good without the foie gras or the truffles. Either or both can be eliminated if you prefer. But I happen to like this dish best with everything just the way it is written.

I have suggested two sauces with this recipe because it really depends on your personal taste. The cream sauce is nice and has the advantage of being fast. The morel sauce takes longer, but is my favorite. It is deep and rich and complements the chicken, the crust and the filling beautifully.

4 to 5 Tbsp. butter
2 shallots, chopped
½ pound mushrooms, finely chopped
salt, pepper
2 double chicken breasts, boned
flour for dredging
1 box frozen puff pastry sheets
4 small slices pâté de foie gras
4 slices truffle
1 or 2 eggs, lightly beaten

Heat one tablespoon of butter in a small frying pan.

Add the shallots, mushrooms, salt and pepper and cook, stirring occasionally until the mixture is dry. Let it cool a little and reserve.

Skin, bone and cut the chicken breasts in half. Season them with salt and pepper and dredge them lightly in flour.

Heat the rest of the butter in a frying pan. Sauté the chicken breasts, turning until they are lightly browned. Remove and let them cool. Be careful not to overcook the chicken breasts, as they will cook again when reheated.

Roll out one-half of the puff pastry sheets a little. Cut out four circles about one inch larger than the chicken breasts. Place the pastry circles onto a floured baking sheet.

Dry the chicken breasts and place one on each circle.

Divide the mushroom mixture and smooth it on the top of each breast.

Place a small slice of foie gras on top of the mushrooms and then a slice of truffle on top of the foie gras.

Roll out the rest of the pastry a little. Cut out four large circles - at least one inch larger than the bottom rounds.

With a pastry brush, paint the outside rim of the bottom circles with a little beaten egg.

Place the top crust over the filling and press down well to seal the edges.

Dip the tines of a fork in flour and press down around the rim of the pastry to both seal and decorate the edges. Be careful not to cut through the pastry completely.

Paint the top crust with the egg wash.

You can make decorations for the top crust with any scraps of leftover pastry, if you like. Put them into place and paint them with egg wash also.

The chicken can be prepared to this point early in the day and refrigerated until baking time. Just make sure your chicken is well dried so that the bottom crust will remain crisp. Also make sure that all of your ingredients are cooled before assembling this dish.

When ready to bake paint the crust again with the egg glaze and place the chicken in a 400 degree oven. Bake until the crust is puffed and browned, about thirty minutes.

Serve immediately with a Morel Sauce, page 54, or Sauce Suprême, page 63, on the side.

If you want to be really fancy, you can leave the first wing joint attached to the chicken breast. Follow the recipe as written up to the point of adding the top crust. When putting it into place, curve one end of the crust back over the tip of the protruding wing bone. Your chicken will look like a little turtle - no one will guess that it is chicken until they cut it open.

CHICKEN LIVERS WITH MADEIRA

Chicken livers are economical and nutritious. If not overcooked, they are absolutely delicious. Try eating them while they are still pink inside and are tender and juicy. They only take a few minutes to cook as you can see by the recipes and make a great last minute dinner.

You can serve chicken livers for an appetizer as well as a main course. They taste wonderful with rice, over toast, or even in a puff pastry shell.

1½ pounds chicken livers
salt, pepper
3 Tbsp. butter or margarine
1 medium onion, chopped
2 small cloves garlic, crushed
1 tsp. flour
¾ cup Madeira
¾ cup chicken stock
2 Tbsp. chopped parsley

Wash and dry the chicken livers. Remove any tough membranes or fat present. Salt and pepper the livers.

Heat the butter or margarine in a large frying pan. Add the livers in one layer. Cook over high heat, turning, until they are just browned on the outside and still very pink on the inside, for about two or three minutes. They will cook again later. Remove the livers from the pan and reserve.

Add the chopped onion to the pan and sauté until golden.

Add the garlic and then the flour to the pan and stir well.

Pour in the Madeira and the chicken stock and scrape the bottom of the pan well. Turn down the heat and simmer the sauce for ten to fifteen minutes.

If the sauce becomes too thick, thin with a little water.

The recipe can be completed to this point an hour or two ahead of time. Do not refrigerate the sauce, let it sit at room temperature until you are ready to continue. Warm the sauce before adding the livers.

Add the livers back to the pan along with the parsley and simmer for three minutes.

Serve immediately. This recipe serves four as a main course or eight as an appetizer.

CHICKEN LIVERS WITH MARSALA AND ONIONS

5 Tbsp. butter or margarine
2 large onions, sliced
salt, pepper
1½ pounds chicken livers
flour for dredging
½ cup dry Marsala
½ cup chicken stock

Heat half the butter or margarine in a large frying pan. Add the onions, some salt and pepper and cook over low heat, stirring every few minutes, until the onions are tender and nicely browned. This will take about fifteen minutes.

Wash and dry the chicken livers. Remove any tough membranes or fat present.

Salt and pepper the livers and dredge them lightly in flour.

Push the onions to the side of the pan and add the rest of the butter or margarine. Turn the heat up high.

Add the livers to the pan and sauté until they are just browned on all sides. This will take only two or three minutes.

Add the Marsala and the chicken stock to the pan, scraping the bottom of the pan well.

Let the livers, onions and sauce simmer for two or three minutes. Test the livers to see if they are cooked. They should be brown outside and still pink inside.

Taste to correct the seasonings and serve immediately.

This recipe serves four as a main course or eight as an appetizer.

CORNISH HENS FARCI

These cornish hens are stuffed with a mushroom, rice and herb combination. Served with a rich morel sauce, they are a wonderful company dish. The stuffing can be cooked ahead of time and the hens prepared for the oven early in the day.

3 or 4 dried morels
½ cup water
4 cornish hens
salt, pepper
Rice Pilaf with Mushrooms, recipe follows
2 Tbsp. oil
1 onion, chopped
1 carrot, chopped
1 stalk celery, chopped
1 bay leaf
½ tsp. thyme
2½ cups chicken stock*
½ cup Madeira

Soak the morels in the half-cup of water for at least thirty minutes.

Wash and dry the hens. Sprinkle them with salt and pepper. Turn the wing tips back.

Stuff the hens with the rice pilaf. Truss them with a string so that they will keep their shape.

Heat the oil in a roasting pan on top of the stove. Brown the hens on all sides, turning them. Remove the hens from the pan.

Add the chopped onion, carrot and celery to the pan. Sprinkle with salt and pepper. Cook for a few minutes.

Add the bay leaf, thyme and one-half cup of the chicken stock.

Return the hens to the pan, breast side up, and place them into a 400 degree oven for forty-five minutes, or until the hens are tender.

Sometimes dried morels can be sandy. Rinse them well if they feel grainy. Dice the morels. Strain and save the soaking water for cooking, it has a lovely flavor.

Remove the hens from the oven once they are done and keep them warm while you make your sauce.

Pour any excess fat out of the roasting pan.

Place the pan on the stove and add one-half cup of stock. Cook and stir over high heat until the liquid is almost evaporated, scraping the bottom of the pan well.

Add the rest of the stock and bring it to a boil, scraping well.

Then strain the sauce into a clean pan. Remove any visible fat from the top of the sauce.

Add the diced morels and simmer the sauce for five minutes.

Add the Madeira and simmer five minutes longer. Taste to correct the seasonings.

If the sauce is too thin, thicken with a teaspoon of cornstarch dissolved in a little cold water. If too thick, add some of the liquid from the dried morels.

Serve the sauce on the side with the hens. This recipe serves four.

The sauce can be enriched with a tablespoon or two of butter, if desired. Stir in right before serving.

*Sometimes I like to substitute one cup of beef stock for an equal amount of chicken stock. It will give the sauce a deeper flavor.

RICE PILAF WITH MUSHROOMS

2 Tbsp. butter or margarine
2 Tbsp. chopped shallots
¼ pound mushrooms, diced
¾ cup rice
1¼ cups chicken stock
2 Tbsp. chopped parsley
1 Tbsp. chopped truffle
salt, pepper

Melt the butter or margarine in a small saucepan. Add the shallots and mushrooms and sauté them for a few minutes.

Add the rice to the pan and stir to coat the grains with the butter or margarine.

Pour in the stock and bring it to a boil.

Stir the rice, cover, and bake in a 375 degree oven for twenty minutes.

Remove the rice from the oven. Stir in the parsley and truffle.

Season to taste with salt and pepper.

Let the rice pilaf cool a little before using it to stuff the hens.

HERBED TURKEY ROLLS

At first taste, you would never believe that the meat used in this recipe is turkey. When prepared this way, it greatly resembles a more expensive cut of veal. The flavor combination of the ham, cheese and herbs complements the meat beautifully.

1 clove garlic, crushed
2 Tbsp. chopped parsley
2 Tbsp. dried bread crumbs
4 Tbsp. oil
8 thin slices raw turkey breast
8 slices boiled ham
8 slices Swiss cheese
flour for dredging
½ cup white wine
½ cup chicken stock

Mix together the garlic, parsley, bread crumbs and two tablespoons of the oil.

Pound the turkey slices a little to both tenderize and flatten them. Sprinkle with salt and pepper.

Divide the parsley and garlic mixture and spread it evenly over the turkey slices. Place a slice of ham and then a slice of cheese on top of the parsley mixture.

Roll up each turkey breast, making sure no cheese sticks out of the rolls. Place a toothpick into each roll to keep it from coming apart while cooking.

The turkey rolls can be prepared to this point early in the day and refrigerated.

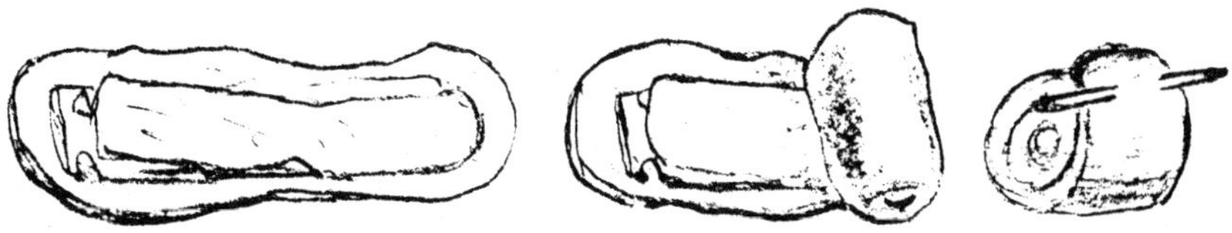

Salt and pepper the outside of the rolls. Dredge them lightly in flour.

Heat the remaining two tablespoons of oil in a frying pan. Brown the turkey rolls on all sides in the oil.

Pour in the white wine and the stock, scraping the bottom of the pan well.

Cover and simmer the rolls until they are tender, about thirty minutes, turning once.

Lift the turkey rolls out of the pan and remove the toothpicks. Strain the sauce over the turkey rolls and serve.

This recipe serves four, two rolls per person.

The Herbed Turkey Rolls can be reheated. They can also be frozen.

BRAISED TURKEY WINGS

Turkey wings are economical and can make a delightful dinner any time of the year. The sauce is wonderful with leftover turkey as well as with the wings. This dish is one of my husband's favorites.

2 Tbsp. oil
4 turkey wings
giblets or extra bones, if available*
salt, pepper
1 medium onion, chopped
1 small leek, chopped
1 carrot, chopped
1 stalk celery, chopped
1 clove garlic, crushed
1 large tomato, diced
1 heaping Tbsp. flour
1 bay leaf
½ tsp. thyme
3 Tbsp. chopped parsley
½ cup white wine
1 cup chicken stock
water, as needed

Heat the oil in a frying pan.

Sprinkle the turkey with salt and pepper. Add the turkey wings and any extra bones or giblets to the oil.

Brown the turkey pieces on all sides, then remove them from the pan.

Add the chopped onion, leek, carrot and celery to the pan. Sprinkle with salt and pepper and cook for a few minutes.

Add the garlic and the tomato to the pan and cook for another minute or two.

Sprinkle the flour on top of the vegetables and stir it in well. Let the flour cook for two minutes.

Add the bay leaf, thyme and parsley to the pan.

Deglaze the pan with the wine and the chicken stock, scraping the bottom well.

Add the turkey and extra bones back to the pan. Check the seasonings, adding more salt and pepper if needed.

Cover the pan and simmer for one and one-half to two hours, or until the turkey wings are tender. Check every half hour or so and add a little water to the pan if needed.

Remove the bay leaf and taste to correct the seasonings. Serve hot with rice, noodles or potatoes.

This recipe serves four.

Alternate: Use leftover cooked turkey for this dish. Make the sauce, using extra bones and giblets only. You can even use the leftover turkey carcass. Simmer for about one hour, until the vegetables are tender and the sauce nicely thickened. Add the cooked turkey, simmer for ten or fifteen minutes and serve.

If you object to the pieces of vegetables present in the sauce, you can remove the turkey after it has been cooked, and purée the sauce in a blender or food processor. Reheat the sauce, return the turkey and then serve.

This dish reheats well and can even be frozen.

*Extra bones are not necessary to this dish, but they will make your sauce taste richer.

DUCK

I like to roast duck and prepare the sauce to be served with the duck separately from each other. Use just the giblets to make a duck stock early in the day or even a day ahead of time. This stock is then used as a base for the duck sauce. The sauce itself can even be partially prepared early in the day, thus getting a messy job out of the way before company arrives.

The duck can be roasted a little ahead of time - see the note at the end of the recipe. Duck is a wonderful company dish. If you break down the preparation into several steps, it can be an easy dish as well.

There are two different sauce recipes given for the duck. The orange sauce is not too sweet and is delicious if you like a fruity taste with your duck. The green peppercorn sauce is rich and spicy and one which I prefer.

ROAST DUCK

2 ducks
salt, pepper
2 cloves garlic
5 or 6 sprigs parsley
2 onions, sliced
1 carrot, chopped
1 stalk celery, chopped
water

Wash and dry the ducks. Remove any excess visible fat. Reserve the giblets for duck stock.

Sprinkle the cavities with salt and pepper. Place one clove of garlic, a few parsley sprigs and a slice or two of onion inside each duck.

Sprinkle the outside of the ducks with salt and pepper.

Fold back the wing tips and place the ducks, breast side down, into a roasting pan.

Place the carrot, celery and remaining onion around the ducks. Fill the roasting pan with about one inch of water.

Roast the ducks in a 425 degree oven for one hour.

Remove the pan from the oven and remove most of the fat and the liquid. Turn the ducks breast side up.

By partially cooking the ducks in the water this way, the fat layer dissolves.

Return the ducks to the oven and continue to roast, basting occasionally, for one more hour, or until the ducks are nicely browned and test done.

Remove the ducks from the oven and let them rest for about ten minutes.

Cut the ducks into quarters and serve with either the orange or the green peppercorn sauce.

Two ducks will serve four to six portions.

The ducks can be completely roasted about an hour or two before serving time. Be careful not to overcook the ducks or they will dry out too much upon reheating. Do not refrigerate the cooked ducks.

Let the ducks rest and then cut them into quarters.

Place the duck quarters onto a rack over a roasting pan. Reheat the duck for about ten minutes in a 425 degree oven, then serve.

DUCK STOCK

giblets from two ducks
2 Tbsp. oil
1 onion, chopped
1 stalk celery, chopped
1 carrot, chopped
2 Tbsp. flour
1 cup white wine
3 cups water or chicken stock
2 tsp. tomato paste
½ tsp. thyme
bay leaf
3 parsley sprigs
salt, pepper

Chop the necks and giblets (not the livers) from the ducks.

Heat the oil in a saucepan. Add and cook the giblets, stirring occasionally, until they are well browned.

Add the chopped onion, carrot and celery to the pan. Cook for about five minutes, stirring occasionally.

Sprinkle the meat and vegetables with the flour and stir it in well.

Deglaze the pan with the white wine, scraping the bottom of the pan well. Stir in the water or stock and the tomato paste.

Bring the liquid to a boil and skim off any foam or scum that rises to the top of the stock.

Add in the thyme, bay leaf, parsley sprigs and salt and pepper.

Cover, leaving the lid ajar, and simmer the stock for one and one-half to two hours.

Strain the stock, pressing the vegetables well to remove all the liquid. Cool and remove any fat that forms on the surface of the stock.

Use this stock as a base to make a sauce for roast duck. This recipe makes about one cup to one and one-half cups stock.

The stock can be refrigerated for a few days, or it can be frozen.

GREEN PEPPERCORN SAUCE

2 Tbsp. butter
4 shallots, chopped
1 Tbsp. green peppercorns
1½ cups duck stock*
¾ cup heavy cream
1 ounce Cognac, optional

Heat the butter in a saucepan. Add the shallots and sauté for a few minutes, until they are tender.

Add the green peppercorns to the pan. Pour in the stock and the heavy cream.

Simmer until the sauce is well reduced and thickened. This will take about ten minutes.

The sauce can be made ahead to this point early in the day and reheated at serving time.

Add the Cognac, if using, and simmer the sauce for a few minutes.

Serve the Green Peppercorn Sauce on the side with roast duck. This recipe makes enough sauce for two ducks, serving four to six.

*If you do not have quite a cup and a half of duck stock, you can make up the difference with chicken stock.

ORANGE SAUCE

segments from 4 oranges
2 Tbsp. butter
2 Tbsp. sugar
2 Tbsp. wine vinegar
1 cup orange juice
1 cup duck stock
¼ cup Grand Marnier
1 ounce Mandarine liqueur*
salt
2 tsp. cornstarch
¼ cup water

Peel and cut the oranges into segments, removing any white membrane. Reserve the segments.

Heat the butter, sugar and vinegar in a saucepan, stirring. The mixture will thicken and turn light brown in just a few minutes.

Add the orange juice and the duck stock as soon as the sugar mixture turns light brown. Stir and bring the liquid to a boil.

Simmer the sauce for ten minutes. Skim the surface as needed to remove any scum that might form.

The sauce can be cooked to this point early in the day and finished right before serving time.

Add the Grand Marnier and the Mandarine to the sauce. Bring the sauce to a boil. Season to taste with salt.

Mix the cornstarch with the water. Stir the cornstarch into the boiling sauce. Simmer the sauce for a few minutes.

Add the orange segments and heat for just a minute longer.

Serve the Orange Sauce on the side with the roast duck. This recipe makes enough sauce for two ducks, serving four to six people.

Margarine can be substituted for the butter in this recipe.

*Mandarine is a tangerine flavored liqueur. If it is unavailable, substitute Apricot Brandy.

DUCK WITH CABBAGE

This dish is so good, it is worth roasting an extra duck just to have enough leftovers to make the Duck with Cabbage. The flavor of the bacon and the cabbage blend beautifully with the duck.

3 to 4 cups cooked duck meat
4 slices double smoked bacon, diced
1 or 2 Tbsp. oil
1 large onion, chopped
1 small head cabbage, shredded
2 carrots, shredded
salt, pepper
1 cup white wine
½ cup duck or chicken stock

If you have any leftover wings or drumsticks, just leave them whole. Cut the rest of the meat into fairly large pieces.

Place the double smoked bacon in a small pot of cold water. Bring it to a boil, drain and rinse the bacon.

Place the drained bacon, oil and onion into a large frying pan.

Sauté until the onion is golden and the bacon turns brown.

Add the cabbage and the carrot and cook and stir until the cabbage wilts a little. Add salt and pepper.

Pour the white wine over the cabbage and stir well.

Cover the pot and simmer, stirring occasionally to keep the cabbage from sticking. Cook until the cabbage is tender - this will take about forty minutes.

Add the duck meat and the stock to the pan. Stir well, cover and simmer for five to ten minutes longer, or until the duck meat is hot.

Taste to correct the seasonings and serve. This dish will serve four.

You can substitute regular bacon for the double smoked bacon called for in the recipe. Do not blanch the regular bacon and use a little less of the oil.

This dish can be reheated and will freeze well, also.

Meat

BEEF RAGOUT

Do not let the amount of wine in this recipe scare you, it is necessary for a rich and delicious sauce. You will not even know the wine is there when your ragoût is finished - the meat will taste just marvelous.

5 ounces double smoked bacon, diced
2 pounds chuck, cut into 1½ inch cubes
salt, pepper
1 medium onion, chopped
1 carrot, chopped
1 stalk celery, chopped
3 cups red wine
1½ cups beef stock
2 cloves garlic, chopped
1 bay leaf
½ tsp. thyme
6 to 8 parsley sprigs
2 tsp. tomato paste
water, as needed
½ pound small whole mushrooms
1 Tbsp. butter or margarine
1 Tbsp. lemon juice

Place the diced bacon in a large saucepan. Cook the bacon until it has rendered some of its fat.

Sprinkle the cubed beef with salt and pepper and add the meat to the bacon. Brown the pieces of beef on all sides then remove them from the pan.

Add the chopped onion, carrot and celery to the pan and cook the vegetables for a few minutes.

Then add the garlic, bay leaf, thyme, parsley and the tomato paste.

Deglaze the pan with the red wine and the stock, scraping the bottom of the pan well. Bring the liquid to a boil.

Add the meat back to the pan, cover and simmer until tender, about one hour to one hour and fifteen minutes. Add water as needed to keep the meat covered for the first forty-five minutes of cooking time.

While the meat is cooking, prepare the mushrooms.

Place two cups of water in a saucepan with the butter or margarine, lemon juice and one teaspoon of salt. Bring the water to a boil.

Add the mushrooms and simmer them for five minutes. Remove the pan from the heat. Let the mushrooms remain in their cooking liquid until you are ready to use them.

When the meat is tender, remove it from the sauce.

Strain the sauce back into a pan. Remove any visible fat from the surface of the liquid.

If you have too much sauce, reduce it a little. If not enough, add water. You will want about a cup and a half of sauce.

Return the meat and the mushrooms to the sauce. Taste and correct the seasonings.

The recipe can be completed to this point and refrigerated for a day or two, or it can be frozen.

When ready to serve, heat the ragoût to the boiling point. Then simmer for five minutes and serve.

Excellent with Noodles with Cream, page 171.

This recipe serves four.

If you like a richer sauce, swirl in a tablespoon or two of butter right before serving.

OLD FASHIONED BEEF STEW

This is a beef stew recipe that I have been making for a long time, one that is perfectly plain and hearty. It is a great change of pace when you have been "sauced" to death and just want something simple and filling.

The stew is made with just meat, vegetables and water, no wine or stock. But you certainly could substitute a little red wine and beef stock for the water, it will only make your sauce richer.

1½ pounds cubed beef chuck
salt, pepper
3 Tbsp. oil
1 large onion, chopped
1 clove garlic, crushed
water, as needed
1 tsp. tomato paste
½ tsp. thyme
2 large potatoes, peeled and cubed
1 carrot, diced
1 cup fresh peas

Trim the beef of any visible fat and cut it into one to two inch cubes. Sprinkle the meat with salt and pepper.

Heat the oil in a frying pan. Add the beef and sauté over high heat, turning, until the cubes are browned. Remove the beef and reserve.

If your pan is small, you may have to do this in two batches.

Make sure your meat is not too crowded or it will not brown properly.

Add the chopped onion to the pan and sauté until it turns golden. Then add the garlic and cook for a few seconds.

Pour in one cup of water, stir and scrape well to deglaze the bottom of the pan.

Stir in the tomato paste and the thyme, then return the browned beef to the pan.

Cover and simmer until the beef is almost tender. This will depend on the qualtiy of the meat and the size of the cubes. Allow about forty-five minutes to one hour.

Add the potatoes and carrots to the pan along with another cup of water. Cover and simmer for fifteen minutes.

Add the fresh peas, cover and cook until they are tender, about ten to fifteen minutes. If using frozen peas, wait to add them until the carrots and potatoes are almost done.

Add more water, if needed, to make a little sauce. This is not a very moist stew but there should be about three-quarters cup of liquid in the pan. Season to taste with salt and pepper and serve hot.

This recipe serves four.

You can, of course, change the vegetables to any that you please. Mushrooms, string beans and even lima beans are nice in this kind of stew. Vary your colors so that you do not use all green vegetables at the same time.

If you plan to reheat the stew, add the peas and then turn off the heat so as not to overcook the vegetables. They will finish cooking when reheated.

The Beef Stew will keep, if refrigerated, for three or four days. Add a little water when reheating. The stew can be frozen, but I find the vegetables tend to get very soft.

STEAK

When cooking steak that is to be served with an accompanying sauce, I prefer to sauté the meat over a very high heat in a pan rather than broiling.

The residue left in the pan gives a marvelous flavor to any sauce that you can make. These flavorful bits and pieces would be lost if the meat were broiled. Steak does not take long to cook when pan sautéed and is much juicier - restaurants cook meat this way most of the time. Besides, you only dirty one pan while making both the meat and the sauce.

In most of the recipes for steak and sauce, an enriched beef stock or Espagnole is used. But if you have any demi-glace around, a spoon or two would be a welcome addition to any of the dishes. As a matter of fact, if you use a demi-glace or a glace de viande to enrich the sauce, a plain beef stock can even be used in place of the enriched version or Espagnole.

BEEF CORDON ROUGE

Extravagance at its best - steak, truffles and foie gras all in one dish.

4 six to eight ounce tenderloin steaks
2 ounces pâté de foie gras
4 slices truffle
salt, pepper
3 Tbsp. oil
2 Tbsp. chopped shallots
½ cup red wine
½ cup Espagnole, page 52, or Enriched Beef Stock, page 53
1 Tbsp. butter

Cut a small pocket in each steak.

Place a slice of the pâté and a slice of truffle into each pocket. Press down well to seal. Salt and pepper the steaks.

Heat the oil in a frying pan. When hot, add the steaks and cook them for three to four minutes on each side.

The amount of cooking time all depends on how you like your steak. The meat will be rare if cooked three to four minutes on each side. If you prefer your steak more well done, just increase the cooking time by a minute or two on each side.

Remove the steaks from the pan, place them on a serving dish and keep warm.

Pour off the extra oil out of the pan. Place the pan back on the heat.

Add the shallots and sauté them for a minute or two.

Deglaze the pan with the red wine and the sauce or stock, scraping well.

Cook and reduce the sauce for a few minutes. Swirl in the butter, pour the sauce over the steaks and serve immediately.

This recipe serves four.

BEEF STEAK STEFANSSON

Hearty and delicious, this recipe is a real favorite with hungry men...and women, too.

4 sirloin strip steaks
salt
coarsely ground black peppercorns
4 Tbsp. Dijon mustard
1 onion, chopped fine
flour for dredging
3 to 4 Tbsp. oil
2/3 cup red wine
2/3 cup Espagnole, page 52, or Enriched Beef Stock, page 53.

Pound the steaks a little to tenderize them. Sprinkle both sides of the meat with a little salt.

On one side of the steaks only, score lightly with a knife on the diagonal, first in one direction, then in the other. You will have formed a diamond shaped pattern on the meat.

Sprinkle the scored side of the steak with lots of coarsely ground black peppercorns. Spread the mustard on top of the pepper.

Divide and place the chopped onion evenly on the top of the mustard coating. Using the heel of your hand, press the onion coating into the steaks.

The steaks can be prepared to this point up to an hour before cooking time.

Dust the top (onion) side of the steak with a light coating of flour. Be careful to leave the onion layer in place.

Heat enough oil in a frying pan to cover the bottom well.

Place the steaks into the hot oil, onion side down, first.

Cook the steaks for about five minutes, then flip the meat over. The onion layer will have formed a thick crust.

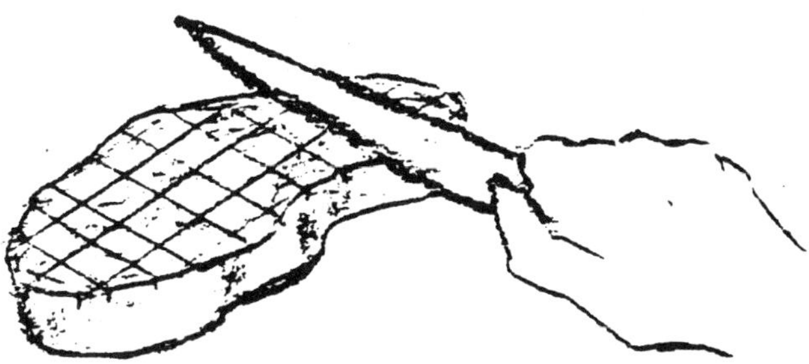

Sauté for another three minutes on the bottom side. The meat should be medium-rare at this point and is best that way.

You can cook the steaks to any degree of doneness you prefer by increasing the cooking time for a few minutes on the second side.

Remove the steaks, place them on a serving plate and keep warm.

Pour the extra oil out of the pan. Place the pan back on the heat.

Add the red wine and the sauce or stock to the pan. Scrape the bottom of the pan well. Cook and reduce the sauce for a few minutes.

Strain the sauce, pour it around the meat and serve immediately.

This recipe serves four.

ENTRECOTE à la MOUTARDE

This is another quick and wonderful recipe when you can afford the luxury of steak for dinner. The sauce has just enough zing to hold up to the meat.

4 sirloin strip or tenderloin steaks, cut about 1 inch thick
salt, pepper
4 Tbsp. oil
3 Tbsp. butter
2 Tbsp. chopped shallots
1 ounce Cognac or brandy
½ cup white wine
½ cup Espagnole, page 52, or Enriched Beef Stock, page 53
3 Tbsp. Dijon mustard
1 Tbsp. chopped parsley

Trim off any extra fat from the steaks. Salt and pepper the meat.

Heat the oil in a frying pan.

When hot, add the steaks and cook them four minutes on each side for meat that will be rare. Cook a minute or two longer if you like your meat more well done.

Remove the steaks and keep them warm.

Pour out any oil remaining in the pan. Place the pan back on the heat.

Add two tablespoons of the butter and the shallots to the pan. Sauté them for a minute or two.

Add the Cognac, wine and stock, scraping the pan well. Simmer for a few minutes.

Whisk the mustard into the sauce. Remove the pan from the heat.

Add the chopped parsley and the remaining tablespoon of butter. Swirl the pan until the butter is melted.

Pour the sauce over the steaks and serve immediately.

This recipe serves four.

If your steaks are very large you may want to increase the amount of sauce. This recipe is enough for four moderate sized steaks.

MEAT LOAF

We prefer meat loaf made with all beef rather than the usual beef, pork and veal combination.

When my children were little, they objected to the taste of diced onion in meat loaf even if it was first sautéed. So I grated it instead - onion flavor without any bits and pieces.

1 medium onion
¼ cup water
1 large clove garlic
2 pounds ground beef (chuck)
1 cup dried breadcrumbs
2 eggs
1 tsp. or more salt
pepper
1 tsp. thyme
2 Tbsp. chopped parsley
8 to 10 slices bacon

Place the onion (coarsely chopped) and the garlic into a food processor or blender along with the water and purée. Or grate the onion by hand and crush the clove of garlic.

Mix all the ingredients except the bacon together in a bowl.

Form the mixture into a large loaf shape with your hands. Place the loaf onto a greased baking sheet with low sides. This will allow the fat to run out of the meat without spilling all over your oven. Cover the top of the meat loaf with slices of bacon, working horizontally.

The meat loaf can be completely prepared ahead of time and refrigerated until ready to bake.

Bake in a 375 degree oven for one hour. The meat should be cooked through and the bacon crisp.

Let the meat loaf rest for a few minutes, then slice and serve. This recipe makes six to eight portions.
Beef fry can be used instead of the bacon on top of the meat loaf. Or just bake plain.

Cooked meat loaf will keep beautifully in the refrigerator for several days. Serve any leftovers cold, or slice and sauté in a little butter or oil. We like meat loaf this way when it is hot and crisp all over even better than when it is freshly baked. Meat loaf can be frozen but the texture will change and it will not be as good as when it is freshly made.

PORCUPINES

This is a dish that my family has always called Porcupines because of the way the meat balls look once they are cooked.

It is a take-off on the usual stuffed cabbage preparation, only we like it better. It is much simpler to prepare than cabbage rolls and tastes every bit as good.

1 head cabbage
1 medium onion, chopped
3 Tbsp. butter or margarine
1 pound ground chuck (beef)
½ cup raw rice
salt, pepper
dash paprika
1 Tbsp. flour
½ cup boiling water
1 ten-ounce can tomato sauce
1½ cups crushed tomatoes (canned)
½ cup sugar
1/8 tsp. sour salt

Cut the cabbage into thin slices and place it in the bottom of a large saucepan.

Sauté the chopped onion in two tablespoons of the butter or margarine until it is soft.

Place the ground meat, rice, salt, pepper and paprika into a bowl. Add the cooked onion and mix well.

Form the mixture into tiny meat balls, about an inch in diameter, with your hands. There should be enough of the meat mixture to make about forty meat balls.

Place the meat balls on top of the cabbage, in a single layer, if possible.

Heat the remaining tablespoon of butter or margarine in a separate saucepan and stir in the flour. Cook for a minute and remove the pan from the heat.

Bring the water to a boil. Stir the boiling water into the cooled roux.

Add the tomato sauce, the crushed tomatoes, salt, pepper, sugar and sour salt to the roux mixture. Stir well.

Pour this sauce over the meat balls and the cabbage.

Bring the sauce to a boil, cover the pan and lower the heat to a simmer.

After the meat balls have been cooking for about twenty minutes, taste the sauce. Adjust the seasonings. If you like your cabbage a little sweeter, add more sugar. If you like it tarter, add a drop more sour salt. Be very careful, sour salt is very strong.

Cook for one hour, or until the meat balls are cooked through and the cabbage is tender.

Serve hot. This recipe serves four.

This dish reheats very well. It tastes as good, if not better, the next day. Porcupines also freeze well.

STUFFED ZUCCHINI

This is a meal in one - beef, zucchini and rice all in a tomato sauce. In the summer you can substitute fresh tomatoes for the canned variety. Economical, especially when zucchini are plentiful.

4 or 5 medium zucchini
3 Tbsp. butter or margarine
1 small onion, chopped
1 pound ground chuck (beef)
¼ cup raw rice
juice of 1 lemon
2 Tbsp. chopped parsley
salt
freshly ground black pepper
1 Tbsp. flour
½ cup boiling water
1 ten-ounce can tomato sauce
1½ cups crushed tomatoes (canned)
1 Tbsp. sugar, or more to taste

Wash the zucchini and trim off the ends. Cut them into three to four inch sections.

Core the zucchini sections, using a zucchini corer or a potato peeler. Be careful not to cut through the skin. Chop the pulp that you have removed.

Heat two tablespoons of the butter or margarine in a small frying pan. Add the onions and cook until they are golden.

In a bowl, mix together the meat, rice, zucchini pulp, cooked onion, lemon juice, parsley, salt and lots of freshly ground black pepper.

Stuff this mixture back into the cored zucchini. There is usually a little bit of stuffing left over.

Place the extra stuffing in the bottom of a saucepan large enough to hold all the zucchini. Layer the filled zucchini on top of the stuffing.

Heat the remaining tablespoon of butter or margarine in a saucepan. Stir in the flour and cook for a minute or two. Remove the pan from the heat.

Whisk the boiling water into the roux. Then stir in the tomato sauce and the crushed tomatoes.

Season with salt, pepper and the tablespoon of sugar. Pour the tomato sauce over the zucchini.

The zucchini can be prepared ahead to this point, then covered and refrigerated until cooking time.

Bring the sauce to a boil, then cover and simmer until the zucchini are tender, about thirty minutes.

While cooking, taste the sauce to see if it needs more salt, pepper or sugar.

Serve hot. This recipe serves four.

Stuffed Zucchini can be reheated. It can even be frozen if necessary, but the zucchini will not remain firm upon thawing.

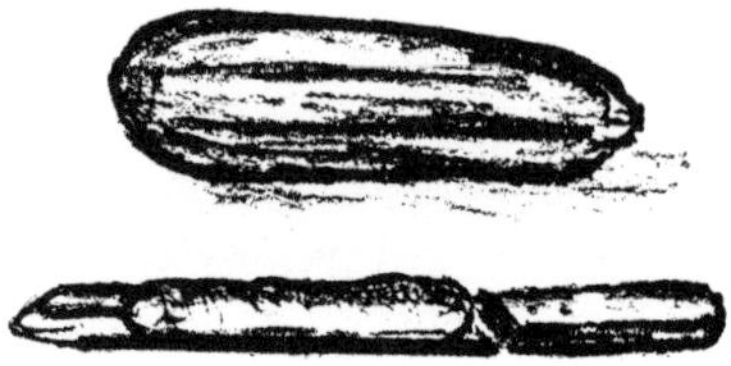

VEAL WITH MORELS

Beautiful thick veal chops with a sauce that is deliciously rich and hearty. Both dried and fresh mushrooms are used for a contrast of flavors and textures - a marvelous treat.

If fresh tarragon is unavailable, substitute fresh parsley in this recipe.

8 or 10 dried morels
½ cup warm water
2 Tbsp. oil
4 thick loin veal chops
salt, pepper
flour for dredging
4 Tbsp. butter or margarine
3 Tbsp. chopped shallots
12 mushrooms, sliced
¼ cup Cognac
½ cup white wine
½ cup chicken stock
2 Tbsp. Demi-Glace, page 57
2 Tbsp. chopped fresh tarragon

Soak the morels in the warm water for one hour. Remove and rinse off any grit that may remain inside the morels. Cut them into thin slices. Reserve both the morels and their soaking liquid.

Heat the oil in a frying pan.

Sprinkle the veal chops with salt and pepper and dredge them lightly in the flour.

Brown the chops on both sides in the oil. Remove the chops from the pan and set aside.

Discard any excess oil that remains, then add two tablespoons of the butter to the pan.

Add the shallots and cook for a minute or two. Then add the sliced mushrooms and the morels. Cook and stir for a few minutes.

Deglaze the pan with the Cognac, white wine and stock. Scrape the bottom well.

Pour in the soaking liquid from the morels, but be careful not to add any grit that has settled to the bottom of the container.

Stir in the demi-glace and add salt and pepper to taste. Bring the sauce to a boil, then reduce the heat.

Return the veal chops to the pan and simmer them for about ten minutes on each side, or until they are tender.

Remove the chops to a serving dish. If the sauce is too thin, reduce a little. If too thick, add water. You only need a few tablespoons of sauce per chop. Correct the seasonings.

Turn off the heat. Add the remaining two tablespoons of butter to the pan along with the tarragon. Swirl until the butter is melted, pour over the chops and serve.

This recipe serves four.

VEAL ROLLS WITH HERBS, HAM AND CHEESE

Veal rolls with a filling are a more economical way to serve what has become a very expensive cut of meat.

The following recipe is a different and delightful change from the usual veal rolls stuffed with a hard boiled egg or bread filling.

4 Tbsp. chopped parsley
1 clove garlic, crushed
4 Tbsp. bread crumbs
4½ Tbsp. oil
8 slices veal tenders
salt, pepper
8 slices boiled ham
8 slices Swiss cheese
flour for dredging
1 cup white wine
1 cup veal or chicken stock

Mix together the chopped parsley, garlic, bread crumbs and one and one-half tablespoons of the oil. This mixture can be chopped in a food processor or by hand.

Pound the veal tenders so that they are nice and thin. Salt and pepper the meat.

Place a slice of ham on each veal tender.

Divide and spread a little of the chopped herb mixture on top of the ham, then top each piece with a slice of cheese.

Roll the veal so that all the filling is enclosed. Use a toothpick to seal the roll.

The veal rolls can be prepared to this point early in the day and refrigerated until time to cook.

Heat the remaining oil in a frying pan.

Dredge the veal rolls in the flour and brown them in the oil on all sides. Lift the browned veal rolls out of the pan and reserve. Discard any remaining oil.

Add the wine and the stock to the pan, scraping the bottom well.

Place the veal back into the pan and cover. Simmer the veal rolls on top of the stove or bake them in a 375 degree oven for thirty minutes or until the meat is tender, turning once while cooking.

Remove the toothpicks. Pour the pan juices over the veal and serve immediately.

This recipe serves four - two veal rolls per person.

The veal rolls can be reheated in the sauce if necessary.

VEAL MARSALA

Veal Marsala is an old favorite and is always good. Using veal or beef stock in this dish gives it a lovely rich flavor.

8 veal scallops
salt, pepper
2 Tbsp. butter or margarine
½ pound mushrooms, sliced
2 Tbsp. oil
flour for dredging
1 cup dry Marsala wine
½ cup veal or beef stock

Pound the veal scallops until they are thin. Sprinkle them with salt and pepper.

Heat the butter or margarine in a frying pan. Add the mushrooms, season with salt and pepper, and cook, stirring, until they are tender.

Remove the mushrooms from the pan and set aside.

Add the oil to the pan. Dredge the veal in the flour so as to lightly coat each piece.

Sauté the veal scallops in two or more batches depending on the size of your pan. Cook for only a minute or two on each side,

just until browned. Add more oil to the pan if needed while cooking.

Remove the browned veal and pour any remaining oil out of the pan.

Deglaze the pan with the wine and the stock, scraping the bottom well.

Add the meat and the mushrooms back to the pan and simmer them for a few minutes in the sauce.

Serve immediately. This recipe serves four, two slices of veal per person.

OSSO BUCCO

We like our Osso Bucco with all of the vegetables left in the sauce and served with saffron flavored rice. You can strain the sauce if you like, but I think the dish then loses some of its charm. The marrow from the bones is wonderful - I like it even better than the meat.

2 veal shanks
3 to 4 Tbsp. oil
salt, pepper
flour for dredging
1 onion, chopped
1 carrot, diced
1 stalk celery, diced
1 or 2 cloves garlic, crushed
2 or 3 tomatoes, peeled, seeded and diced
2 Tbsp. tomato paste
2 Tbsp. fresh basil, chopped
½ tsp. rosemary
1 bay leaf
1 cup red wine
1¼ cup veal or beef stock
2 Tbsp. chopped parsley

Have your butcher saw the veal shanks into four or five pieces, each about two inches thick.

Heat the oil in a large pan. Salt and pepper the veal shanks and dredge them lightly in the flour.

Add the shanks to the pan, bone side down, and brown well. Turn and brown the other side. Remove the veal from the pan and reserve.

Add the chopped onion, carrots and celery to the pan and cook the vegetables for a few minutes.

Add the garlic, diced tomatoes, tomato paste, basil, rosemary and bay leaf to the vegetables.

Deglaze the pan with the red wine, scraping the bottom well. Then add the stock.

Return the meat to the pan and bring the sauce to a boil. Cover and cook until the meat is tender. This should take about one hour to one hour and fifteen minutes.

If there is a lot of liquid left in the pan once the shanks are tender, just remove the meat and reduce the sauce over high heat until about two cups remain. If you prefer your sauce without vegetables, strain at this point. Discard the bay leaf even if you do not strain the sauce. Add the meat back to the pan.

The Osso Bucco can be completed to this point and refrigerated for a day or two. It can even be frozen.

Heat, garnish with the chopped parsley and serve with rice.

This recipe serves four to six.

Most Osso Bucco recipes call for a Gremolada to be served with the meat. I find that this detracts from the taste of the veal. However, if you like a Gremolada, one made of equal parts of lemon rind and pistachios chopped together go best with this dish.

STUFFED VEAL BREAST

Most veal breast recipes call for a bread stuffing but this recipe uses a delightful combination of ground veal, rice and spinach instead. The filling is extraordinarily good and has been a family favorite for years.

½ large veal breast, about 3½ pounds
salt, pepper
2 to 3 Tbsp. oil
water, as needed
1 onion, chopped
1 carrot, chopped
1 stalk celery, chopped
1 clove garlic, crushed
1 tomato, diced
1 bay leaf
1 tsp. thyme
6 to 8 parsley sprigs
½ cup white wine
1 cup veal or chicken stock
1 Tbsp. cornstarch

Stuffing:

1 ten-ounce package frozen spinach leaves, or 1 lb. fresh
3 Tbsp. butter or margarine
1 medium onion, chopped
¼ cup rice
scant ½ cup chicken stock
½ pound ground veal
salt, pepper
2 Tbsp. chopped parsley
1 egg

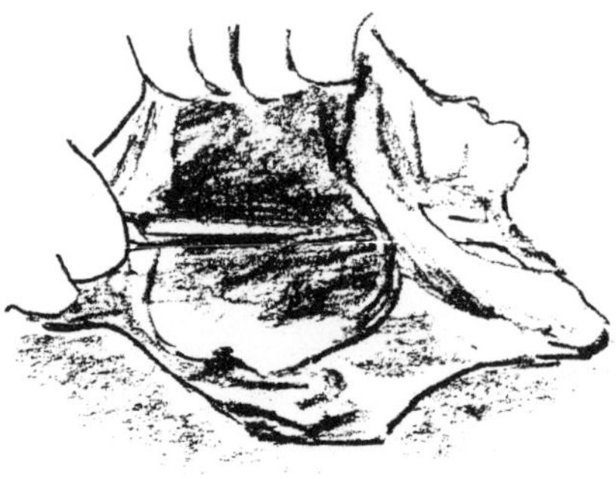

Have your butcher crack the tops of the bones in the veal breast for easier serving. Cut a large pocket in the meat and trim off any visible fat.

Prepare the stuffing. Blanch the spinach in boiling salted water. Refresh under cold water, squeeze dry and chop.

Heat one tablespoon of the butter or margarine in a small saucepan. Add two tablespoons of the chopped onion and sauté until the onion is golden.

Add the rice to the pan and stir to coat all the grains with the butter.

Add the stock and bring it to a boil. Stir the rice and cover with a lid. Bake the rice in a 375 degree oven for eighteen minutes. Do not overcook the rice, it will cook again. Cool.

Sauté the remaining onion in the two tablespoons of butter or margarine until golden.

Add the ground veal, sprinkle with salt and pepper and stir and cook until the meat is well browned. Cool the meat a little.

Mix the cooked meat, rice, spinach, parsley and the egg together. Taste to correct the seasonings.

The stuffing can be completely prepared ahead of time and refrigerated, covered, for a day or two.

Place the stuffing evenly into the pocket you have prepared in the veal breast. It is not necessary to sew it closed.

Salt and pepper both sides of the meat.

Pour about two tablespoons of oil on the bottom of a shallow roasting pan. Place the meat in the pan, bone side down, and rub the top with the remaining tablespoon of oil.

Place the veal into a 400 degree oven. Add water as needed to keep the meat from sticking and baste the meat occasionally as it roasts. Cook for one and one-half hours and remove the pan from the oven.

Add the onion, carrots, celery, garlic, tomato, bay leaf, thyme and parsley to the pan, around the meat. Return the veal to the oven.

Add water as needed to keep the vegetables from sticking to the bottom of the pan. Baste the meat every ten or fifteen minutes for another hour, or until the veal is tender.

Total roasting time for the veal should be two to two and one-half hours. The top will be very dark and crusty. We like it that way. If you do not, just keep the meat lightly covered with a piece of aluminum foil as it cooks.

Remove the meat from the pan and keep warm.

Pour the excess fat out of the roasting pan.

Place the pan on top of the stove and deglaze it with the wine and the stock, scraping well.

Strain the sauce, pressing the vegetables well to extract their juices, into a small saucepan.

Bring the sauce to a boil and skim as much fat off the top as possible using a small ladle or spoon.

Taste and correct the seasonings.

Dissolve the cornstarch in a little water. Stir the cornstarch into the boiling sauce slowly. Use only as much as is needed to make a sauce which will coat the back of a spoon. You do not want glue.

Slice the veal and serve with the sauce on the side.

This recipe serves four to five.

This recipe may be doubled and a whole veal breast used. The roasting time will be just about the same.

You can use leftover cooked rice instead of making the pilaf for the stuffing. You will need about one-half cup of cooked rice.

You can also use leftover cooked veal instead of the ground veal in the stuffing. Chop it very finely and sauté the meat for only a minute or two with the onions.

If you have any veal breast left over, it can be reheated in the sauce.

CALVES LIVER WITH GREEN PEPPERCORNS

The calves liver used in this recipe is treated just as if it were a steak. We like ours about an inch thick and cooked so that it is rare on the inside. The liver is juicy and tender and has a completely different taste prepared this way.

2 tsp. green peppercorns
½ cup butter, softened
5 Tbsp. chopped parsley
juice of ½ lemon
salt, pepper
4 very thick slices of calves liver
2 Tbsp. oil

Crush the green peppercorns.

Mix the softened butter with the peppercorns, parsley, lemon juice and salt and pepper to taste.

Form the butter into a roll. Wrap and chill until serving time.

This herb butter will keep for a few days in the refrigerator or it can be frozen.

Wash and dry the liver slices. Remove any membranes from the outside edges of the meat so that the liver will not curl up when it is cooked.

Sprinkle the liver with salt and pepper and rub the meat with the oil.

Place the liver under a hot broiler and cook for just a few minutes on each side. Broiling time will depend on the thickness of the meat. It should be crusty and brown on the outside and very pink on the inside. Liver does not take long to cook, so be careful not to dry out the steaks.

Place a slice of green peppercorn butter on each liver steak and serve immediately.

This recipe serves four.

Alternate: The liver can be pan sautéed instead of being broiled. I prefer to do this if the slices of liver are not too thick. Salt and pepper the liver slices and dredge them very lightly in flour. Heat a few tablespoons of oil in a frying pan and cook the meat over high heat for just a few minutes on each side. You still want your liver to be very pink on the inside. Serve immediately topped with some of the herb butter.

CALVES LIVER WITH SHALLOTS AND VINEGAR

The whole secret of this dish is not to overcook the liver. Very thin calves liver takes no more than one minute to cook or else it will toughen. Try it this way for a really tender and delicious treat.

8 very thin slices of calves liver
3 Tbsp. butter
2 Tbsp. oil
salt, pepper
flour for dredging

2 Tbsp. chopped shallots
¼ cup water
2 Tbsp. Sherry wine vinegar
2 Tbsp. Demi-Glace*
1 Tbsp. chopped parsley

This dish only takes two to three minutes to cook, so assemble all the ingredients before you begin.

Trim off any membranes visible on the outside of the liver slices so that they will not curl when cooked. Rinse and dry the meat well.

Heat two tablespoons of butter along with the oil in a large frying pan.

Salt and pepper the liver slices and dredge them very lightly in the flour.

Add the liver to the pan (you will probably have to do this in two or three batches) and sauté over high heat for about thirty seconds on each side.

Remove the liver slices to a serving plate and keep them warm.

Pour the extra oil and butter out of the pan.
Add the shallots and cook them for one minute, just until they soften and begin to turn brown.

Add the water, vinegar and the Demi-Glace, scraping the bottom of the pan well.

Cook for a minute or two until the sauce begins to thicken. Taste to correct the seasonings.

Add the remaining tablespoon of butter and remove the pan from the heat. Swirl the pan until the butter is melted.

Pour the sauce over the liver, sprinkle with the chopped parsley and serve immediately.

This recipe serves four, two slices of liver per person.

*If you do not have Demi-Glace, use an Espagnole, page 52, or an Enriched Beef Stock, page 53.

Margarine can be substituted for butter in this recipe, but the sauce will not have as much flavor.

Try to use Sherry wine vinegar, it has a wonderfully mellow flavor.

RACK OF LAMB en PERSILLADE

The combination of the mustard and crumb topping with the persillade gives the lamb a wonderful flavor.

The persillade, or parsley stuffing, used with a rack of lamb in this recipe will work equally well with either a shoulder or a leg of lamb. The walnuts in the persillade are used for texture as well as taste.

1 rack of lamb
2 Tbsp. walnuts, chopped
3 Tbsp. chopped parsley
1 tsp. butter or margarine
½ tsp. lemon juice
1 slice lemon rind, cut into dice
½ clove garlic
salt, pepper
1 to 2 Tbsp. oil
1 or 2 Tbsp. Dijon mustard
¼ cup dried bread crumbs

Leave the rack of lamb in one piece, but have your butcher crack the bones at the back so that you can cut it into chops for serving. Trim off all the extra fat from the meat.

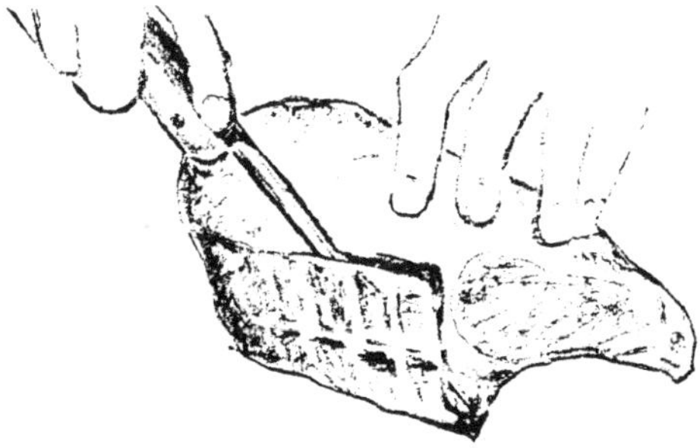

Cut to free the meat from the bone just at the backbone area, leaving the meat in place on the bone.
Place the walnuts, parsley, butter or margarine, lemon juice and rind, garlic, salt and pepper into a food processor or blender. Process until the mixture is well blended. Or chop the nuts, parsley, lemon rind and garlic finely by hand. Mix with the butter or margarine, lemon juice, salt and pepper.

Place this stuffing mixture between the meat and the bone where you cut it free at the back end of the rack.

The lamb can be stuffed with the persillade and refrigerated early in the day before roasting. Bring the meat to room temperature before cooking.

Sprinkle the outside of the rack with salt and pepper and rub with a little oil on all sides.

Oil the bottom of a roasting pan. Place the meat in the pan, bone side up.

Roast the lamb in a 425 degree oven for fifteen minutes.

Turn the lamb so that the bone side is now down and continue to roast for another fifteen minutes.

Remove the rack from the oven and let it cool for a few minutes.
Spread the mustard onto the top of the rack and sprinkle it with the bread crumbs.
Place the lamb back into the oven for another ten to fifteen minutes, or until the crumbs are browned.

At this point the meat should still be a little pink inside and well done on the outside. If you like your lamb more well done, roast it a few minutes longer.

If the meat is done to your liking but the crust is not browned, place the rack under a hot broiler for a minute or two but be careful not to let it burn.

Remove the meat from the oven and let it rest for five to ten minutes, covered lightly.

Slice into chops and serve. One whole rack serves three.

The lamb can be prepared a half-hour or so before serving time, up to the point of putting it back into the oven with the crumb topping. Just let it sit at room temperature until you are ready to continue. Do not refrigerate the lamb.

ROAST STUFFED LEG OF LAMB

A roast leg of lamb makes a wonderful dish for company or a delicious Sunday family dinner. You could also use the persillade on page 144 as a stuffing. Double the amount given for a leg of lamb.

1 leg of lamb, 6 to 7 pounds
salt, pepper
stuffing (recipe follows)
3 Tbsp. oil
water, as needed
1 medium onion, chopped
1 carrot, chopped
1 clove garlic
1 bay leaf
½ tsp. thyme
3 to 4 parsley sprigs
½ cup white wine

Cut the shank end off the leg of lamb and save it for braising. Bone and butterfly the lamb. Ask for the bones if your butcher does this for you as you will need them to make the sauce,

Remove as much of the fat and thick white outer skin as possible from the lamb. Lamb fat has a terrible taste.

Flatten the roast into a rectangular shape, boned side up, as best you can. Salt and pepper the meat.

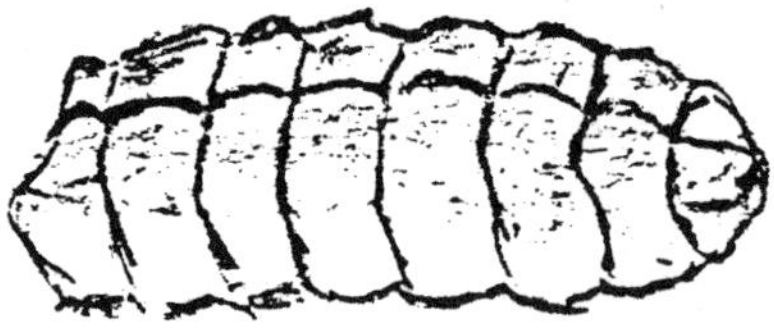

Prepare whichever stuffing you prefer and spread the filling evenly over the meat. Leave the edges clear on all sides.

Roll the lamb and tie it securely so that it keeps its shape while cooking.

Salt and pepper the outside of the roast and rub it with one tablespoon of the oil.

The lamb can be prepared to this point early in the day and refrigerated.

Heat the remaining oil in a shallow roasting pan on top of the stove.

Brown the lamb roll on all sides, turning. Add the extra bones to the pan and pour in one-half cup of water.

Place the lamb into a 375 degree oven and roast for forty-five minutes.

Turn the lamb over and add the onion, carrot, garlic, bay leaf, thyme and parsley to the pan.

Return the meat to the oven and continue roasting until the lamb is done. Add more water to the pan as needed to keep the vegetables from sticking while the lamb cooks.

Total roasting time for the leg of lamb should be about one hour and thirty minutes to two hours. The lamb should feel tender when tested with a fork and the juices should run clear. The lamb tastes best if it is still a little pink on the inside.

Remove the lamb from the oven and let it rest for at least ten or fifteen minutes while you prepare the sauce.

Pour off any extra fat from the roasting pan. Place the pan on top of the stove and heat.

Add the white wine and one-half cup water to the roasting pan. Scrape to loosen all the sediment from the bottom of the pan. Simmer for a few minutes.

Do not be afraid to add more water if your sauce cooks down too much.

Remove the bones from the pan and strain the sauce into a small saucepan.

Remove as much fat as possible from the top of the sauce. If too thick, add water. If too thin, thicken by adding a teaspoon of cornstarch mixed with a little water to the boiling sauce. Add salt and pepper to taste.

Remove the strings from the lamb and cut it into thick slices. Serve on a platter with the sauce on the side.

This recipe serves six to eight.

WESTPHALIAN HAM STUFFING

Of all the stuffing recipes I have ever tried, this one is my favorite for a leg of lamb.

1 Tbsp. butter
1 medium onion, chopped
2 ounces Westphalian ham or
  Canadian bacon, diced
2 cloves garlic, crushed
1 cup fresh bread crumbs

2 Tbsp. chopped parsley
1 tsp. oregano
1 tsp. lemon juice
1 egg
salt, pepper

Heat the butter in a small frying pan.

Add the onion and the ham and sauté for a few minutes until the onion is golden.

Add the garlic and continue to cook for one more minute. Remove the pan from the heat and cool a little.

Place the bread crumbs, parsley, oregano and lemon juice into a bowl. Add the contents of the frying pan to the bowl. Add the egg and mix the stuffing well. Add salt and pepper to taste.

This recipe is enough to stuff one boned leg of lamb.

The stuffing can be prepared a day ahead of time and refrigerated.

LEFTOVER CURRY

This dish can be made with almost any leftover meat you have around - beef, lamb, pork, chicken. Shrimp curry is good, too. Use up any odds and ends, or combination of them that you have in the refrigerator.

2 Tbsp. oil or butter
1 large onion, chopped
½ cup mushrooms, sliced
1 green pepper, diced
1 red pepper, diced
3 cups cooked diced meat
2 cups cooked rice*
2 tsp. Madras curry powder
½ cup white wine
1 cup leftover meat gravy or stock
½ cup raisins
2 cups fresh pineapple, diced, or 1 can (with juice)
1 banana, diced
4 to 6 Tbsp. mango chutney
salt, pepper

Heat the oil or the butter in a large frying pan.

Add the onion and cook for a few minutes.

Then add the mushrooms, peppers, meat and rice. Cook and stir for two or three minutes.

Sprinkle on the curry powder and stir it in well.

Immediately add the wine and the stock to the pan and mix well.

Stir in the raisins, diced pineapple, banana and the chutney.

Season to taste with salt and pepper. Add more curry powder if you like your dish spicier.

Simmer the curry for ten to fifteen minutes and serve hot.

This recipe serves six.

*If you do not have any leftover rice, you can make some right along with the curry. Sauté the onion and the mushrooms in the butter or oil for a few minutes. Add ¾ cup raw rice to the pan and stir to coat the grains in the butter. Add 1¼ cups chicken stock to the pan and bring the liquid to a boil. Cover and bake the rice in a 375 degree oven for fifteen minutes. Remove the pan from the oven and place back on top of the stove. Stir in the diced meat and the peppers. Continue with the rest of the recipe as instructed.

WESTPHALIAN PORK CHOPS

Plain breaded pork chops will never taste as good after you try them this way. The flavor combination of the pork with the ham and herbs is fantastic.

2 tsp. chopped parsley
1 clove garlic, crushed
½ tsp. freshly ground black pepper
½ tsp. rosemary, chopped
¼ tsp. salt
2 tsp. bread crumbs
2 tsp. oil

4 loin pork chops, ¾ inch thick
4 slices Westphalian or boiled ham
salt, pepper
flour for dredging
1 egg
dried bread crumbs, about 1 cup
oil for frying chops

Mix together all the ingredients in the first column. This will be your herb stuffing mix.

Trim off all visible fat and cut a pocket in each pork chop.

Place the ham slices in front of you. Divide the herb mixture evenly onto the ham slices and roll them into half or thirds.

Place the rolled ham packet inside the pocket you have cut in the pork chops and press with the palm of your hand to seal.

Salt and pepper the chops. Dredge them in flour.

Beat the egg with a teaspoon or two of water. Dip the floured chops into the egg wash.

Spread the crumbs onto a flat plate. Dredge the chops in the crumbs.

The pork chops can be prepared to this point and refrigerated for a few hours.

When you are ready to cook the chops, heat a scant one-quarter inch of oil in a large pan.

When hot, add the chops and cook at a medium high heat for about five minutes on each side.

This is enough time to cook the pork yet still have it remain juicy. The outside crust should be nice and brown. Serve immediately.

This recipe serves four, one chop per person. If your family eats larger portions, just increase the recipe.

PIQUANT PORK CHOPS

The sauce used on these chops has a smokey barbeque taste. For those who like that kind of flavor, this recipe is fast and easy.

4 loin pork chops
salt, pepper
flour for dredging
3 Tbsp. oil
¼ cup red wine
½ cup beef stock
1 tsp. tomato paste
1½ tsp. Dijon mustard
1 Tbsp. brown sugar
pinch thyme

Trim the pork chops of all visible fat. Season them with salt and pepper and dredge the chops lightly in flour.

Heat the oil in a frying pan.

Add the pork chops to the hot oil and cook them for just three to four minutes on each side, only until they are nicely browned.

Remove the chops to an ovenproof platter and place them into a 375 degree oven while you make your sauce. This way the chops will finish cooking at the same time that your sauce is ready.

Pour the extra fat out of the frying pan.

Add the wine and the stock, scraping the bottom of the pan to dislodge any brown particles which may be stuck there.

With a whisk, mix in the tomato paste, mustard, sugar and thyme.

Bring the sauce to a boil, then turn the heat down and let the sauce simmer for about five minutes.

The sauce will reduce in volume and become thicker and dark brown in color. Add salt and pepper to taste.

When the sauce is thick, remove the chops from the oven, pour the sauce over them and serve.

This recipe serves four, one chop per person.

Vegetables

ACORN SQUASH AND APPLE CASSEROLE

The flavors of acorn squash and apples blend beautifully together. Serve with chicken or turkey instead of the usual sweet potatoes - a nice change.

2 medium acorn squash
2 large apples
¼ cup brown sugar
1 tsp. cinnamon
2 Tbsp. butter
¼ cup water

Cut the squash in half and remove the seeds.

Cut it in half again (quarters). Then cut the squash lengthwise into slices about one-third to one-half inch thick.

Peel the slices, using a potato peeler or a paring knife. It is much easier to peel the squash in slices than to try and peel it when it is whole.

Peel and core the apples. Cut them in half and slice thinly. You can do this easily in a food processor.

Butter well the bottom of a large casserole.

Place slices of the squash and apples alternately in a circular pattern in the pan.

Sprinkle them with the sugar and the cinnamon.

Dot the top of the casserole with the two tablespoons of butter.

Pour the quarter-cup of water into the bottom of the pan, around the squash and apples.

Cover the casserole and place it in a 375 degree oven for thirty minutes.

Remove the cover and continue to bake for an additional fifteen to twenty minutes, or until the squash is tender and the liquid has evaporated.

This recipe serves four to six.

Margarine can be substituted for the butter in this recipe, if necessary.

STUFFED ACORN SQUASH

This is a wonderful recipe to use when your acorn squash does not have a lot of flavor. The ingredients used in this filling would make anything taste good.

4 small to medium acorn squash
2 Tbsp. butter
1 small onion, finely chopped
2 Tbsp. chopped parsley
½ cup sour cream
3 Tbsp. brown sugar
½ tsp. cinnamon
salt, pepper
1 to 1½ cups dried bread crumbs

Cut the acorn squash in half and remove the seeds.

Place the squash, skin side up, in a pan and fill with one-half inch of warm water.

Bake the squash in a 350 degree oven until they are tender, about forty to fifty minutes.

Cool the squash for a few minutes - until you can handle them easily.

Scrape out the pulp with a spoon, being careful not to puncture the shells. Mash or purée the pulp.

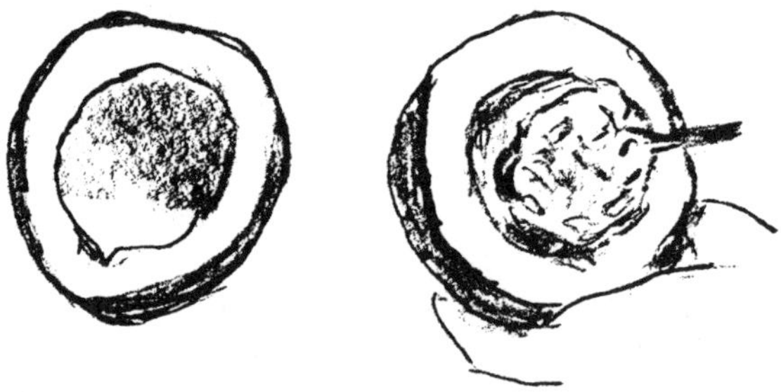

Heat the butter in a small frying pan. Add the onion and sauté until it is golden.

In a bowl, mix together the mashed squash, onion, parsley, sour cream, sugar, cinnamon, salt, pepper and one cup of the bread crumbs.

Stir well and add more bread crumbs, if needed, to make a fairly firm mixture.

Taste and correct the seasonings. You may need to add more sugar, depending upon the natural sweetness of the squash. Three spoons are enough if the squash are sweet, but you will need more if they are not.

This mixture will be enough to fill six squash halves. Pick out the six best looking shells and fill them.

The squash may be readied to this point early in the day and refrigerated until serving time.

Place the squash, filled side up, into a buttered casserole and bake in a 375 degree oven until piping hot, about thirty minutes.

This recipe serves six.

BEETS WITH SOUR CREAM AND HORSERADISH

Do not be put off by the title of this recipe. You will not taste the horseradish, it merely spices up the sauce a little.

2 bunches fresh beets (about 8)
2 Tbsp. butter
1 tsp. salt, or more
freshly ground black pepper
2 Tbsp. flour
1 cup sour cream
2 tsp. grated white horseradish
2 tsp. lemon juice

Wash the beets well but do not peel them. Cut off the tops, leaving about a half inch of the stems attached to the beets. Leave the tips attached also.

Cook the beets in lots of boiling water until they are tender, about an hour to an hour and a half. Add more water as needed to keep the beets covered while cooking.

Drain the beets and place them under cold running water. As soon as they are cool enough to handle, slip off the skins.

The beets can be cooked ahead and refrigerated.

At serving time, slice the beets.

Heat the butter in a frying pan. Add the beets, the teaspoon of salt and lots of pepper.

Sauté for a few minutes.

Mix the flour into the sour cream and stir this into the beets.

Add the horseradish and the lemon juice. Cook for about five minutes, stirring occasionally.

Serve hot. This recipe serves four to six.

The horseradish can be left out and just the sour cream and flour combination used in this recipe. Taste and add the lemon juice if you want your beets to have a little more tang.

CARROTS WITH MADEIRA

Carrots take on a delightful flavor when cooked with a little Madeira. The hazelnuts can be eliminated if you do not like them, as the carrots are perfectly delicious alone. The hazelnuts, however, do lend a lovely flavor and a little bit of crunch to the carrots.

6 to 8 carrots
2 Tbsp. butter
2 Tbsp. chopped shallots
salt, pepper
½ cup Madeira
1 cup water
2 Tbsp. chopped toasted hazelnuts

Peel the carrots and cut them into very thin slices.

Heat the butter in a saucepan, add the shallots and cook them for a minute or two.

Add the carrots to the pan and season with salt and pepper. Stir to coat all the carrots with the butter.

Add the Madeira and the water and bring the liquid to a boil.

Cover the pan and simmer until the carrots are tender, about fifteen to twenty minutes.

Add more water, if needed as the carrots cook, to keep them from sticking.

Stir in the toasted hazelnuts and cook for another minute or two.

Serve hot. This recipe serves four.

Margarine can be substituted for the butter in this recipe, if necessary.

CARROT PUDDING

Sugar and spice and everything nice - what more could a carrot need.

6 large carrots
1 tsp. sugar
salt
½ cup butter
½ cup brown sugar
2 eggs
1 tsp. lemon juice
¾ cup flour
1 tsp. baking powder
¼ tsp. grated nutmeg

Peel the carrots and cut them into large pieces. Cook them in boiling water with a teaspoon of sugar and some salt added until they are tender.

Drain the carrots well and purée them.

The carrots can be cooked and puréed a day ahead of time. Store covered in the refrigerator.

Cream the butter with the brown sugar until light and fluffy.

Add the eggs to the butter-sugar mixture one at a time, beating well.

Then stir the puréed carrots and the lemon juice into this mixture.

Mix together the flour, the baking powder and the nutmeg and stir the dry ingredients into the carrot mixture.

Taste and correct the seasonings.

Pour the carrot pudding into a well-buttered small casserole.

Bake in a 350 degree oven for about forty-five to fifty minutes, or until firm and browned.

Serve directly from the casserole.

This recipe serves four.

EGGPLANT CASSEROLE

Eggplant, topped with a tomato and herb sauce, topped again with a rich and creamy layer - a deliciously different do-ahead combination.

1 medium eggplant
salt, pepper
½ cup oil or more
1 onion, chopped
1 clove garlic, crushed
1 cup canned plum tomatoes
1 Tbsp. tomato paste
1 Tbsp. chopped parsley
1 Tbsp. chopped fresh dill
2/3 cup sour cream
¼ cup heavy cream

Peel and slice the eggplant into rounds about one-half inch thick.

Sprinkle the slices with salt and let them sit for thirty minutes. Then wipe the eggplant slices dry.

Line two baking sheets with aluminum foil and place the eggplant slices onto the sheets.

Using a pastry brush, brush both sides of each slice with a little oil.

Bake the eggplant in a 350 degree oven for about twenty minutes or until fairly tender, turning once.* Reserve.

Meanwhile, heat one tablespoon of oil in a small frying pan.

Add the onion, sprinkle with salt and pepper and sauté until golden.

Add the garlic and the plum tomatoes along with the juice from the can. Break apart the tomatoes with your spoon.

Stir in the tomato paste. Simmer the sauce for fifteen minutes.

Stir the parsley and dill into the sauce and taste to correct the seasonings.

Place the cooked eggplant slices in an even layer in the bottom of a large buttered casserole.

Smooth the tomato sauce over the eggplant.

Mix together the sour cream and the heavy cream and pour this mixture over the tomato sauce.

The casserole can be completed to this point and refrigerated until serving time.

Bake the casserole in a 375 degree oven for about twenty minutes or until hot and the topping set.

Serve hot. This recipe serves four.

A layer of grated cheese can be used either on top of or instead of the cream topping. The dish is good either way.

*The eggplant slices could also be sautéed in butter or oil instead of being baked. I just find it easier and less greasy to bake the eggplant this way.

GLAZED PEARL ONIONS

24 small white pearl onions
3 Tbsp. butter
1 Tbsp. sugar
pinch salt
water to cover

Peel the pearl onions.

Place them in a frying pan with the butter, sugar and a pinch of salt. Add water to the pan so that the onions are covered.

Bring the water to a boil and cook uncovered until the water evaporates and the sugar and butter form a glaze. This should take about fifteen to twenty minutes.

Shake the pan often as the glaze begins to form to keep the onions from sticking.

By cooking them this way, the onions should be both tender and nicely browned at the same time.

Serve hot. This recipe serves four.

Margarine can be substituted for the butter in this recipe, if necessary.

LAYERED SPINACH AND CHEESE PUFF

This is a beautiful company dish that can be completely prepared early in the day, then refrigerated until time to bake. Not quite a soufflé, but close. It is much easier to prepare and is foolproof.

Spinach Layer:

1 ten-ounce package frozen spinach, or 1 pound fresh
2 Tbsp. chopped shallots
2 Tbsp. butter
1 Tbsp. flour
¼ cup heavy cream
salt, pepper
dash nutmeg

Cheese Layer:

2 Tbsp. butter
2½ Tbsp. flour
1½ cups milk
2 eggs
½ cup grated Swiss cheese
salt, white pepper

Topping:

¼ cup grated Swiss or Parmesan cheese
1 Tbsp. butter

First prepare the spinach layer. Blanch the spinach in boiling salted water for a few minutes.

Refresh under cold water, drain and squeeze dry. Chop the the spinach.

Sauté the shallots in the butter for a minute or two.

Sprinkle the shallots with the flour. Stir and cook for one minute longer.

Pour in the cream and then add the spinach. Season to taste with the salt, pepper and nutmeg. Mix well and set aside.

Next, prepare the cheese layer. Melt the butter in a saucepan and stir in the flour.

Cook for a minute or two and remove from the heat.

Heat the milk to the boiling point in a separate saucepan. Stir the hot milk into the cooled roux.

Remove the pan from the heat and cool for just a few minutes.

Mix the eggs, one at a time, into this cream base. Stir in the cheese and season to taste with the salt and pepper.

Butter a one and one-half quart soufflé dish.

Pour a thin layer of the cheese mixture into the bottom of the dish.

Spread the spinach layer over this. Then pour in the rest of the cheese mixture.

Sprinkle with the grated cheese for the topping and dot with butter.

This dish can be completely prepared before baking and refrigerated until serving time.

Bake in a 400 degree oven for fifty-five minutes to one hour.

Serve immediately. This recipe serves four to six.

STRING BEANS WITH MUSHROOMS

A delightful flavor combination, especially when tomatoes are in season. Good with fish or fowl.

1 pound string beans
salt
2 Tbsp. butter
2 tomatoes
2 Tbsp. chopped shallots
¼ pound mushrooms, sliced
juice of ½ lemon
pepper

Cook the string beans in lots of boiling salted water until they are barely tender. Refresh under cold water and drain them well.

The cooked string beans can be refrigerated for a day or two.

Seed and dice, but do not peel the tomatoes. Reserve until needed.

At serving time, heat the butter in a large frying pan.

Add the shallots and the mushrooms and stir and cook for a few minutes just until the mushrooms are tender.

Add the string beans to the pan and cook for another minute.

Stir in the diced tomatoes and the lemon juice. Add salt and pepper to taste.

Cook and stir for just a minute to heat the tomatoes. They should be just hot, not cooked.

Taste to correct the seasonings. You may need a little more lemon juice.

Serve immediately. This recipe serves four.

Margarine can be substituted for the butter in this recipe, if necessary.

BAKED ZUCCHINI

Zucchini prepared this way is wonderful with barbequed meat or poultry.

4 zucchini
salt
2 cloves garlic, crushed
juice of 1 lemon
4 Tbsp. oil
pepper
2 Tbsp. chopped parsley

Do not peel the zucchini. Cut them in half lengthwise and score the top of the flesh diagonally with a knife.

Sprinkle the zucchini with a little salt and let them sit for thirty minutes. Wipe the zucchini dry.

Crush the garlic to a very fine paste. Mix the garlic with the lemon juice and the oil.

Place the dried zucchini into a greased baking pan, flesh side up.

Spoon the garlic mixture over the zucchini and sprinkle them with a little pepper and the parsley. Cover the pan.

The zucchini can be prepared to this point early in the day and refrigerated until serving time.

Bake the zucchini in a 400 degree oven for twenty minutes, or until they are tender.

Serve hot. This recipe serves four.

Olive oil can be substituted for the plain oil if desired.

ZUCCHINI CASSEROLE au GRATIN

This is a delicate and beautifully flavored casserole that is just right for that special company dinner. A real favorite in our house any time.

7 medium zucchini
salt
4 Tbsp. butter
1 medium onion, chopped
pepper
1 heaping Tbsp. flour
1½ cups milk
2 Tbsp. sour cream
3 Tbsp. grated Swiss cheese
2 Tbsp. butter

Topping:

¼ cup fresh white bread crumbs
¼ cup grated Swiss or Parmesan cheese

Wash but do not peel the zucchini. Trim off the ends and cut the zucchini into julienne.

Sprinkle the julienned zucchini with a little salt. Mix and let the zucchini sit for thirty minutes.

Squeeze well to get rid of the extra moisture.

Heat two tablespoons of the butter in a frying pan.

Add the onion, sprinkle with salt and pepper and cook until golden.

Add the zucchini and the remaining two tablespoons of butter to the pan and sauté, stirring, for five minutes.

Sprinkle the flour over the zucchini and mix it in well.

Pour in the milk, one-half cup at a time, stirring until it is well absorbed before adding more.

Stir the sour cream and the grated cheese into this mixture and add salt and pepper to taste.

Pour the zucchini mixture into a well buttered small casserole. Smooth down the top.

Sprinkle with the bread crumbs and the grated cheese for the topping. Dot with butter.

The casserole may be prepared to this point early in the day and refrigerated until needed. Remove from the refrigerator thirty minutes before baking.

Bake the casserole in a 375 degree oven for thirty-five to forty minutes. The zucchini should be very hot and the topping well browned.

This recipe serves six.

Starches

CHEESE TOPPED POTATO SLICES

Crunchy and delicious, these cheese-topped potato slices are a favorite with children as well as with adults.

4 Idaho baking potatoes
½ cup butter, softened
1 egg
4 ounces grated Swiss cheese
salt, pepper

This dish can be prepared with either peeled or unpeeled potatoes. Naturally, I like them better unpeeled. If leaving the skins on, scrub and dry the potatoes. If not, then peel them.

Cut the raw potatoes horizontally into one-half inch round slices.

Mix together the butter, egg, grated cheese and some salt and pepper. I find this easiest to do with my hands.

Place about a teaspoon of the mixture on top of each potato round and flatten it out evenly to coat the top of the potato slice.

Butter a large baking dish. Place the potatoes, cheese side up, into the dish.

The potatoes can be prepared to this point and refrigerated for a little while, only. If left for too long, they will turn brown.

Bake the potatoes in a 375 degree oven for forty minutes. The potato slices should be tender and the topping nicely browned.

Serve hot. This recipe serves four to six.

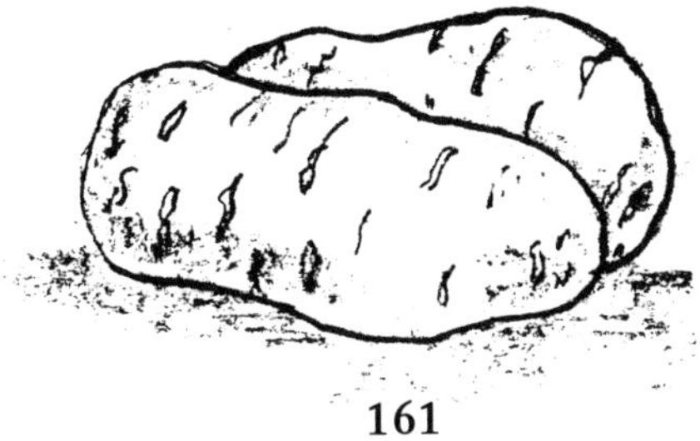

POMMES de TERRE au GRATIN

This rich and delicious dish goes well with almost any type of meat or fowl.

1 small clove garlic
2 Tbsp. butter
3 large potatoes, sliced thin
salt, white pepper
1 cup half and half
3 Tbsp. grated Swiss cheese
2 Tbsp. dried bread crumbs

Cut the garlic clove in half. Rub it around the bottom and sides of a wide ovenproof casserole, pressing hard to extract the juices.

Discard the garlic. Let the pan dry for a few minutes. Then coat the pan well with butter.

Slice the potatoes very thin - the food processor does a great job.

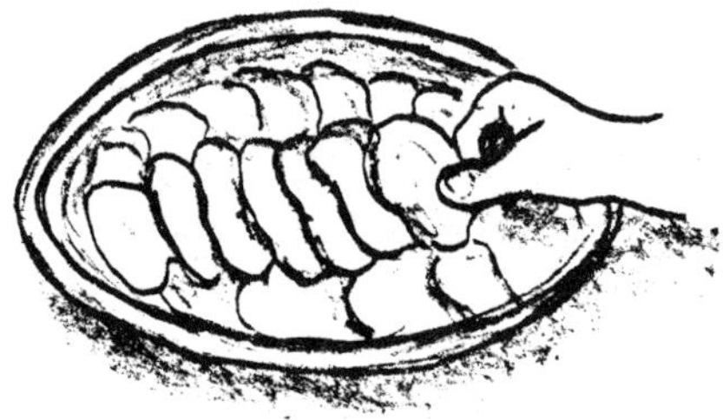

Place one-third of the potatoes into the pan in an even layer. Sprinkle with salt and pepper.

Repeat two more times, until all the potatoes are layered in the pan. Then pour the half and half over the potatoes.

Sprinkle the top of the casserole with the grated cheese and the bread crumbs. Dot with the butter.

These potatoes cannot sit once they are prepared or they will turn brown. When the casserole is ready, place it directly into the oven to bake.

Bake in a 375 degree oven for fifty to sixty minutes or until the potatoes are tender and the top of the casserole is browned.

Serve hot. This recipe serves four to six.

You can substitute whole cream for the half and half in this recipe if you like your potatoes to have a richer flavor. Parmesan cheese can be substituted for the Swiss cheese.

The potato casserole must be cooked immediately once it is prepared. But it can be allowed to sit at room temperature for a half hour or so after it is baked. Reheat briefly before serving. The casserole is best, however, when fresh.

BAKED STUFFED POTATOES

You can use leftover baked as well as fresh potatoes to make this dish. Be careful when you scoop out the potatoes to leave enough shell to fill. If they break, you can always bake the filling alone in a buttered casserole. Baked stuffed potatoes are marvelous with grilled meat.

2 large Idaho baking potatoes
1 Tbsp. butter
¼ cup sour cream
2 Tbsp. milk or cream
3 Tbsp. grated Swiss cheese
½ tsp. salt
white pepper
½ tsp. paprika

Scrub and dry the potatoes. Prick them once with a fork, then bake the potatoes in a 400 degree oven for one hour, or until they feel tender when pressed with your fingers.

Let the potatoes cool a little, then cut them in half, lengthwise.

Scoop out the potato pulp with a spoon. Try not to make a hole in the skins.

Mash the potato pulp. You can use either a ricer, a potato masher, a food mill or a mixer with a flat blade. Do not use a food processor, it will ruin the consistency of the mixture.

I find that the easiest way to prepare this dish is to use a mixer fitted with a flat blade attachment.
Beat the butter into the mashed potatoes.

Add the sour cream, milk, cheese, salt and pepper. Beat until the mixture is very smooth.

Fill the potato shells with this mixture. Do not mound the potatoes. Keep them flat as they will puff when baked.

Sprinkle the potatoes with the paprika.

The potatoes can be readied to this point and refrigerated until serving time.

Place the potatoes in a buttered shallow pan and bake them in a 400 degree oven for twenty minutes or until they are hot and browned.

This recipe serves four, one stuffed potato half per person.

LAYERED POTATO CAKE

Potato cakes are both easier to handle and turn out better if you bake rather than boil the potatoes used. I find that the consistency of baked Idahos are just perfect for these recipes. Never use a food processor or blender to mash the potatoes. You will end up with potato soup - it purées them much too finely for the potato cake recipes. I prefer to use a potato ricer - they are inexpensive and handy gadgets that always work well.

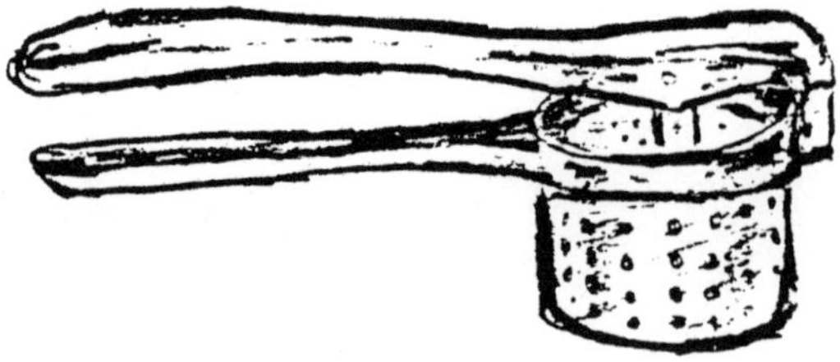

You have an added bonus with both this and the following recipe - potato skins. In my house we bake the skins separately with a little butter and salt and serve the baked skins right along with the potato cakes. There are some people, like me, who would rather have the crunchy skins anytime.

3 large Idaho baking potatoes
3 Tbsp. butter
salt, pepper
3 ounces sour cream
3 ounces light cream
3 to 4 Tbsp. grated Swiss cheese

Scrub and dry the potatoes. Prick them once with a fork. Bake the potatoes in a 400 degree oven for one hour or until they feel tender when pressed with your fingers.

Let the potatoes cool for just a few minutes, then cut them in half and scoop out the pulp. Mash the potato pulp.

Add the butter to the potatoes, sprinkle with some salt and pepper and mix well.

Butter well an eight inch round pan or a small casserole. Place the mashed and seasoned potatoes into the pan and press them down well.

Stir the sour cream and the light cream together until they form a smooth mixture. Pour this mixture on top of the potato layer.

Sprinkle with the grated cheese.

The recipe can be prepared to this point ahead early in the day and the casserole refrigerated until time to bake.

Place the casserole into a 375 degree oven for twenty minutes (or longer if refrigerated). The potatoes should be hot, the topping set and the cheese melted.

Serve immediately. This recipe serves four or five.

Do not reheat or freeze the potato cake.

POMMES MACAIRE

2 large Idaho baking potatoes
1 very small onion, chopped
3 to 4 Tbsp. butter
1 Tbsp. chopped parsley
salt, pepper
dash nutmeg
1 egg yolk
flour for dredging

Scrub and dry the potatoes. Prick them once with a fork. Bake the potatoes in a 400 degree oven for one hour or until they feel tender when pressed with your fingers.

Let the potatoes cool for just a few minutes.

Sauté the onion in one tablespoon of the butter until it is golden and set aside.

Split the potatoes in half lengthwise and scoop out the pulp.

Put the potato pulp through a ricer or a food mill. You can also use a hand masher or a mixer, but not a food processor.

Add the sautéed onion, parsley, salt, pepper, nutmeg and the egg yolk to the mashed potatoes. Mix well and correct the seasonings. Set the potato mixture aside to cool.

When cool enough to handle easily, form the potatoes into small patties. You will have enough potatoes to make eight to ten cakes.

The potatoes can be readied to this point and refrigerated until serving time.

Heat the remaining butter in a frying pan.

Dredge the potato cakes lightly in the flour. Do not do this ahead of time as the patties will get sticky.

Sauté the potato cakes in the butter for a few minutes on each side, until they are nicely browned. Serve immediately. Serves four - two patties per person.

Margarine can be substituted for the butter in this recipe.

Alternate: You can add bacon to the potato cakes for an equally delicious treat. Dice two slices of bacon and sauté along with the onions, eliminating the one tablespoon of butter. Continue with the rest of the recipe.

CANDIED SWEET POTATOES

These potatoes are boiled, lightly covered with a sauce and then baked in the oven. They come out crunchy and coated with a glaze rather than swimming in a lot of sticky sauce.

4 sweet potatoes
2 Tbsp. butter
¼ cup dark brown sugar
¼ cup orange juice
dash cinnamon

Boil the sweet potatoes until they are almost tender. Do not overcook them as they will bake again later. Cool the potatoes. Peel and cut them into quarters.

Heat the butter in a wide ovenproof pan.

Stir the sugar, orange juice and cinnamon into the butter. Cook and stir until the sugar is melted.

Remove the pan from the heat and place the potatoes into the pan. Turn to cover all sides of the potatoes with the sauce.

The potatoes can be readied to this point and refrigerated until serving time.

Place the potatoes in a 375 degree oven and bake for thirty minutes. The sauce will be absorbed by the potatoes and they will be lightly glazed and delicious.

Serve hot. This recipe serves four to six.

Margarine can be substituted for the butter in this recipe.

PLAIN RICE PILAF

I like to use one and one-half cups of stock to every cup of rice cooked rather than the standard two cups found in most pilaf recipes. The grains are always dry and separate when prepared my way. Rice is much too wet for my taste when cooked with double the amount of liquid.

Chicken stock is usually used to make a rice pilaf. However, other stocks can be substituted. Try using a fish stock when you are serving the rice with fish - the flavors blend well together. A vegetable stock can also be used when you want a completely meatless meal. Veal stock or beef stock work too - or even water in a pinch.

1 small onion, chopped
1 Tbsp. butter
1 cup rice
1½ cups stock
salt, pepper

Heat the butter in a saucepan. Add the onion and cook for just a few minutes.

Add the rice to the pan and stir to coat all the grains with the butter.

Pour the stock into the pan and bring it to a boil. Stir well.

Cover the pan with a lid and place it into a 375 degree oven for twenty minutes.

Remove the pan from the oven and let it sit for five minutes with the lid on.

Then stir the rice, add salt and pepper to taste, and serve hot. If you are using a canned stock, the rice may not need any additional seasoning.

This recipe serves four.

Margarine can be substituted for the butter in all rice pilaf recipes.

Herbs can be added to the basic pilaf to perk up the flavor. For example, try a little pinch of thyme and a piece of bay leaf when you add the stock to the rice. Remove the bay leaf before serving.

To make a saffron rice pilaf, add a pinch of saffron to the rice along with the chicken stock.

To make a green rice pilaf, stir one-half cup of chopped parsley into the cooked rice before serving.

Rice is best when freshly prepared. It can be reheated if necessary. Add a little water to the pan, cover the rice and reheat in the oven just until hot. Additional butter or margarine can be added to the rice if needed. Rice can be frozen. I don't like the taste or texture nearly as well as freshly cooked rice.

CURRIED RICE PILAF

The combination of the curry powder with the tomato paste gives this rice dish a beautiful color as well as a delightful flavor.

2 Tbsp. butter
1 small onion, chopped fine
1 Tbsp. tomato paste
1 tsp. curry powder
1 cup rice
1½ cups chicken stock
salt, pepper

Heat the butter in a saucepan. Add the onion to the pan and cook until it turns golden.

Mix the tomato paste and the curry powder into the cooked onion.

Add the rice. Cook and stir for a few minutes to coat the grains of rice with the butter.

Pour in the chicken stock and bring the liquid to a boil. Stir well, then cover the pan. Place the rice in a 375 degree oven and bake for twenty minutes.

Remove the pan from the oven and let the rice sit, covered, for five minutes. Stir the rice, add salt and pepper if desired, and serve.

This recipe serves four to six.

SPICED RICE PILAF

Beautifully aromatic and flavorful, this recipe has the color, taste and smell of an Indian rice pilaw.

1 small onion, minced
2 Tbsp. butter
1 cup rice
½ tsp. cinnamon
¼ tsp. ground cardomon
2 whole cloves
1½ cups chicken stock
½ cup fresh peas
salt, pepper

In a saucepan, sauté the onion in the butter until it is golden.

Add the rice to the pan, stirring to coat all the grains with the butter.

Mix the cinnamon, cardomon and cloves into the rice. Cook for a minute or two, to release the aroma of the spices.

Add the chicken stock and bring the liquid to a boil. Stir the rice well. Add the peas, stir once more and cover the pan.

Place the rice in a 375 degree oven and bake for twenty minutes. Remove the rice from the oven and let it sit, covered, for five minutes.

Stir the rice with a fork, add salt and pepper to taste and serve hot.

This recipe serves four.

If you are using frozen peas instead of fresh, add them after the rice has baked in the oven for ten minutes. Frozen peas need less cooking time than fresh.

WILD RICE WITH MUSHROOMS

Wild rice has a wonderfully nutty and distinctive flavor all its own. This recipe can be used either as a vegetable with or as a stuffing for fowl. Marvelous with little Cornish game hens or good even with duck or chicken.

1 cup wild rice
¼ cup butter
1 onion, finely chopped
salt, pepper
1 cup sliced mushrooms
½ cup double-strength beef stock

Wash the wild rice well in lots of running water. Drain.

Cook the rice in a pot of boiling salted water for thirty minutes, or until the rice is just tender. Drain well.

Heat the butter in a frying pan. Add the onion and cook until it is soft and golden, seasoning with salt and pepper.

Add the sliced mushrooms to the onion and cook until the mushrooms are dry.

Stir the cooked rice into the pan.

Add the beef stock and cook slowly until all the liquid is absorbed. This should take about ten minutes.

Season to taste with salt and pepper and serve hot.

This recipe makes six servings.

Margarine can be substituted for the butter in this recipe.

The rice can be reheated if necessary. Add a little additional water or stock to the pan, cover and heat on top of the stove or in the oven until warm. An extra spoon or two of butter will not hurt this dish, either.

WHITE BEAN CASSEROLE

This is a very French way of cooking beans. Only in France they would add creme fraiche to the beans instead of the mixture of sour cream and heavy cream. Wonderful with roast lamb.

1 cup dried great northern beans, cooked
3 slices bacon, diced
1 small onion, chopped
1 clove garlic, crushed
3 Tbsp. butter
salt, pepper
¼ cup heavy cream
½ cup sour cream
1 tsp. flour

Soak and cook the beans according to the package directions in boiling water with no salt added. Salt will make the beans tough. Drain them well.

The beans can be cooked and refrigerated for a few days, until needed.

Sauté the bacon and the onion together until the onion is golden. Add the garlic and cook for one minute longer.

Add the butter to the pan and stir in the cooked beans. Add salt and pepper to taste.

When the beans are hot, stir in the heavy cream and the sour cream, which has been mixed with the flour. Simmer for ten to fifteen minutes, stirring occasionally. Serve hot.

This recipe serves six.

Canned beans can be substituted for the dried beans. You will need two and one-half cups of beans for this recipe.

NOODLES WITH CABBAGE

For this dish I like to use a very firm noodle, preferably the little square variety that are found in many ethnic food stores (Hungarian, in this case). Use a thick noodle - even a good brand of dried fettuchini will work. Noodles and cabbage are a wonderful taste combination and are excellent with plain roast duck or even roast goose.

1 head cabbage
3 Tbsp. butter, or more if needed
1 large onion, chopped
salt
freshly ground black pepper
pinch of sugar
1 pound package of noodles

Shred the cabbage by using the thin slicing disc of a food processor or cut it into very thin slices by hand.

Heat the butter in a large frying pan.

Add the onion, salt, pepper and sugar and cook until the onion is golden.

Add the cabbage to the pan and stir well. Cover the pan and cook slowly.

Stir the cabbage every five minutes or so until it is tender and golden brown in color. Add more butter, if needed, to keep the cabbage from burning while it cooks. It should take about thirty to forty minutes to cook the cabbage.

The cabbage can be cooked ahead and refrigerated for a day or two.

Cook the noodles until they are barely tender in lots of boiling salted water. Pour the noodles into a colander.

Rinse the noodles with hot water to remove any extra starch and drain well.

Add the drained noodles to the cooked cabbage. Stir and cook until they both are hot.

Add lots of freshly ground black pepper and salt to taste. The noodles should be spicy.

This recipe serves eight or more.

Margarine can be substituted for the butter in this recipe.

The Noodles with Cabbage can be reheated but is best when freshly prepared.

NOODLES WITH CREAM

Rich and delicious - Noodles with Cream tastes like the fresh noodle and creme fraiche combination served in many restaurants in France. Excellent with the Beef Ragoût.

Use either medium or broad egg noodles for this dish. The recipe even works very well with fettuchini if you prefer the taste of a firmer noodle.

1 eight-ounce package noodles
1 to 2 Tbsp. butter
¼ cup heavy cream
½ cup sour cream
1 tsp. flour
salt, pepper

Cook the noodles in lots of boiling salted water until they are barely tender. The noodles will cook again, so do not overcook them. There is nothing worse than mushy noodles.

Pour the noodles into a colander and rinse them with hot water to remove the extra starch. Drain well.

Melt the butter in a frying pan. Add the noodles and toss to coat them with the butter.

Pour the heavy cream into the pan and stir it into the noodles.

Mix the sour cream and flour together and add them to the noodles.

Toss and stir until hot and thick. Add salt and pepper to taste and serve immediately.

This recipe serves four to six.

NOODLES WITH A MUSHROOM SAUCE

Mushrooms, cream and noodles always make a delightful combination. Fresh parsley can be substituted for the chives if they are unavailable.

1 eight-ounce package noodles
2 to 3 Tbsp. butter
2 Tbsp. chopped shallots
½ pound sliced mushrooms
½ cup heavy cream
salt, pepper
1 Tbsp. chopped chives

Use medium-sized noodles for this dish. Either egg noodles or fettuchini are fine.

Cook the noodles in lots of boiling salted water until barely tender. They will cook again.

While the noodles are cooking, heat the butter in a frying pan. Add the shallots and sauté for a minute or two.

Add the mushrooms, sprinkle with a little salt and pepper and continue to cook for a few minutes. Set aside until the noodles are ready.

When the noodles are cooked, pour them into a colander. Rinse the noodles under hot water to remove the extra starch and drain well.

Heat the partially cooked mushrooms and shallots and add the cooked noodles to the frying pan.

Pour in the heavy cream and toss and cook for a few minutes.

When very hot, season with salt and pepper to taste. Add the chives, toss again and serve immediately.

This recipe serves four to six.

CURRIED SCALLOPS WITH PASTA

I prefer the sweet taste of tiny bay scallops for this dish. Sea scallops will work as well, but you may want to cut them in half. Curried Scallops with Pasta makes a both delicious and quick dinner. They could even be served as an appetizer course or as a lunch.

½ pound pasta
2 shallots, chopped
4 Tbsp. butter
¾ pound scallops
¼ cup white wine
1 tsp. curry powder
½ cup heavy cream
1 egg
salt, pepper

Any spaghetti-type pasta can be used. I prefer a thin spaghetti for this dish.

Cook the noodles in a large pot of boiling salted water until they are al dente.

When the noodles are almost cooked, heat two tablespoons of the butter in a small pan. Add the shallots and cook them for just a minute.

Add the scallops and the wine to the pan. Sauté the scallops only until they are done. This will take just a minute or two, depending on the size of the scallops.

Remove the scallops from the pan with a slotted spoon and keep them warm.

Add the curry powder and the cream to the liquid remaining in the pan. Cook and reduce the sauce a little.

Once the pasta is cooked, drain well. Place the hot noodles into a serving bowl and toss them with the remaining two tablespoons of butter and the raw egg. Season well with salt and pepper.

Place the cooked scallops on top of the noodles and pour the hot curry sauce over all.

Toss and serve immediately. This recipe serves three to four.

PASTA WITH MUSHROOMS AND PEAS

A wonderfully filling and fairly inexpensive dinner that can be prepared quickly - for variations see the end of the recipe.

2 cups peas
½ cup butter
1 pound mushrooms, diced
salt
freshly ground black pepper
1 pound spaghetti or linguine
2 cups light cream
1 cup grated Parmesan cheese

If the peas are frozen, just thaw them and reserve. If they are fresh, cook in boiling water with a pinch of salt and sugar added until they are tender. Refresh, drain and reserve.

Heat three tablespoons of the butter in a very large frying pan.

Add the mushrooms, salt and pepper and cook for a few minutes until the mushrooms are soft.

Add the peas to the pan, stir and set it aside.

Cook the noodles in lots of boiling salted water until they are barely tender. They will cook again.

Pour the noodles into a colander. Rinse the noodles with hot water and drain.

Add one cup of the cream and the Parmesan cheese to the pan containing the mushrooms and heat.

When hot, stir in the cooked noodles and lots of freshly ground black pepper.

Toss and stir until the noodles are well coated with the sauce.

Add the rest of the cream and taste to correct the seasonings. Toss well and when hot, serve.

Pass some extra grated cheese and a pepper mill with the pasta.

This recipe serves six as a main course.

Alternates:

1. A quarter pound of sliced Proscuitto or diced ham can be added to the noodles along with the mushrooms and peas. Add the diced ham to the butter and sauté for a few minutes. Then add the mushrooms and proceed with the recipe.

2. Half spinach noodles and half regular noodles can also be used. The dish looks beautiful this way. If the noodles are not the same thickness, cook them separately.

PASTA WITH A WALNUT SAUCE

This is a most unusual and rich tasting sauce. You would never believe that it contains nuts - it is different and delicious.

Regular noodles can be used instead of the spinach noodles. The contrast of colors between the white sauce and the green noodles look prettier, that is why the recipe calls for them. The taste is just about the same.

¾ cup butter
1 clove garlic, crushed
1 Tbsp. chopped parsley
1 Tbsp. chopped fresh basil
6 ounces walnuts, chopped fine
1 Tbsp. finely chopped almonds
2 cups heavy cream
½ cup grated Parmesan cheese
salt, pepper
1 pound spinach pasta
½ cup cooking water from pasta

Melt all but two tablespoons of the butter in a saucepan.

Add the garlic, parsley and basil to the pan and cook for just a minute or two.

Add the finely chopped walnuts and almonds, then pour in the cream. Cook, stirring, until the mixture comes to a boil.

Add the one-half cup of cheese and some salt and pepper to taste. Let the sauce simmer for ten to fifteen minutes.

The recipe can be completed to this point early in the day and the sauce finished right before serving.

Cook the pasta in a large pot of boiling salted water until it is al dente.

Reserve one-half cup of the cooking water, then pour the pasta into a colander. Rinse under hot water and drain well.

Place the hot noodles onto a large serving platter and toss with the remaining two tablespoons of butter.

Add the reserved cooking water from the noodles to the walnut sauce and heat until the sauce is boiling.

Pour the sauce over the cooked pasta and serve immediately.

Pass some additional grated cheese and a peppermill with the pasta.

This recipe serves six as a main course.

Salads

AVOCADO AND PINEAPPLE SALAD

This is a nice light way to begin a heavy meal. The taste of avocado and pineapple go well together, especially with just a hint of curry.

Except for the avocado, the salad can be readied early in the day. The salad will hold up without discoloring, if mixed with dressing, for an hour or two. Keep it refrigerated and covered.

2 large ripe avocados
2 cups diced ripe pineapple
salt, pepper
½ tsp. curry powder
2 Tbsp. wine vinegar
¼ cup salad oil
lettuce leaves

Peel and dice the avocados.

If using canned pineapple, drain and dice the pineapple into pieces the same size as the avocado.

Place the diced pineapple and avocado into a bowl.

In a separate bowl, mix together the salt, pepper, curry powder, vinegar and oil.

Toss the salad with the dressing. Serve the salad on lettuce leaves garnished with a sprig of parsley.

Serve cold. This recipe will serve four.

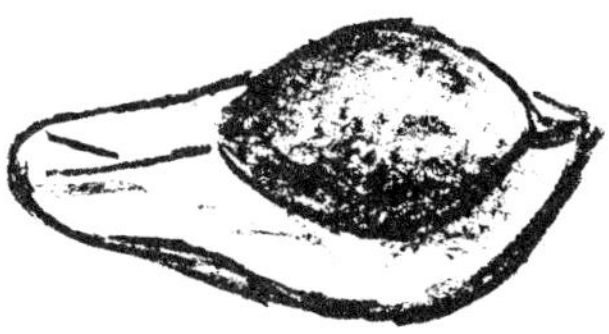

BROCCOLI SALAD

The marinade recipe for the broccoli can be used for many other vegetables as well. Good with leftover string beans, cauliflower, asparagus, etc.

1 bunch broccoli, cooked
1 clove garlic, crushed
1 tsp. Dijon mustard
¼ cup lemon juice
1 tsp. capers. chopped
salt, pepper
½ cup salad oil
lettuce leaves
1 hard-boiled egg

Cook the broccoli in boiling salted water until it is just tender. Refresh under cold water and drain well.

Leftover cooked broccoli can be used for this salad.

In a small bowl, mix together the garlic, mustard, lemon juice, capers and salt and pepper.

Whisk the oil into the bowl and beat until the mixture thickens.

Pour the dressing over the broccoli, turning to coat all of the pieces. Then cover and refrigerate the broccoli for at least thirty minutes.

The broccoli can be left in the dressing overnight, if covered and refrigerated.

When ready to serve, place the broccoli on lettuce leaves. Chop the hard-boiled egg and sprinkle it over the broccoli. Spoon any extra dressing over the egg and serve.
This recipe serves four or more.

The salad can be completed early in the day and refrigerated. This recipe works well for buffets. You may want to cut your vegetables into bite-sized pieces.

CUCUMBER SALAD WITH CREAM

This is a delightful salad to accompany fish. I sometimes like to add a tablespoon of chopped dill or parsley to the cucumbers right before serving.

3 cucumbers
salt
juice of 1 lemon
white pepper
½ cup heavy cream

Cut off the ends of the cucumbers, as they are sometimes bitter. Peel the cucumbers and slice them in half, lengthwise.

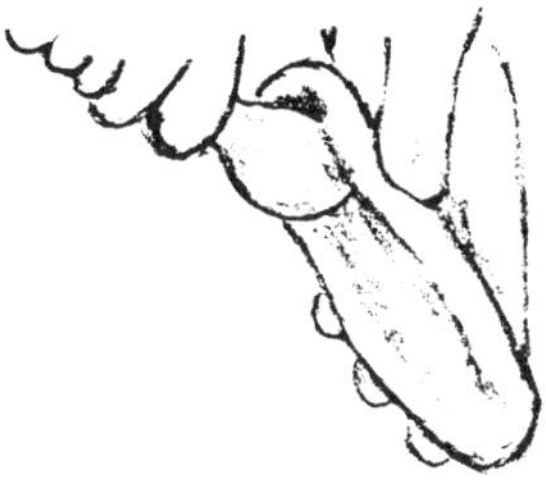

Remove the seeds, using a spoon. Thinly slice the cucumbers. A food processor is perfect for this.

Sprinkle the sliced cucumbers with salt and let them sit for thirty minutes. Rinse well, then dry the cucumbers.

Place the cucumbers into a bowl and add the lemon juice and the pepper. Mix in the cream.

Refrigerate the cucumber salad for a few hours.

When ready to serve, taste the salad and correct the seasonings.

Serve cold. This recipe serves four.

An alternate would be to use cooked string beans instead of cucumbers. Add a spoon or two of chopped chives to the dressing.

ORANGE AND ENDIVE SALAD

The avocado in the dressing gives a beautiful color and flavor contrast to both the oranges and the endive. This salad is also good as an appetizer.

2 Belgian endive
4 oranges
½ ripe avocado
1 Tbsp. lemon juice
2 Tbsp. mayonnaise
2 Tbsp. heavy cream
salt, pepper
lettuce leaves

Cut the Belgian endive in half, lengthwise, and remove the core.

Slice the endive into half-inch rounds and place them in a dish of cold water for a half hour.

Peel and cut the oranges into segments, removing the white membranes from between the sections. Reserve the oranges.

Mash the avocado with the lemon juice, mayonnaise, heavy cream and salt and pepper to taste. You can do this by hand or use a blender or a food processor.

Drain the endive well. Mix the endive with the avocado dressing.

Arrange lettuce leaves decoratively on four salad plates and spoon the endive-avocado mixture on top of the lettuce.

Arrange the orange segments in a row on top of the endive.

Serve the salad cold. This recipe serves four.

The salad can be arranged and refrigerated for an hour or two before serving time.

If you do not like Belgian endive, just leave it out of the salad. The avocado dressing is wonderful on plain orange segments.

TOSSED GREEN SALAD

I like to use a mixture of greens in a tossed salad for variety of both taste and texture. There are no rules - use what is available in any combination you like.

The list below is my favorite combination of greens. I am not fond of iceberg lettuce so I leave it out of my salads for the most part. If you like the taste, add it by all means.

I like to add a few raw sliced mushrooms, some Belgian endive and cherry tomatoes to my salad if they are in season.

A tossed green salad is also a wonderful place to use up bits and pieces of cooked vegetables. Cooked asparagus spears or string beans are an excellent addition. Many times I will cook a little extra just so that I have some left for my salad the next day.

Wash and dry all salad greens well. I like to wash mine when I bring them in from the market. I drain the greens well, wrap them in paper towels and place them in plastic bags in the refrigerator. They will keep dry and crisp for a few days and are ready when I need them. Tossed green salads should always be served cold.

Boston lettuce
Bib lettuce
Leaf or garden lettuce
Romaine
Watercress

Dressing:

1 clove garlic
½ tsp. Dijon mustard
2 Tbsp. wine vinegar
¼ cup oil
salt, pepper

Break the salad greens into bite-sized pieces.

Place the greens and vegetables, if you are using any, into a salad bowl. Keep the bowl in the refrigerator until serving time.

Prepare the salad dressing. Crush the clove of garlic lightly. This is easiest to do by whacking the garlic with the side of a large chef's knife.

Place the garlic into a small bowl along with the mustard, salt, pepper and vinegar. Stir, pressing the garlic with your fork.

Whisk the oil into the bowl and let the dressing sit until serving time.

When you are ready to toss your salad, remove and discard the garlic from the dressing. Enough garlic flavor will have been absorbed by the dressing by now.

Mix the dressing well, pour it over the salad, toss and serve immediately.

This recipe makes enough dressing for four small servings.

ROMAINE SALAD MIMOSA

Both the crumb topping and the greens can be readied early in the day. At serving time all you have to do is put everything together. A delightfully crisp and crunchy combination.

1 head romaine lettuce
1 large clove garlic
2 Tbsp. butter
½ cup coarse bread crumbs
2 Tbsp. wine vinegar
¼ cup oil
salt, pepper
1 hard-boiled egg, chopped

Wash and dry the lettuce and cut or tear it into bite size pieces. Place the lettuce into a salad bowl and chill until serving time.

Crush the clove of garlic lightly with your knife.

In a small frying pan, heat the butter. Add the partially crushed garlic to the butter and press well while cooking to release the juices.

When the garlic begins to turn brown, remove and discard the the clove.

Add the bread crumbs to the butter and sauté them over low heat for a few minutes, just until they turn light brown.

Remove the crumbs from the heat and reserve until serving time.

When ready to serve, beat the vinegar and oil together in a small bowl.

Sprinkle the salad greens with salt and pepper.

Add the vinegar and oil, the browned bread crumbs and the chopped hard-boiled egg to the greens. Toss well and serve immediately.

This recipe serves four.

SPINACH SALAD WITH FOIE GRAS

Warm salads are now the latest "in" dish all over Europe. Definitely a last minute dish, this salad takes only a few minutes to prepare and is usually served as a first course. Spinach, foie gras and calves liver, with croutons for crunch, in a hot fresh herb vinagrette dressing make a delightful combination.

spinach leaves
4 ounces pâté de foie gras
1 cup croutons
4 ounces calves liver
salt, pepper
4 Tbsp. butter
3 Tbsp. chopped shallots
¼ cup white wine
¼ cup vermouth
2 Tbsp. sherry wine vinegar
1 Tbsp. chopped parsley
1 Tbsp. chopped chives
1 Tbsp. chopped dill

Arrange the spinach leaves on four individual salad plates. Slice the foie gras into cubes and divide them evenly among the four plates. Sprinkle with the croutons.

The calves liver takes only a minute to cook, so have all the rest of the ingredients measured out and ready before you begin. Slice the liver into very thin julienne strips. Sprinkle with salt and pepper.

Heat one tablespoon of the butter in a small frying pan. Add the liver and sauté quickly over high heat. The liver will only take one minute to cook. Remove the liver and divide it among the salad plates.

Heat another tablespoon of butter in the frying pan. Add the shallots and cook for a minute or two.

Pour in the white wine, vermouth and vinegar, scraping well to deglaze the pan. Let the dressing cook for a minute. Add salt and pepper to taste.

Add the parsley, chives and dill along with the remaining two tablespoons of butter to the pan. Remove the pan from the heat and stir the dressing just until the butter melts.

Spoon the hot dressing evenly over the salads and serve immediately. This recipe serves four.

WATERCRESS AND MUSHROOM SALAD

The peppery taste of the watercress complements the mild flavor of the mushrooms. Combined with a garlic dressing, this is a wonderful salad.

1 cup sliced mushrooms
1 bunch watercress
½ clove garlic, crushed
½ tsp. Dijon mustard
salt, pepper
2 Tbsp. wine vinegar
¼ cup oil

Wash, dry and slice the mushrooms thinly. Place them into a salad bowl.

Break off the tough stems attached to the watercress. Use just the thin stems with the leaves. Add the cress to the salad bowl.

Refrigerate the salad until you are ready to serve, but not for more than an hour or two, or the mushrooms will discolor.

Make the dressing by crushing the garlic finely.

Place the crushed garlic in a small bowl along with the mustard, salt, pepper and the vinegar. Mix well.

Add the oil and whisk until the dressing thickens a little.

Set the dressing aside until serving time.

When ready to serve, toss the salad with the dressing.

This salad serves four.

For this salad I prefer two parts cress to one part mushrooms, but you can add more mushrooms if you like.

SALAD ESCOFFIER

Any leftover cooked meat can be used for this salad - beef, pork, veal or even chicken. You can also use more than one kind of meat at a time, depending on what you have leftover.

2 cups sliced cooked meat
½ cup finely sliced onion
½ cup finely sliced green pepper
½ cup finely sliced tomato
½ cup finely sliced dill pickle
½ cup cooked string beans
½ cup ketchup
2 Tbsp. wine vinegar
few drops Tabasco
salt, pepper

Slice the meat, onion, green pepper, tomato and pickle. Place them into a bowl, along with the string beans.

Stir the ketchup, vinegar and Tobasco into the salad. Season to taste with salt and pepper.

Cover and refrigerate the salad for a few hours, it will taste better.

Serve this salad cold or at room temperature. This recipe serves four.

This salad can be served on lettuce leaves and garnished with tomato wedges and a sprig of parsley. If you have any leftover hard-boiled eggs around, slice them into rounds or cut them into wedges and serve with the salad.

ONIONS à l'ORIENTALE

This is a very piquant cold relish - not really a salad - that is wonderful tasting with almost any pâté or terrine. It is easy to make and will keep fresh for a very long time.

1 bag frozen pearl onions	2 Tbsp. oil
3 ounces raisins	¼ cup water
½ cup sugar	1 bay leaf
1/3 cup wine vinegar	½ tsp. thyme
1/3 cup white wine	½ tsp. salt
3 Tbsp. ketchup	½ tsp. pepper

Place all of the ingredients into a saucepan and mix them well. Bring to a boil and mix well again.

Simmer the relish uncovered, for fifty to sixty minutes, stirring occasionally to keep the onions from sticking.

When finished, the sauce should be thick and the onions tender. Remove the bay leaf, taste to correct the seasonings and chill.

Serve the relish cold or at room temperature with meat pâtés. This recipe makes approximately two cups of relish.

Onions à l'Orientale will keep for up to two weeks in the refrigerator, if well covered.

Quick Breads

CREAM CHEESE BISCUITS

Quick and easy, these hot biscuits are a tasty treat any time of the day.

¼ cup butter
¼ cup cream cheese (2 ounces)
¼ cup sour cream
1 egg
1½ cups flour
1 tsp. baking powder
1 tsp. baking soda
½ tsp. salt

You will need two plain baking sheets. Preheat the oven to 450 degrees.

Whip the butter and the cream cheese together until they are well blended.

Add the sour cream and the egg and mix well.

Mix the dry ingredients together and stir them into the creamed mixture. The dough will be very sticky at this point.

Pat - do not attempt to roll the dough onto a floured surface, one-third to one-half inch thick.

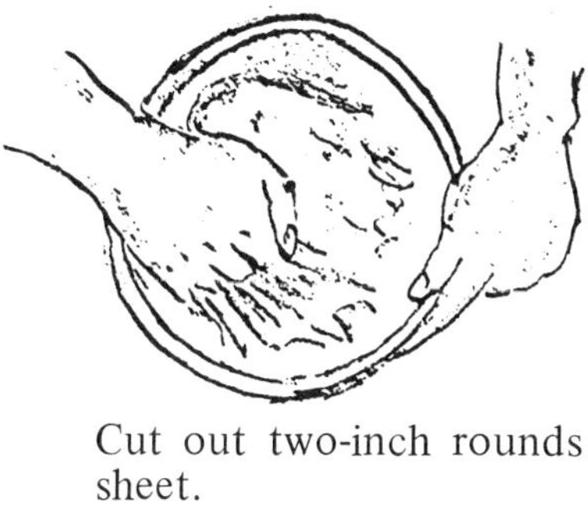

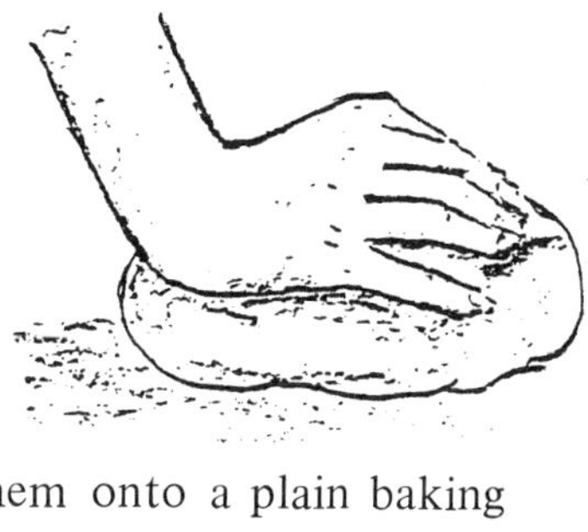

Cut out two-inch rounds and place them onto a plain baking sheet.

The biscuits can be prepared a few hours ahead and refrigerated until baking time.

Bake the biscuits in a 450 degree oven for eight to ten minutes or until they are puffed and browned. Serve hot.

This recipe makes twenty-four two inch biscuits.

LIGHT BISCUITS

These are incredibly light and tasty biscuits. Once baked, you cannot tell that they are made with farmer cheese - they have great flavor and texture. And they are easy to make.

6 ounces farmer cheese
1 egg
1½ cups flour
½ tsp. salt
2 tsp. baking powder
2 Tbsp. butter, melted

You will need two floured baking sheets. Preheat the oven to 450 degrees.

Cream together the farmer cheese and the egg until they are well blended.

Mix together the flour, salt and baking powder.

Add the dry ingredients to the cheese mixture and blend well to form a dough.

Either pat or roll out the dough so that it is one-third to one-half inch thick. Cut out two-inch rounds and place them onto the floured baking sheets.

The biscuits can be made ahead to this point and kept for a few hours in the refrigerator before baking.

Brush the tops of the biscuits with the melted butter.

Bake them in a 450 degree oven for fifteen minutes or until they are puffed and browned. Serve hot.

This recipe makes about twenty biscuits that are two inches in diameter.

ENGLISH CREAM SCONES

This is a very delicate dough and should be made by hand. A food processor would work the dough far too much and produce very tough scones.

The scones are quick, easy and have a wonderfully mild sweet flavor. If you would prefer them to taste more like a biscuit, then add less sugar. You could also add some raisins to the dough and make raisin cream scones.

2 cups flour
3 Tbsp. sugar
2 tsp. baking powder
1 Tbsp. cream of tartar
½ tsp. salt
6 Tbsp. butter
2 eggs
½ cup heavy cream
egg wash

You will need a buttered baking sheet. Preheat the oven to 450 degrees.

Mix the flour, sugar, baking powder, cream of tartar and salt together in a bowl.

Work the butter into the dry ingredients with your fingers until the mixture forms small crumbs.

Mix the eggs and the cream together and stir them into the dry ingredients, using a fork. Work the dough very gently.

With your hands, form the dough into two flat circular rounds about one inch thick.

Cut the circles into quarters and place the pieces onto the prepared cookie sheet.

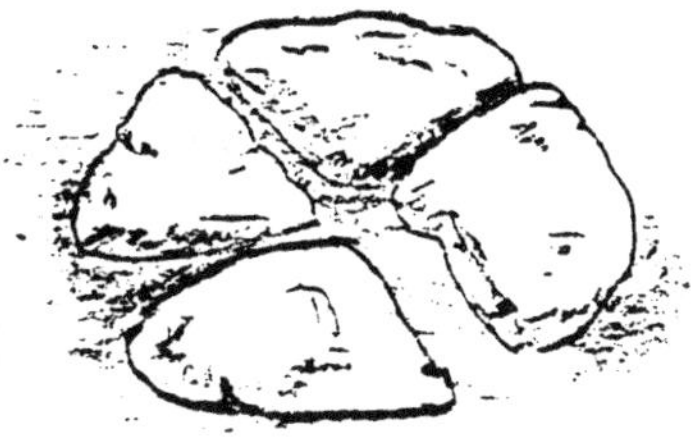

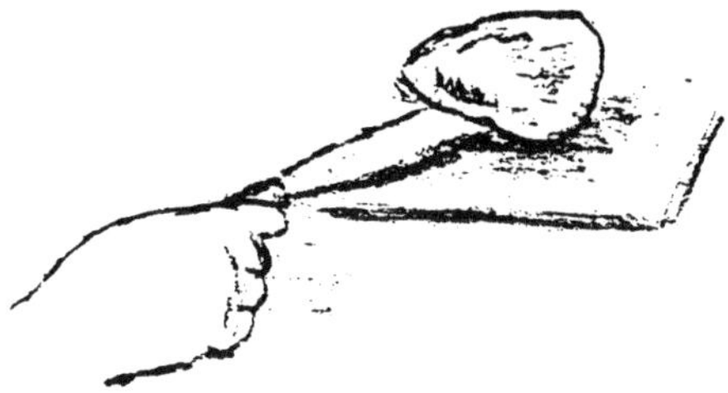

Brush the tops of the scones with a little egg wash.

Bake the scones in a 450 degree oven for fifteen minutes, or until done.

Serve hot with butter and jam. Scones are only good when they are hot and fresh, so only make as many as you will need per serving each time.

This recipe makes eight large scones.

CORNBREAD WITH PARSLEY

Corn Bread with Parsley is wonderful hot and fresh from the oven served with butter. Any leftovers make an excellent stuffing for fowl. Freeze the bread to use for a stuffing until needed.

¼ cup butter
½ cup cornmeal, yellow or white
¾ cup flour
1 tsp. baking powder
1 tsp. baking soda
1 Tbsp. sugar
1 tsp. salt
¾ cup sour cream
2 eggs
½ cup milk
2 Tbsp. chopped parsley

Butter an eight or nine inch square pan. Preheat the oven to 375 degrees.

Melt the butter and let it cool a little. I do this right in the baking pan and add an extra teaspoon of butter. This way I have greased my pan and melted the butter at the same time without using an extra pot.

Mix the cornmeal, flour, baking powder, baking soda, sugar and salt together in a bowl.

In a separate bowl, mix the sour cream with the egg. Blend in the milk and the melted butter.

Stir the liquid mixture into the dry ingredients. Mix in the parsley.

Do not overbeat, just mix to incorporate all the ingredients.

Pour the batter into the prepared pan and bake in a 375 degree oven for thirty-five minutes.

Serve hot with butter. This recipe serves four or more.

The recipe can be doubled and baked in a seven and one-half by twelve inch pan. Baking time will be about the same.

WHOLE WHEAT CORN BREAD

I prefer this bread made with white cornmeal, as the flavor is more delicate. But either white or yellow will work, so use whichever you have.

Leftovers are no problem as this bread is excellent the next day sliced, toasted and served with butter and jelly. It makes a great breakfast bread.

1 Tbsp. butter
½ cup cornmeal, white or yellow
½ cup whole wheat flour
3 Tbsp. sugar
1½ tsp. baking powder
¾ tsp. salt
1 egg
½ cup light cream

Butter and flour an eight or nine inch square pan. Preheat the oven to 350 degrees.

Melt and cool the butter a little.

Mix the cornmeal, flour, sugar, baking powder and salt together in a bowl.

In a separate bowl, beat the eggs just to mix, then stir in the melted butter and the cream.

Add the liquid to the dry ingredients, stirring just to incorporate everything. Do not overbeat.

Pour the batter into the prepared pan and bake in a 350 degree oven for twenty to twenty-five minutes or until done. The bread should be firm to the touch and lightly browned on top.

Let the bread sit for ten to fifteen minutes before slicing.

Serve warm, with butter. This recipe serves four or more.

The recipe can be doubled and the bread baked in a seven and one-half by twelve inch pan. Baking time is about the same.

QUICK WHOLE WHEAT BREAD

This is a wonderful bread with a full rich flavor from the addition of the whole wheat flour. Easy to make, you can have fresh hot bread in less than an hour from start to finish.

1 cup whole wheat flour
1½ cups regular flour
¾ tsp. baking soda
1 tsp. cream of tartar
1 tsp. salt
2 Tbsp. butter
1 cup milk

You will need an ungreased baking sheet. Preheat the oven to 400 degrees.

In a bowl, mix together the flours, baking soda, cream of tartar and the salt.

Add the butter and work it into the flour mixture using your fingers or a pastry cutter until small crumbs form.

Make a well and add the milk. Stir the milk into the dry ingredients until a dough is formed.

Turn the dough out onto a lightly floured board and work it with your hands into a ball.

Flatten the ball of dough into a circular shape, about one and one-half inches thick.

Place this circle on your baking sheet. With a knife, score the top of the dough with a large X.

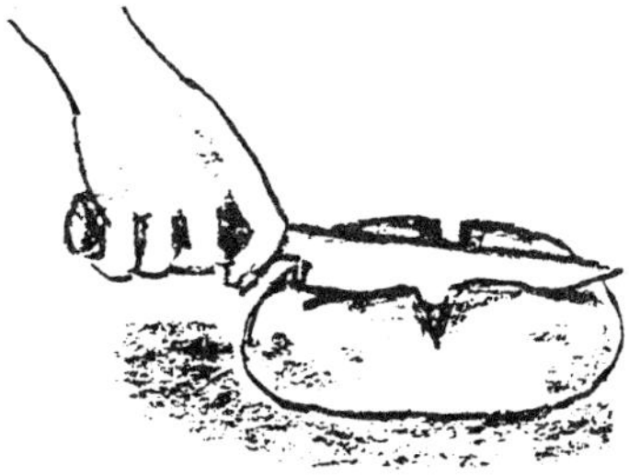

Bake the bread in a 400 degree oven for thirty minutes or until it tests done. Serve hot.

This recipe makes one loaf of bread, serving four to six.

This bread is best when hot and fresh. Serve directly from the oven with butter. If you would like a shiny crust on your bread, you can paint the top with an egg wash before baking.

You can use this recipe to make a walnut bread. After you have added the milk, work one-half cup of chopped walnuts into the dough. Then form and bake. Walnut bread is especially good when served with cheese.

ALMOND WHOLE WHEAT BREAD

Contrary to most fruit or nut bread recipes, this Almond Bread is delicious even while still fresh and warm. Crunchy, with lots of flavor, this is always a winner in our house.

Any nuts you prefer can be substituted for the almonds. This bread is good when made with walnuts, pecans or even macadamia nuts.

1 cup flour
1 cup whole wheat flour
2 tsp. baking powder
1 tsp. salt
½ cup ground almonds
¼ cup butter
¾ cup sugar
1 egg
1 cup sour cream or yogurt
¼ cup milk
½ cup chopped almonds

Butter and flour a nine inch bread loaf pan. Preheat the oven to 350 degrees.

Mix together the flours, baking powder, salt and ground almonds.

In a separate bowl, cream the butter with the sugar until it is light and fluffy.

Beat the egg into the butter and sugar mixture.

Add half the dry ingredients and stir well.

Mix in the sour cream or yogurt and the milk.

Add the rest of the dry ingredients and mix well. Stir in the chopped almonds.

Pour the batter into the prepared pan.

Bake in a 350 degree oven for one hour and fifteen minutes, or until the bread feels firm and springy to the touch.

Cool the bread in the pan for five to ten minutes. Then turn the bread out on a rack to finish cooling. Serve while warm or at room temperature.

This recipe makes one loaf of bread.

The bread will keep for several days if wrapped and refrigerated. It also freezes well.

BANANA BREAD

For a change of pace, try substituting chocolate chips for the nuts in this bread - a favorite with children. The older and riper the bananas, the better your bread will taste.

1½ cups flour
1¼ cups whole wheat flour
1 Tbsp. baking powder
½ tsp. salt
1 egg
¾ cup sugar
2 Tbsp. butter, melted
1¼ cups mashed bananas (about 3)
¾ cup milk
¾ cup chopped pecans or walnuts

Butter and flour a nine inch bread pan. Preheat the oven to 350 degrees.

Mix together the flours, baking powder and salt and reserve.

In the bowl of a mixer, beat the sugar and the egg until they become thick and light in color.

Mix in the melted butter, then the mashed bananas and the milk.

Stir in the dry ingredients and the chopped nuts.

Pour the batter into the prepared pan and bake in a 350 degree oven for about one hour and ten minutes, or until the bread tests done.

Cool the bread in the pan for ten minutes. Then turn out onto a rack to finish cooling. The bread can be served warm or cold.

This recipe makes one loaf of bread.

Banana Bread will keep for a few days if well wrapped. It also freezes well.

CARROT BREAD

This is an excellent carrot bread and will rival the best carrot cakes in both flavor and texture. The amounts of spices given are correct and are needed in this recipe.

¾ pound carrots
1½ cups flour
¾ tsp. baking powder
¾ tsp. baking soda
½ tsp. salt
2 tsp. cinnamon
2 tsp. nutmeg
1 cup sugar
1 egg
¾ cup oil
¼ cup water

Grease and flour a nine inch bread loaf pan. Preheat the oven to 350 degrees.

Peel the carrots and trim off the ends. Shred the carrots using the grating blade of a food processor. Or use a grater.

Mix together the flour, baking powder, baking soda, salt, cinnamon and nutmeg and set aside.

Put the sugar and the egg into the bowl of a mixer. Beat until they become very thick and light in color.

Continue to beat, adding the oil gradually, then the water.

Stir the grated carrots into this mixture. Then gradually blend in the dry ingredients.

Pour the batter into the prepared pan and bake in a 350 degree oven for one hour and fifteen minutes or until your bread tests done.

Cool a little, then turn out of the pan to finish cooling on a rack.

This recipe makes one loaf of bread.

This bread will keep for several days if wrapped and refrigerated. It also freezes well.

DRIED FRUIT AND NUT BREAD

This is a wonderful way to use up little bits and pieces of stale dried fruits even if they are as hard as rock. Save them to make this bread.

Any combination of fruits can be used for this bread, depending on what you have at hand. Dried figs are excellent. So are dried prunes, apricots, raisins, etc.

This is one of my favorite fruit and nut breads, I even prefer it to cake.

3 cups chopped dried fruit
2 cups orange juice
½ cup butter
½ tsp. salt
2 eggs
1 cup sugar
2 Tbsp. Grand Marnier
3 cups flour
1 tsp. baking powder
1 tsp. baking soda
1½ cups chopped nuts

Butter two nine-inch bread loaf pans. Preheat the oven to 350 degrees.

Place the cut up dried fruits into a saucepan. Add the orange juice, butter and salt. Cook at a simmer until the fruit is tender.

Add water to the pan, if needed, as the fruit cooks. The amount of liquid absorbed depends upon the dryness of the fruit.

Remove the pan from the heat and cool the fruit.

The cooked fruit can be refrigerated for a day before continuing with the recipe.

Beat the eggs with the sugar until they become light and fluffy.

Add the cooled dried fruits and the Grand Marnier to the eggs and stir until blended.

Mix the flour, baking powder and baking soda together.

Add the dry ingredients to the egg-fruit mixture and blend well. Stir in the chopped nuts.

Pour the batter into the prepared pans and bake in a 350 degree oven for fifty-five minutes to one hour or until the bread tests done.

Remove from the oven and cool the bread in the pans for ten minutes. Then turn out to finish cooling on a rack.

Dried Fruit and Nut Bread is even better if allowed to sit overnight and mellow before slicing.

This recipe makes two loaves of bread.

Margarine can be substituted for the butter in this recipe, but it will not taste as good.

This bread will keep well for a week, if wrapped and refrigerated. It also freezes beautifully.

ZUCCHINI BREAD

The instructions for making this bread are given for using a food processor. It makes such fast work of all the shredding and mixing that your batter will be ready to bake in less than five minutes. Instructions for baking this bread without a processor follow the recipe.

If you like, one cup of raisins can be stirred into the batter before baking. Also, a cup of drained crushed pineapple can be added for a nice fruity variation of the Zucchini Bread.

2 cups shredded zucchini, (2 medium)
grated rind ½ lemon
1½ cups sugar
1 cup oil
2 tsp. vanilla
3 eggs

3 cups flour
1 tsp. baking powder
1 tsp. baking soda
1 tsp. salt
1 Tbsp. cinnamon
1 cup walnuts, chopped

Butter and flour two nine-inch bread loaf pans. Preheat the oven to 350 degrees.

Wash, then trim the ends off the zucchini.

Shred or julienne the zucchini using the shredding blade of a food processor. Remove the zucchini, drain it well and squeeze dry to remove the extra moisture.

Place the lemon rind and the sugar in a food processor bowl fitted with the metal blade, and process until well blended.

Add the oil, vanilla and eggs and turn the machine on and off until well blended.

Add the shredded zucchini back to the bowl and again process until well blended.

Mix the flour, baking powder, baking soda, salt and the cinnamon together.

Remove the cover of the food processor and place the dry ingredients on top of the mixture already in the bowl.

Process, turning the machine on and off just until the dry ingredients are absorbed.

If you like, you can add the chopped nuts at this point and process for a few seconds. Your bread will have a nice nutty taste this way.

Or you can remove the batter from your processor and then stir in the nuts.

Pour the batter into the prepared pans and bake in a 350 degree for one hour or until the bread is done.

Remove from the oven and let the bread cool in the pans for five to ten minutes. Then turn out and let the bread finish cooling on a rack.

This recipe makes two loaves of bread.

Zucchini bread freezes beautifully and also will keep for three or four days if well wrapped and refrigerated.

Instructions for making Zucchini Bread without a food processor:

Grate the zucchini coarsely and let it drain in a strainer. Then press dry to remove the extra moisture.

Beat the eggs and sugar in the bowl of a mixer until they are light and fluffy.

Slowly add the oil to the egg mixture, beating constantly.

Then stir in the vanilla, the lemon rind and the drained zucchini.

Mix the flour, baking powder, baking soda, salt and cinnamon together and stir the dry ingredients into the batter.

Add the nuts and raisins or pineapple if desired, mix well and bake as instructed.

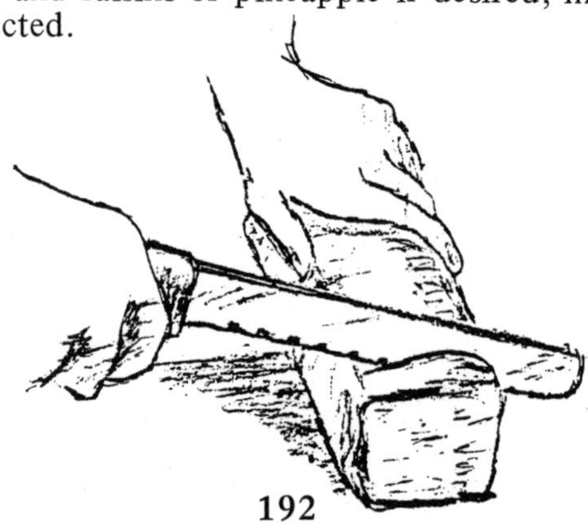

Desserts

CARROT-PINEAPPLE CAKE

This is a wonderfully moist carrot cake with a rich and spicey flavor. It is one of my favorites. Instructions are first given for making the cake in a food processor as this is the fastest and easiest way to prepare a carrot cake. Instructions for an alternate method of preparation follow the recipe.

¾ cup raisins
2 Tbsp. Grand Marnier
1 small can crushed pineapple
2 cups flour
1½ tsp. cinnamon
½ tsp. nutmeg
1 tsp. salt
2 tsp. baking powder
1 tsp. baking soda
¾ pound carrots
1½ cups brown sugar
1 cup butter
4 eggs
1 tsp. vanilla
¾ cup pecans or walnuts
Pineapple Cream Cheese Frosting
1 to 1½ cups chopped nuts, optional

Butter and flour a nine-inch tube pan. Preheat the oven to 350 degrees.

Soak the raisins in the Grand Marnier for at least thirty minutes.

Drain the pineapple, reserving the juice for the frosting.

Mix the flour, cinnamon, nutmeg, salt, baking powder and baking soda together. Set aside.

Peel the carrots. Using the shredding disc of a food processor, place the carrots in the feed tube and process.

Remove the carrots from the bowl and set them aside for a few minutes. Replace the shredding disc with the metal knife.

Place the sugar and the butter into the processor bowl. Process until they form a smooth mixture.

Stop the machine and add two eggs. Turn the machine on and off until the eggs are blended into the batter. Repeat, adding the other two eggs and the vanilla and blend well.

Add the grated carrots back to the bowl, one-third at a time, and process until the shreds disappear.

Place the dry ingredients on top of the carrot mixture and process, turning the machine on and off until they are incorporated.

Add the nuts and process again.

Remove the batter from the machine and pour it into a bowl. Stir in the raisins along with the Grand Marnier and the drained pineapple.

Pour the batter into the prepared pan and bake in a 350 degree oven for one hour and ten minutes or until the cake tests done.

Cool the cake before removing it from the pan.

Frost the top and the sides of the carrot cake with the cream cheese frosting.

Press the chopped nuts onto the sides of the cake for decoration. Use the same kind of nuts you used in the cake. Refrigerate the cake until serving time. This cake will serve twelve to sixteen.

The carrot cake will keep for several days in the refrigerator. It also freezes very well.

Alternate recipe: Leave the pineapple out of the cake for a plain carrot-raisin cake. Substitute one-half cup of orange juice for the liquid used in the frosting.

Oil can be used in place of the butter in this cake.

Instructions for the Carrot Pineapple Cake without a food processor:

Follow the food processor instructions for soaking the raisins, draining the pineapple and mixing the dry ingredients.

Grate the carrots using a hand grater and set them aside. Chop the nuts finely and reserve.

Place the butter and sugar into a mixing bowl and cream until they are light and fluffy.

Add the eggs, one at a time, to the butter-sugar mixture, beating well between each addition.

Stir in the vanilla and the grated carrots.

Gradually mix the dry ingredients into the batter.

Then stir in the raisins along with the Grand Marnier, the drained pineapple and the chopped nuts.

Pour the batter into the prepared pan and bake as instructed.

PINEAPPLE CREAM CHEESE FROSTING

This is a wonderful frosting for almost any fruit or nut cake. Not too sweet, yet full of flavor, it complements the carrot cake perfectly.

- Juice from canned crushed pineapple
- Water, as needed
- 1/3 cup sugar
- 8 ounces cream cheese, softened
- 1½ Tbsp. butter

Place the drained juice from the crushed pineapple into a measuring cup. Add enough water to total one-half cup of liquid.

Place this liquid and the sugar into a small saucepan.

Heat to the boiling point, then simmer, stirring occasionally, for about five minues. Cool the syrup.

Beat the butter together with the cream cheese until they are very light and fluffy.

Gradually beat in the cooled syrup. Continue to beat the frosting until it is very smooth, then ice the cake.

This recipe makes enough frosting to ice the top and sides of a nine-inch tube cake.

FRENCH CHOCOLATE CAKE

This has to be the richest chocolate cake ever! It has become a favorite with everyone who has tried the recipe. Don't be fooled by the size, just a small portion is enough for most people.

The addition of the honey and the brandy keeps this cake moist and soft for a long time, if you have any left over. We never do, it gets eaten very quickly in my house.

Another advantage, this cake must be made a few days ahead of time.

½ cup raisins
¼ cup brandy
7 ounces semi-sweet chocolate
3 Tbsp. very strong coffee
½ cup butter, softened
  (4 ounces)
¼ cup sugar (2 ounces)
3 eggs, separated
¼ cup honey
2/3 cup ground almonds
  (3 ounces)
5 Tbsp. cake flour (1 ounce)
pinch salt
Mocha Ganache

Butter a deep eight-inch cake pan. Line the bottom with waxed or parchment paper. Butter the paper liner, then flour the whole pan. Preheat the oven to 350 degrees.

Soak the raisins in the brandy for one hour.

Melt the chocolate and the coffee in a double boiler, or in a metal bowl placed over a pan of boiling water.

Once the chocolate is melted, remove it from the heat and gradually begin to stir in the half cup of butter, one tablespoon at a time. If the butter stops melting, place the bowl back over the boiling water for just a minute, then remove it and continue adding the butter. Cool a little.

Reserve one tablespoon of sugar. Beat the egg yolks with the rest of the sugar until they are thick and light. Stir the chocolate mixture into the egg yolks, then mix in the honey.

Mix the ground almonds with the flour and stir them into the batter. Add the raisins along with any remaining brandy. Mix well.

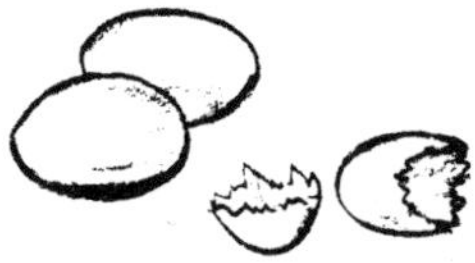

Beat the egg whites until they are foamy. Add a pinch of salt and continue beating. When they turn white, add the reserved tablespoon of sugar. Beat until the whites are stiff.

Stir one-quarter of the egg whites into the chocolate mixture, then carefully fold in the rest.

Pour the batter into the prepared pan and bake in a 350 degree oven for forty to forty-five minutes. Do not overbake this cake - it should remain moist in the center.

The sides of the cake will begin to shrink in a little, and the cake will test firm to the fingers around the sides when it is done.

Let the cake sit in the pan on a rack until it is completely cool. This will take an hour or two. Then turn the cake out of the pan.

Wrap the cake well and refrigerate it at least overnight. It will mellow and taste much better after a few days. The cake can also be frozen at this point instead of being refrigerated.

The day you plan to serve the cake, frost it with the Mocha Ganache. Refrigerate the cake until thirty minutes before serving time.

Cut into thin slices to serve. This cake is very rich and will serve twelve or more.

This cake is best if frozen without the ganache, as freezing will make it lose its shine.

If it is necessary to freeze the cake once it is iced, place the cake in the freezer unwrapped.

Once the cake is frozen, remove, wrap well and return the cake to the freezer. To defrost, unwrap first so that the frosting will not stick to the wrapper.

MOCHA GANACHE

5 ounces heavy cream
1 tsp. instant coffee powder
5 ounces semi-sweet chocolate, chopped fine

Place the cream into a saucepan and heat until it comes to a boil.

Remove the pan from the heat and stir in the coffee powder and the chocolate. Continue to stir until the chocolate is dissolved and the mixture is smooth.

Let the Ganache cool, stirring occasionally. The mixture will thicken a little.

To frost, place the cake on a rack with a pan underneath.

Pour the icing over the cake, smoothing with a large metal spatula or palette knife. Try to touch the top of the cake as little as possible with your knife. Smooth the icing onto the the sides of the cake.

Let the cake dry, remove it from the rack, and refrigerate.

MOCHA HAZELNUT TORTE

Loving hazelnuts as much as I do, this is one of my favorite cakes. The variety of flavors and textures of the cake, filling and frosting all contrast and complement each other beautifully.

2 cups hazelnuts, ground
2 Tbsp. cocoa powder
1 tsp. baking powder
1 tsp. cinnamon
1 tsp. instant coffee powder
1 Tbsp. brandy
6 eggs, separated
2/3 cup sugar
pinch salt
Hazelnut Cream Filling
Mocha Buttercream
Decoration: ¾ cup chopped hazelnuts

Butter and flour a nine-inch springform pan. If you use a regular deep cake pan instead, line the bottom with waxed or parchment paper which has also been buttered and floured. Preheat the oven to 350 degrees.

Place the hazelnuts into the oven and toast for fifteen minutes to loosen the skins. Let them cool for a few minutes. Then rub the nuts well to remove the brown outer skins.

Once the nuts are cold, grind the two cups needed for the cake. Chop and set aside the three-quarter of a cup to be used for decoration.

Mix the ground hazelnuts, cocoa powder, baking powder and the cinnamon together and set aside.

Dissolve the instant coffee powder in the brandy and reserve.

Beat the egg yolks with one-third cup of the sugar until they are very thick and light in color.

Stir the nut mixture into the beaten egg yolks. Blend the dissolved coffee into the batter.

Beat the egg whites until they are foamy. Add a pinch of salt and continue to beat until they form peaks. Gradually add the rest of the sugar to the egg whites and continue to beat until they are very stiff.

Stir one-quarter of the beaten egg whites into the batter. Then carefully fold in the rest of the whites. Pour the batter into the prepared pan.

Bake in a 350 degree oven for forty-five to fifty minutes, or until the cake tests done. Turn the cake out of the pan to cool.

This cake improves in flavor if allowed to sit overnight before filling and frosting. It will keep well in the refrigerator for a few days. The cake freezes beautifully. Fill and ice after defrosting.

When you are ready to ice the cake, slice it in half. Spread the filling on the bottom layer of the cake and then set the top layer in place over the filling.

Frost the top and sides of the cake with the Mocha Buttercream, reserving some of the icing for decoration.

Press the chopped hazelnuts onto the sides of the cake.

Use a pastry bag fitted with a star tube to decorate the top of the cake with the remaining frosting.

This cake will serve twelve.

The finished cake will keep fresh for a few days. Store in the refrigerator.

HAZELNUT CREAM FILLING

½ cup milk
4 Tbsp. ground hazelnuts
3 Tbsp. sugar
3 Tbsp. butter, softened
¼ tsp. instant coffee powder
1 Tbsp. brandy

Place the milk, hazelnuts and sugar into a saucepan. Heat, stirring occasionally, until the mixture has thickened. Remove the pan from the heat and cool for a few minutes.

Gradually stir the softened butter into this cooked mixture. Dissolve the coffee powder in the brandy and blend into the filling.

Chill the filling for about twenty minutes before spreading it onto the cake.

This recipe makes enough filling to cover one eight or nine-inch cake layer.

The filling can be prepared a day ahead of time and refrigerated.

MOCHA BUTTERCREAM

¾ cup confectioners sugar
1½ cups butter, softened
3 egg yolks
1 heaping tsp. instant coffee powder
1½ Tbsp. brandy

Sift the confectioners sugar to remove any lumps.

Beat the butter with the sugar until they are light and fluffy. Add the egg yolks and continue to beat until the mixture is very smooth.

Dissolve the coffee powder in the brandy. Add to the frosting and stir until well incorporated.

Chill the frosting for a few minutes if it is too soft to use immediately.

This recipe makes enough frosting for the top and sides of two eight or nine-inch cake layers.

COFFEE AND WALNUT CREAM CAKE

Instead of butter, heavy cream is used to give this cake both a rich flavor and a light texture. A good dessert for both family and company.

¾ cup flour
¾ cup ground walnuts
¾ cup sugar
2 tsp. baking powder
½ tsp. salt
½ tsp. cinnamon
2 tsp. instant coffee powder
1 Tbsp. brandy or rum
1 tsp. vanilla
1 cup heavy cream
2 eggs
confectioners sugar or
Chocolate Glaze, page 203

Butter a deep eight-inch cake pan. Line the bottom of the pan with a circle of parchment or waxed paper. Then butter the paper as well and flour the pan. Preheat the oven to 350 degrees.

Mix together the flour, walnuts, sugar, baking powder, salt and cinnamon and reserve.

Dissolve the coffee powder by mixing it into the brandy or rum and the vanilla and set aside.

Whip the cream until it is just lightly stiff.*

Beat the eggs, one at a time, into the whipped cream, just until they are incorporated.

Stir in the brandy mixture into the cream. Then fold in the dry ingredients.

Pour the batter into the prepared pan and bake in a 350 degree oven for forty-five minutes. The cake will begin to pull away from the sides of the pan when it is done.

Let the cake cool until you can touch the pan without burning your hands. Then turn out to finish cooling on a rack.

When the cake is cool, sprinkle with confectioners sugar or spread the Chocolate Glaze over the top.

If you used rum in the cake, use rum in the glaze. Or use brandy in both, whichever you prefer.

This cake serves eight to ten.

This cake will keep well for a few days. It can also be frozen. Freeze without the glaze, if possible.

*Be very careful not to overbeat the cream, you want a cream cake, not a butter cake.

CHOCOLATE CHIP SOUR CREAM CAKE

The sour cream gives this cake a rich and mellow flavor. Chocolate chips are a favorite with kids of all ages.

½ cup butter
1 cup sugar
2 eggs
1 tsp. vanilla
2 cups flour
1 tsp. baking powder
1 tsp. baking soda
pinch salt
1 cup sour cream
1 cup chocolate chips

Butter a nine inch tube pan. Preheat the oven to 350 degrees.

In a mixer, cream the butter with the sugar until it is light and fluffy. Add the eggs, then the vanilla and beat well.

Mix together the flour, baking powder, baking soda and salt.

Add half of these dry ingredients to the batter and stir until they are incorporated.

Blend in the sour cream, then add the rest of the dry ingredients and mix well.

Stir in the chocolate chips.

Pour the batter into the prepared pan and bake in a 350 degree oven for one hour, or until the cake tests done.

Remove from the oven and let the cake sit until the pan is cool enough to handle. Then turn the cake out onto a rack to finish cooling.

This cake can be served plain or drizzled with the Chocolate Glaze, page 203.

This cake will serve twelve.

Chocolate Chip Cake will keep fresh for a few days. It also freezes very well.

CHOCOLATE RAISIN SQUARES

I like to call these my adult brownies. They can be addictive and have been a favorite in many classes. Easy too, as the batter is made all in one saucepan.

1 cup raisins
¼ cup rum or brandy
1¼ cups flour
¾ tsp. baking soda
pinch salt
¾ cup dark brown sugar
½ cup water
½ cup butter
6 ounces semi-sweet chocolate, chopped
2 eggs
1 cup milk
1 cup chopped walnuts
Chocolate Glaze

Line a jelly roll pan with waxed or parchment paper. Preheat the oven to 350 degrees.

Soak the raisins in the rum or brandy for at least thirty minutes.

Mix together the flour, baking soda and salt and reserve.

In a medium-sized saucepan, combine the brown sugar, water and butter. Bring this mixture to a boil, stirring occasionally.

Remove the pan from the heat and stir in the chocolate. Continue to mix until all the chocolate is melted.

Add the eggs to the pan, stirring well until they are incorporated.

Add the dry ingredients alternately with the milk, mixing well.

Stir the raisins along with the brandy and the walnuts into the pan.

The batter will be very liquid - it is supposed to be. Pour the batter into the prepared jelly roll pan.

Bake in a 350 degree oven for twenty-five minutes or until the cake tests done.

Let the cake cool a little before frosting with the Chocolate Glaze.

Once the glaze has set, cut the cake into squares and serve.

This recipe makes sixteen to twenty brownies, guaranteed not to last very long.

These brownies will stay fresh for a few days, if covered. They can be frozen.

Pecans can be substituted for the walnuts in this recipe.

CHOCOLATE GLAZE

8 ounces semi-sweet chocolate
½ cup butter
2 Tbsp. rum or brandy

Put the chocolate into a metal bowl and place the bowl on top of a small pot of boiling water. You can use a double boiler, but this way is easier.

Once the chocolate is melted, remove the bowl from the heat. Add the butter, a little at a time, to the melted chocolate. Beat until each bit of butter is absorbed before adding more. Then stir in the brandy.

Pour the warm glaze over the cake, smoothing with a metal spatula.

ALMOND CREME TART

Not too sweet, with a lovely mild almond flavor and contrasting textures, this tart has been a favorite of ours for many years.

Crust:

¼ cup ground toasted almonds (1½ ounces)
¾ cup flour
1 Tbsp. sugar
pinch salt
6 Tbsp. butter
2 Tbsp. ice water

Filling:

1½ tsp. gelatin (½ package)
1/8 cup water
¼ cup flour
¼ cup sugar plus 1 Tbsp.
4 eggs, separated
1 cup heavy cream
3 Tbsp. Amaretto
pinch salt
1 cup toasted almond slices
6 Amaretti cookies, crushed

You will need a deep nine inch tart pan with a removable bottom. Preheat the oven to 400 degrees.

First make the crust, using a food processor or the hand method (see page 18). Grind the one-quarter cup of almonds in a food processor or blender.

Add the flour, sugar and a pinch of salt to the ground nuts and mix well.

Work the butter into the dry ingredients until small crumbs are formed.

Add enough water to form the dough into a ball. Wrap the dough and refrigerate for thirty minutes before rolling.

The dough can be made a day ahead and refrigerated overnight. Remove from the refrigerator to soften a little before rolling.

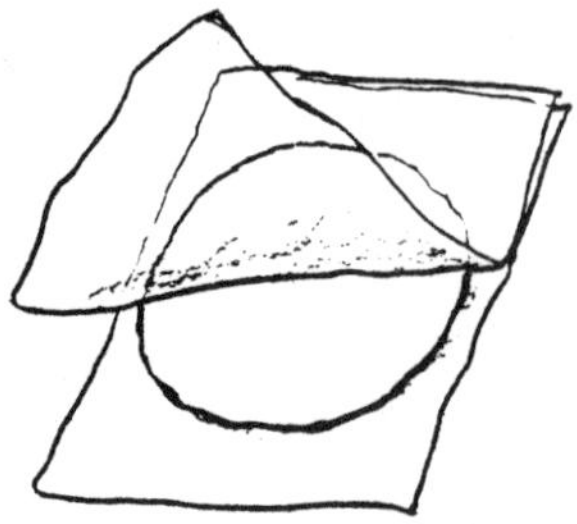

Roll out the chilled dough between two sheets of waxed paper. Lift and turn the paper if the dough sticks, using a little flour if necessary.

Line the tart shell with the dough. Trim the top edge evenly.

Cover the dough with a piece of aluminum foil. Press the paper into the bottom and sides of the crust. Fill the pan with weights. Place on a baking sheet and bake the crust in a 400 degree oven for fifteen minutes.

Remove the paper and the weights and continue to bake the crust for twenty to twenty-five minutes, or until it is done. The crust should be light brown in color.

Let the crust cool on a rack right in the pan.

While the crust is baking, you can begin to assemble the filling.

Toast and cool the almond slices.

Pour the water into a small dish. Sprinkle the gelatin over the water and let it sit for a few minutes to soften.

Place the flour and a quarter cup of the sugar into a saucepan. Add the egg yolks to the pan and stir them in well.

Gradually add the heavy cream to this mixture, stirring until smooth. Mix in the softened gelatin.

Place the saucepan over a low heat and cook, stirring, until the mixture becomes very thick.

Pour the cooked filling into a bowl to cool. When the filling reaches room temperature, stir in the Amaretto.

Beat the egg whites until they are foamy. Add a pinch of salt and continue to beat. When soft peaks form, add the tablespoon of sugar and beat until stiff.

Stir a quarter of the beaten egg whites into the cooled filling. Add the sliced toasted almonds to the filling along with the rest of the egg whites and fold them all together.

Remove the baked crust from the pan and place it onto a serving tray. Pour the filling into the crust, smoothing the top evenly. Sprinkle the top of the filling with the crushed Amaretti cookies.

Chill until serving time. Serve the tart cold or at room temperature. This tart will serve ten to twelve portions.

Almond Creme Tart will hold up well in the refrigerator overnight. Do not freeze.

APPLE CUSTARD TART

The apples baked in the custard filling blend beautifully with the cookie-like crust in this tart. This tart can be made with pears also, but I find that the apples taste better.

Shortcrust:

1¼ cups flour
1 Tbsp. sugar
pinch salt
6 ounces butter
1 egg
1 Tbsp. water

Filling:

3 Tbsp. dried bread crumbs
4 apples
¼ cup sugar
1 Tbsp. cornstarch
2 eggs
½ cup sour cream
1 tsp. vanilla
1 tsp. lemon juice
1 cup heavy cream

You will need a tart pan with a removable bottom, nine inches by one and one-quarter inches deep. Preheat the oven to 375 degrees.

First make the crust using a food processor or the hand method (see page 18).

Mix the flour, salt and sugar together. Work the butter into the dry ingredients until small crumbs are formed.

Mix the egg with the water. Add this liquid to the butter-flour mixture and work together just until a dough is formed.

Shape the dough into a ball. Flatten a little, wrap and chill for at least thirty minutes before rolling.

The dough can be made a day ahead and refrigerated. Remove to soften a little before rolling.

Roll out the crust and fit it into the tart pan, cutting off any excess dough from around the edges. Place the tart back into the refrigerator and chill for ten minutes. Chilling the crust right before baking should reduce any shrinkage.

Sprinkle the bread crumbs in an even layer over the bottom of the crust. They will absorb the extra liquid from the apples and keep the crust from getting soggy.

Peel and core the apples. Slice them thinly. Stand the apple slices in rows in the prepared crust.

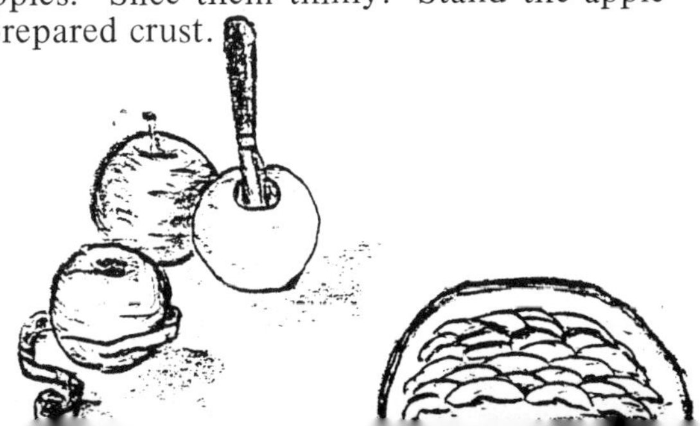

Place the tart onto a baking sheet and bake in a 375 degree oven for thirty minutes.

While the crust and apples are baking, prepare the custard filling.

Mix the sugar and the cornstarch together in a bowl. Beat the eggs into this mixture.

Then stir in the sour cream, vanilla and lemon juice and beat until smooth.

Add the cream and mix well. Refrigerate the custard until it is needed.

After thirty minutes of baking time, remove the tart from the oven. Pour the custard over the apples and return the tart to the oven. Bake until the custard is set, about fifty minutes.

Serve the tart at room temperature or chilled. This tart will serve ten to twelve.

The apple tart is best the day it is made, but it will keep for a day or two in the refrigerator. Do not freeze - the custard becomes watery.

APPLE-PEAR PECAN PIE

This is a delightful taste combination. The apples and pears blend beautifully with the crunchy streusel topping.

Crust:

¼ cup pecans, ground
1 cup flour
1 Tbsp. sugar
pinch salt
¼ pound butter
2 Tbsp. water

Streusel Topping:

½ cup chopped pecans
¼ cup flour
¼ cup sugar
1½ tsp. cinnamon
3 Tbsp. butter
½ tsp. vanilla

Filling:

3 apples, sliced
3 pears, sliced
½ cup sugar
2 Tbsp. flour
¼ tsp. cinnamon
1 tsp. lemon juice

You will need a nine inch pie pan. Preheat the oven to 400 degrees.

First make the crust, using a food processor or the hand method (see page 18).

Grind the pecans in a blender or food processor, then mix together the ground nuts, flour, sugar and salt.

Work the butter into the dry ingredients just until the mixture forms small crumbs.

Add the water and work until a dough forms. Form the dough into a ball. Flatten, wrap in waxed paper and chill for thirty minutes.

The dough can be made a day or two ahead of time and refrigerated. Remove from the refrigerator to soften a little before rolling.

Next, make the streusel. Place the chopped nuts, flour, sugar and cinnamon into a bowl. Add the butter and the vanilla and work them into the dry ingredients to make small crumbs. Try to use your hands for this, as streusel never tastes as good when it is made in a food processor or blender. Reserve until needed.

The streusel can be made a day ahead of time and refrigerated until needed.

Roll out the crust to fit the pie pan and flute the edges decoratively.

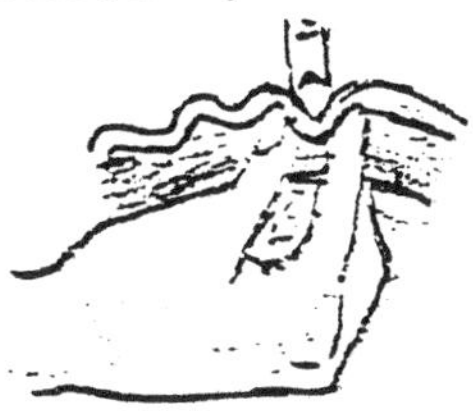

Peel, core and cut both the apples and the pears into very thin slices. The food processor is great for this job.

Mix the sliced fruit with the sugar, cinnamon, flour and lemon juice. Pack the fruit evenly into the prepared crust.

Sprinkle the streusel evenly on top of the fruit.

Place the pie on a baking sheet and cover it loosely with a piece of aluminum foil. This will allow the crust and fruit to cook thoroughly without danger of the streusel burning.

Bake the pie in a 400 degree oven. Remove the aluminum foil cover after forty-five minutes.

Continue to bake until the pie is done, about another thirty minutes. Total baking time is about one hour and fifteen minutes. The streusel and the crust will be browned and the juices from the fruit will just begin to bubble over the edge of the pie.

Remove the pie from the oven. Serve warm or cool, do not attempt to cut this pie while it is still very hot.

This recipe makes one nine-inch pie, serving about ten portions.

Apple-Pear Pecan Pie is good served plain, with vanilla ice cream or even with sweetened whipped cream. I prefer this pie just plain.

Margarine can be substituted for the butter in this recipe.

The pie is best when fresh, but it will keep well for a day or two. Remove from the refrigerator about an hour before serving.

If it is necessary to freeze this pie, do so before baking. Place the pie into the oven while it is still frozen allowing at least an extra ten minutes of baking time.

DRIED FRUIT PIE

This pie filling has a deliciously mild and creamy flavor - just the perfect complement for the dried fruits and nuts. I like the proportion and combination of fruits given in the recipe, but you can alter them to your own taste. If you like an all raisin pie, then just use the raisins, or all apricots, etc. If you like more nuts, add a little more in place of some of the fruits. You can use whatever combination of fruits or nuts you have on hand that you think will taste good together.

Crust:

1 cup flour
1 Tbsp. sugar
pinch salt
½ cup butter
2 Tbsp. ice water

Filling:

½ cup diced prunes, pitted
½ cup diced dried apricots
½ cup chopped walnuts
½ cup raisins
2 cups sour cream
2 eggs
1 cup sugar
¼ cup flour
pinch salt
1 tsp. vanilla

Topping:

¼ cup flour
½ cup brown sugar
¼ cup chopped walnuts
¼ cup butter

You will need a deep nine-inch pie pan. Preheat the oven to 400 degrees.

First make the crust, using a food processor or the hand method (see page 18). Mix together the flour, sugar and salt. Work the butter into the dry ingredients until the mixture forms small crumbs.

Add the water and mix until the dough will form into a ball. Wrap and chill the dough while you prepare the filling.

The crust can be prepared a day or two ahead and refrigerated.

Chop the dried prunes, apricots and walnuts into pieces so that they are all about the same size as the raisins.

In a bowl, mix together the sour cream, eggs, sugar, flour, salt and vanilla.

Stir the chopped fruits and nuts into this sour cream mixture. Set aside.

Prepare the topping next. Mix together the flour, sugar, walnuts and butter until they form small crumbs. Reserve the topping until needed.

The topping can be made a day ahead of time and refrigerated until needed.

Roll out the crust and place it into the pie pan. Flute the edges of the crust decoratively.

Pour the sour cream and fruit filling into the crust. Set the pie onto a baking sheet, place in a 400 degree oven and bake for thirty minutes.

Remove from the oven and sprinkle the topping evenly over the surface of the pie. Return the pie to the oven and continue to bake until the filling is set and the topping browned, about another forty minutes.

Serve the pie at room temperature. This pie serves ten to twelve.

You can substitute half the recipe for streusel topping found on page 206 in place of the topping used here, if you prefer.

If refrigerated, the Dried Fruit Pie will keep fresh for up to a week. Remove from the refrigerator a half hour before serving.

Return the remainder of the pie to the refrigerator directly after serving. Do not freeze this pie.

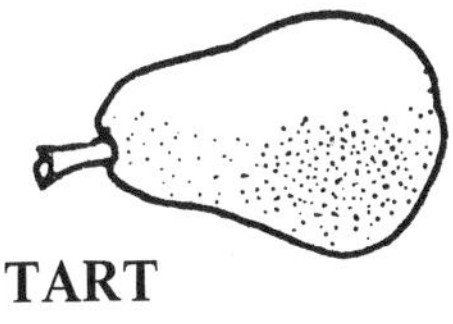

CHEESE AND PEAR TART

This is a wonderfully light tasting cheese tart. The farmer cheese is just perfect here. Do make an effort to get some, there is really no substitute. If you don't have any pears, you can use apples. This cheese tart is even good plain, without any fruit topping. This tart will keep well, if refrigerated, for a few days. Do not freeze.

Crust:

1 cup flour
2 Tbsp. sugar
pinch salt
½ cup butter
2 Tbsp. half and half

Filling:

¼ cup white raisins
1 Tbsp. brandy
8 ounces farmer cheese, softened
8 ounces cream cheese, softened
1 Tbsp. flour
6 Tbsp. sugar
1 egg
¼ cup sour cream
1 tsp. lemon juice
1 tsp. vanilla
2 or 3 pears
2 Tbsp. cinnamon-sugar

You will need a nine or ten inch tart shell with a removable bottom. Preheat the oven to 400 degrees.

First make the crust, using the food processor or by hand (see page 18). Mix together the flour, sugar and salt. Work the the butter into the dry ingredients until small crumbs are formed.

Stir in the half and half. Form the dough into a ball with your hand and flatten the ball a little. Wrap the dough in waxed paper and refrigerate for at least thirty minutes.

The dough can be prepared a day or two ahead of time. Remove it from the refrigerator to soften a little before rolling.

Roll out the dough and fit it into the tart shell. Cut off the excess dough from around the edges of the tart. Chill the crust while you are preparing the filling.

Soak the raisins in the brandy for a little while.

Do not use a food processor to prepare the filling, it will make the cheese much too soupy. Use a mixer fitted with a flat beater or use a wooden spoon.

Place the farmer cheese and the cream cheese into a bowl and mix well. Stir the flour and the sugar into the cheese mixture.

Add the egg, sour cream, lemon juice and the vanilla and mix well. Then stir in the raisins and the brandy.
Pour the filling into the prepared crust.

Peel, core and thinly slice the pears. Place them in a decorative pattern around the top of the tart.

Do not peel the fruit ahead of time as it will discolor.

Sprinkle the pears with the cinnamon-sugar. Use two tablespoons of sugar mixed with a little cinnamon.

Place the tart onto a baking sheet and bake in a 400 degree oven until the crust is browned and the filling set, about fifty to fifty-five minutes.

If the pears start to turn brown too quickly, cover the tart loosely with a piece of aluminum foil and continue to bake until the crust is done.

Serve the cheese tart at room temperature or chilled. This tart will serve ten to twelve portions.

PUMPKIN-PECAN PIE

An unusual pumpkin pie chock full of spices and brandy, with a hidden pecan layer in the bottom. Good any time of year, not just on Thanksgiving.

Crust:

1¼ cups flour
1 Tbsp. sugar
pinch salt
10 Tbsp. butter
2 Tbsp. ice water

Nut Layer:

½ cup chopped pecans
¼ cup brown sugar
2 Tbsp. butter, softened

Filling:

½ cup brown sugar
½ tsp. salt
¾ tsp. cinnamon
½ tsp. ginger
½ tsp. nutmeg
1½ cups cooked or canned pumpkin
2 eggs
1 ounce brandy or rum
1 cup light cream

You will need a nine inch pie pan. Preheat the oven to 400 degrees.

First make the crust using a food processor or by hand (see page 18). Mix the flour, sugar and salt together. Work the butter into the dry ingredients until small crumbs are formed. Add the water and work the dough into a ball. Wrap and re-refrigerate the dough for thirty minutes before rolling.

The dough can be made a day or two ahead of time and refrigerated.

Roll out the dough and line the pie pan. Crimp the edges of the crust decoratively.

Mix together the pecans, sugar and the butter. Pat the nut layer evenly into the bottom of the crust.

For the filling, stir together the sugar, salt, cinnamon, ginger, nutmeg and the pumpkin.

Add the eggs, one at a time, and mix well. Stir in the brandy or rum and the cream.

Pour the pumpkin filling into the nut filled crust, set onto a baking sheet and bake in a 400 degree oven for about fifty minutes, or until the crust is browned and the filling set.

Chill the pie before serving. This recipe makes one nine inch pie, serving about ten portions.

Best the day it is made, this pie will, however, keep well for a day or two if refrigerated.

LINZER TORTE

This is my version of an old European favorite. It will keep fresh for a very long time and tastes even better after a week or so, if you have any left that long. It is a really super do-ahead party dessert.

1 cup plus 6 Tbsp. butter (11 ounces)
2/3 cup sugar (5 ounces)
3 hard-boiled egg yolks
1 1/3 cups flour (11 ounces)
¼ cup cocoa powder (1 ounce)
½ cup almonds, toasted and ground (3 ounces)
grated rind of 1 lemon
½ tsp. cinnamon
½ tsp. cardamom
1 to 2 Tbsp. Kirsch
2/3 jar red raspberry preserves
1 egg, mixed

In a bowl, work together the butter, sugar and hard-boiled egg yolks until they are very well blended.

Mix in the flour, cocoa powder, ground almonds, lemon rind, cinnamon and cardamom. Add enough Kirsch to form a smooth dough.

Blend well, you cannot overwork this dough. I find it easiest to begin making the dough in a mixer fitted with a flat beater, but I like to finish it with my hands.

Wrap the dough well in waxed paper. Put it into a plastic bag and refrigerate the dough for several hours, or overnight. Remove the dough from the refrigerator about an hour before needed.

Butter and flour a nine or ten inch shallow tart pan with a removable bottom. Preheat the oven to 375 degrees.

You can either roll out half the dough on a lightly floured board or pat it into place directly in the pan, covering the bottom and sides with a fairly thick layer.

Spread the torte with the raspberry preserves, smoothing it into a thin layer. You may not need all the preserves, it is better to use too little than too much. You only need about a quarter-inch layer of the jelly.

Roll out the rest of the dough into a rectangle and cut it into half-inch strips. I like to use a ravioli cutter for this as the scalloped cutting edge gives the torte a pretty finish.

Form the strips into a lattice pattern on top of the torte. I also like to place a narrow strip of dough around the outside rim of the torte covering the lattice edge.

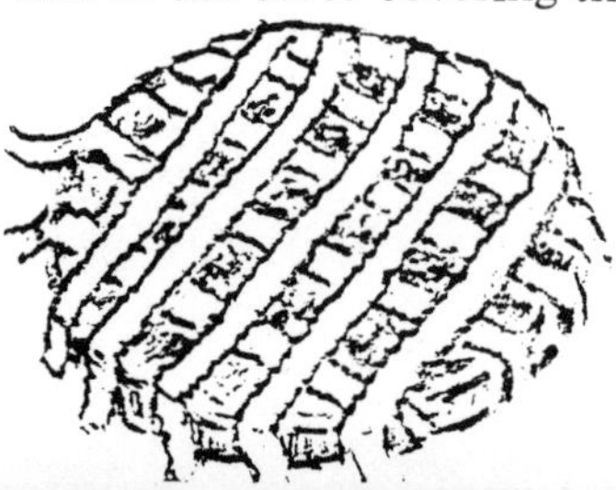

Brush the top of the lattice crust with a little of the beaten egg, using a narrow brush.

Place the torte onto a baking sheet as sometimes butter will leak out of the bottom of the tart pan as it bakes. Bake in a 375 degree oven for thirty-five to forty-five minutes.

The top of the crust will turn a little darker in color and begin to feel firm when the torte is done.

Remove the pan from the oven and let the torte cool in the pan until it reaches room temperature. Once cool enough to handle easily, remove the torte from the pan.

When it is cold, wrap the torte well and store in the refrigerator for at least a day or two to mellow before serving.

Serve Linzer Torte at room temperature either plain or with sweetened whipped cream. This recipe makes ten to twelve portions.

This torte can be stored for as long as two weeks, if well wrapped, in the refrigerator. It can also be frozen.

Sometimes at holiday time, I like to double the recipe and bake Linzer Torte in a jelly roll pan. Cut the torte into lots of little squares - it makes a delicious cookie as well as a torte.

BRANDY CIRCLES

These are holiday cookies that I now bake year round. The brandy flavor disappears once they are baked and gives the cookies a wonderful keeping quality. Brandy Circles stay fresh for a very long time, if there are any left, that is.

They are very firm and crisp little cookies.

1 1/3 cups butter
¾ cup confectioners sugar
3½ cups flour
½ tsp. salt
6 Tbsp. brandy
1 egg white

Cream the butter with the sugar until it is light and fluffy.

Add the flour and salt to the butter-sugar mixture, blending well to incorporate all the flour.

Add the brandy and the egg white and mix well. The cookie dough will be very thick.

The dough is easier to handle if it is chilled. Wrap well and refrigerate for at least a half hour.

I even like to make up the dough a day ahead of time and chill it overnight in the refrigerator.

If so, remove the dough and allow it to soften for at least a half hour before rolling.

Butter a few baking sheets. Preheat the oven to 350 degrees.

On a lightly floured board roll out half the dough so that it is about an eighth of an inch thick. Cut out small ring shapes. Use two circular cutters, one smaller than the other, or a small doughnut cutter.

Place the rings onto the prepared baking sheets and bake for about ten minutes, or until the cookies are very lightly browned. Check the bottoms of the cookies to see if they are done.

Remove the cookies from the baking sheets and place them on a rack to cool.

The dough from the centers of the circles can be re-rolled or they can be baked as miniature cookies. Children adore these tiny cookies.

Repeat rolling, cutting and baking the cookies until all the dough is used.

This recipe will yield about twelve dozen cookies.

Brandy circles will keep fresh for several days. Store in an airtight container. They also freeze beautifully.

CINNAMON PECAN BALLS

Rich and buttery, these are one of my husband's favorite cookies. Handle carefully, as they break easily. They are soft and crumbly, but an utterly delicious cookie.

½ cup ground pecans
1 cup flour
2 Tbsp. sugar
1 tsp. cinnamon
½ cup butter
1 tsp. vanilla
½ cup chopped pecans
confectioners sugar

Butter a baking sheet. Preheat the oven to 325 degrees.

These cookies can be made easily in a food processor. To do so, place half a cup of pecans in a food processor and grind until they are finely chopped.

Add the flour, the two tablespoons of sugar and the cinnamon to the bowl and process again to mix.

Cut the butter (cold) into small pieces and place it on top of the flour mixture. Process until the dough is smooth.

Add the vanilla and the remaining pecans. Process just until the vanilla is blended into the dough and the nuts are coarsely chopped. Remove the dough from the machine.

To make the dough without a processor, first grind half the pecans using a blender. Coarsely chop the rest of the nuts.

Cream the butter (room temperature) with the sugar until it is light and fluffy. Mix in the vanilla.

Mix together the flour, cinnamon and both the ground and chopped pecans. Stir the dry ingredients into the butter mixture until they are well incorporated.

Pinch off walnut sized pieces of the cookie dough and roll them into one-inch balls. Place the balls of dough on the prepared baking sheet.

Bake the cookies in a 325 degree oven for thirty to thirty-five minutes. They will be a light brown color on the bottom when they are done.

Remove the cookies from the oven and let them cool for a minute or two. Then roll the cookies in the confectioners sugar to coat them well and place them back onto the cookie sheet.

Return the cookies to the oven for five to ten minutes. Remove the cookies from the baking sheet and place them on a rack to cool.

This recipe makes about thirty-two cookies.

These cookies are best when fresh. They can be stored for a few days in an airtight container. They can be frozen, but crumble easily, so handle them carefully.

CHOCOLATE MERINGUES

Meringues are a favorite with most people. The addition of the grated chocolate and pecans cuts some of the sweetness usually associated with this cookie and gives them more character. These are firm on the outside, chewy on the inside and very easy to make.

2 egg whites
dash salt
½ cup sugar

4 ounces semi-sweet chocolate, grated
½ cup chopped pecans
½ tsp. vanilla

Butter two baking sheets. Preheat the oven to 350 degrees.

Beat the egg whites until they are foamy. Add the salt and beat them until they turn white.

Gradually add the sugar and continue to beat until the meringue is stiff and shiny.

Fold the grated chocolate, the nuts and the vanilla into the meringue.

Drop the batter by teaspoonfuls onto the prepared baking sheets.

Bake in a 350 degree oven for fifteen minutes, or until the cookies are firm and shiny. Remove the cookies and place them on a rack to cool.

This recipe makes thirty-six cookies.

The meringues can be stored in an airtight container for two or three weeks. Do not refrigerate these cookies.

NUT ROLLS

I like to double this recipe and bake four nut rolls at a time as they freeze beautifully once baked. Pop directly into the oven from the freezer to both defrost and warm for unexpected company. This recipe has been a family favorite for many years.

4 ounces butter
4 ounces cream cheese
1 cup flour
½ cup apricot preserves
1 tsp. cinnamon
¼ cup sugar
1 cup chopped walnuts

You will need a plain baking sheet. Preheat the oven to 375 degrees.

Whip the butter and the cream cheese together until they are light and fluffy.

Blend the flour into this mixture and form the dough into a ball. Wrap and chill the dough for at least thirty minutes.

The dough can be prepared to this point and refrigerated for a day or two, or it can be frozen. Remove from the refrigerator for a little while to soften before rolling.

Cut the dough into half. Roll out half the dough into a rectangle approximately ten by twelve inches in size.

Spread the dough with half of the apricot preserves, leaving an inch clear around the edges.

Mix the cinnamon and sugar together and sprinkle half of this mixture evenly over the preserves. Spread a half cup of the chopped walnuts over the sugar.

Roll the dough lengthwise into a log shape. Fold and tuck the ends of the dough under the roll.

Place the roll onto an ungreased baking sheet. Repeat, using the rest of the dough and the filling.

Bake the nut rolls in a 375 degree oven until they are nicely browned, about forty minutes.

Remove the rolls from the cookie sheet. I find this easiest to do using two large pancake turners.

I like to set the nut rolls directly onto a piece of aluminum foil placed on a cake rack to cool. This way I can wrap them right in the foil without having to transfer them again for freezing.

Cool the nut rolls a little before slicing. They are good either warm or cold. This recipe makes two rolls, or about twenty-four slices.

The baked nut rolls freeze beautifully. Slice after defrosting.

OATMEAL RAISIN COOKIES

An old fashioned favorite made all in one saucepan - no dirty bowls or mixers. They are easy and good, too. Use regular or quick cooking oatmeal, not the instant variety.

2/3 cup butter
1 cup brown sugar
1 egg
1 cup flour
1 tsp. baking powder
1 tsp. vanilla
2 cups oatmeal
1 cup raisins

Butter two baking sheets. Preheat the oven to 350 degrees.

In a saucepan, heat the butter until it melts. Stir the sugar into the butter until it dissolves and remove the pan from the heat.

Let the pan cool for a minute or two, then beat in the egg.

Mix together the flour and the baking powder and stir the flour mixture into the pan.

Then blend the vanilla into the batter. Add the oatmeal and the raisins and mix well. The batter will be very stiff.

Drop the batter, by teaspoonfuls, onto the prepared sheets. Flatten the cookies with a fork.

Bake in a 350 degree oven for fifteen minutes. Even though they are baked, these cookies will still be soft, they harden as they cool. The bottoms of the cookies should be light brown when they are done.

Remove the baking sheets from the oven and let the cookies sit for a few minutes to harden. Then place the cookies on a rack to finish cooling.

This recipe makes about four dozen cookies.

These cookies will remain fresh for several days. They also freeze beautifully.

Chocolate chips can be substituted for the raisins in this recipe. Or use part chips and part raisins - or even chopped nuts.

Margarine can be substituted for the butter in this recipe.

SCHNECKEN

Any nuts you prefer can be used to make these cookies. I am especially fond of hazelnuts but walnuts or pecans work well. Schnecken is the closest thing there is to heaven!

4 ounces butter
4 ounces cream cheese
1 cup flour
1 Tbsp. melted butter
1 tsp. cinnamon
1/3 cup sugar
2/3 cup finely chopped nuts
1 egg yolk

Butter two cookie sheets. Preheat the oven to 400 degrees.

Whip the cream cheese with the butter until soft and fluffy. Mix in the flour and form the dough into a ball.

Wrap and chill the dough for at least thirty minutes for easier handling.

The dough can be prepared a day or two ahead and refrigerated, or it can be frozen. Remove from the refrigerator to soften a little before rolling.

Cut the dough into five pieces. Roll the dough, one piece at a time, into eight inch circles.

Using a pastry brush, paint the round with a little of the melted butter.

Mix the cinnamon and sugar together. Sprinkle the circle with about one tablespoon of this mixture.

Spread about two tablespoons of the finely chopped nuts on top of the sugar and pat them down, using the plam of your hand.

Cut the circle into eight pie-shaped sections. The easiest way to do this is to use a pizza cutter. Roll up each triangular piece of dough, starting with the wide end of the triangle. Form the rolled cookie into a crescent shape.

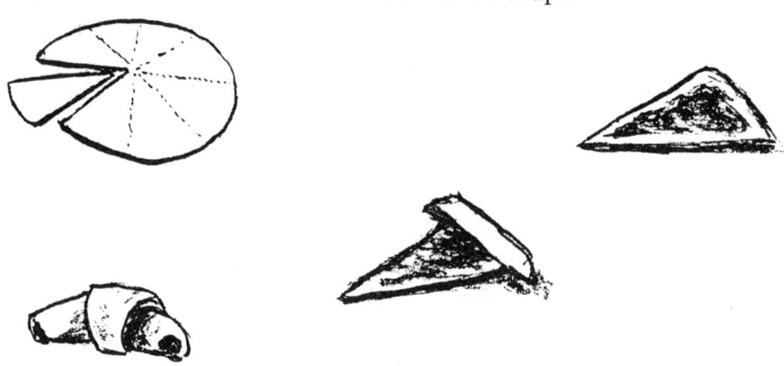

Place the cookies as they are completed onto the prepared baking sheets. Repeat until all the dough and the filling is used.

Paint the tops of the cookies with a little of the egg yolk, using a small pastry brush.

Bake the cookies in a 400 degree oven until they are golden, about fifteen minutes. Remove the cookies and let them cool on a wire rack.

The Schnecken are wonderful either warm or cold. This recipe makes about forty cookies.

The Schnecken will keep fresh for a few days. They also freeze beautifully.

BREAD, APPLE AND NUT PUDDING

More like a soufflé than a pudding, no one will ever believe you made this dessert from leftover bread. It is even delicious cold, if you have any left.

½ cup ground hazelnuts
1½ cups soft bread crumbs (no crusts)
½ cup half and half
1/3 cup butter
3 Tbsp. sugar
1 egg yolk
2 egg whites
1 ounce heavy cream
1 tsp. grated lemon rind
1 large green apple
2 Tbsp. cinnamon-sugar

Butter a one quart casserole or soufflé dish. Preheat the oven to 375 degrees.

Toast the hazelnuts and remove their skins. Grind the nuts. Other nuts can be used as well - try almonds or even walnuts in this pudding.

Soak the bread crumbs in the half and half for about ten or fifteen minutes.

Cream the butter with two tablespoons of the sugar in a bowl. Add the egg yolk, heavy cream and lemon rind and mix well.

Stir in both the bread crumb mixture and the ground nuts.

Beat the egg whites until they turn white in color. Add the remaining tablespoon of sugar and continue to beat until they are stiff.

Stir a quarter of the beaten egg whites into the bread mixture, then fold in the rest.

Pour half of this mixture into the prepared dish.

Peel, core and thinly slice the apple. A food processor is wonderful for this. Place the apple slices into the dish in an even layer. Sprinkle with the cinnamon-sugar.

Cover the apple slices with the rest of the bread mixture.

Bake in a 375 degree oven for forty-five to fifty minutes or until the pudding feels firm, is puffed and well browned on top.

Serve hot. This pudding will serve four to six portions.

If allowed to cool, the pudding will deflate a little. Don't worry - it will still taste great.

NOODLE AND APRICOT PUDDING

These two noodle puddings can be served either with a meal or by themselves. I love them as an afternoon or late night snack with hot coffee or tea. Try them for brunch or lunch - as a matter of fact, they are good anytime.

1 eight ounce package medium egg noodles
2 eggs
½ cup sugar
½ tsp. cinnamon
dash nutmeg
1 apple
1/3 cup raisins
½ cup chopped walnuts
1 cup Apricot Sauce, page 230

Butter a nine inch round or square pan. Preheat the oven to 350 degrees.

Cook the noodles in boiling salted water until they are barely tender as they will cook again. Pour them into a colander and rinse with hot water. Drain the noodles well.

Leftover cooked noodles can be used to make this pudding.

In a bowl, mix together the eggs, sugar, cinnamon and nutmeg. Add the cooked noodles to the bowl, mixing them in well.

Peel, core and dice the apple. Mix the diced apple, raisins and nuts into the noodles.

Pour half of the noodle mixture into the prepared pan.

Spread with the cup of Apricot Sauce, then smooth the rest of the noodle mixture over the sauce.

Bake in a 350 degree oven for one hour and fifteen to twenty minutes. The pudding should be set and the top lightly browned.

Serve hot or warm, cut into wedges. This recipe will serve six to nine portions, depending on how it is cut.

Prune jelly or lekvar can be substituted for the Apricot Sauce in this recipe. However, I think it tastes best with the apricot.

Although best when fresh, the noodle pudding will keep well for a few days if wrapped and refrigerated. The pudding can be reheated. Add a little extra butter to the bottom of the pan. Cover the pudding with a piece of aluminum foil and heat in a 350 degree oven for fifteen minutes or until hot. Noodle pudding can also be frozen.

NOODLE, CHEESE AND APPLE PUDDING

I am really not sure which of these two puddings I prefer; they are both great.

1 eight ounce package medium egg noodles
8 ounces farmer cheese
1 cup sour cream
1 egg
½ cup sugar
½ tsp. cinnamon
dash nutmeg
1/3 cup raisins
1 or 2 apples
1 Tbsp. cinnamon-sugar

Butter a nine inch square or round pan. Preheat the oven to 350 degrees.

Cook the noodles in boiling salted water until they are barely tender, as they will cook again. Pour them into a colander and rinse with hot water. Drain the noodles well.

Cooked leftover noodles can be used to make this pudding.

In a bowl, mix the farmer cheese with the sour cream. Stir in the egg, then add the half-cup of sugar, the cinnamon and the nutmeg.

Blend the cooked drained noodles into this cheese mixture. Spread half the noodles into the prepared pan.

Peel, core and thinly slice the apple. Layer the apple slices evenly over the noodles and sprinkle with the cinnamon-sugar mixture.

Smooth the rest of the noodles over the apple layer.

Bake in a 350 degree oven for one hour and fifteen to twenty minutes. The pudding should be set and the top lightly browned.

Serve hot or warm, cut into wedges. This recipe serves six to nine portions, depending on how it is cut.

If farmer cheese is unavailable, substitute half cream cheese and half small curd cottage cheese. Farmer cheese does make the best noodle pudding, so try to find some if you can.

This pudding both reheats and freezes well. See the previous recipe for instructions on reheating.

HOT ORANGE RICE MOLD

This is a delightfully different hot rice pudding recipe flavored with orange and almond and served with a warm orange sauce.

1 Tbsp. butter	¼ cup flour
¾ cup rice	rind of one orange
3 cups milk	4 eggs, separated
10 Amaretti cookies	pinch salt
½ cup sugar	Orange Sauce, page 231

Butter a two quart soufflé dish and dust it with granulated sugar to coat. Chill until needed. Preheat the oven to 400 degrees.

Heat the butter in a saucepan. Add the rice and stir until all the grains are coated with the butter. Add the milk and bring the mixture to a boil. Stir.

Lower the heat and simmer, stirring occasionally, until all the milk is absorbed by the rice. This will take about forty minutes. Cool the rice a little.

If using a food processor, grind the Amaretti cookies together with the sugar, flour and orange rind. If using a blender, first grate the orange rind by hand, then add it to the mixture and blend until fine crumbs are formed.

Stir the egg yolks into the cooled rice, then blend in the cookie mixture.

Beat the egg whites until they are foamy. Add the salt and continue to beat until stiff. Stir a third of the egg whites into the rice, then fold in the rest.

Pour this mixture into the prepared soufflé dish and bake in a 400 degree oven for thirty-five to forty minutes or until the mold is firm and lightly browned.

Allow the mold to rest for ten minutes before serving. The pudding can be served directly from the soufflé dish or it can be unmolded.

Serve the mold hot or warm with the Orange Sauce. This recipe will serve eight.

BRANDIED CHOCOLATE MOUSSE

No, there is no mistake. There is no sugar in this recipe - it does not need any. This has to be the most devastatingly rich chocolate mousse recipe ever! You only need a little bit to satisfy that chocolate urge. It was one of the most popular desserts I made at the restaurant.

Nice served with a little sweetened whipped cream and some shaved chocolate curls on top.

12 ounces semi-sweet chocolate
5 eggs, separated
1 Tbsp. instant coffee powder
3 Tbsp. brandy
1½ cups heavy cream
pinch salt

Chop the chocolate into small pieces. Place into a metal bowl and set the bowl over a pot of boiling water. Stir occasionally until the chocolate has melted. You can use a double boiler but a bowl is easier.

Remove the bowl from the heat and allow the chocolate to cool. Stir the egg yolks into the cooled chocolate one at a time, beating until they are well incorporated.

Dissolve the coffee powder in the brandy. Then blend this mixture into the chocolate.

Whip the cream until it is firm but not stiff and set it aside for a few minutes (refrigerate).

Beat the egg whites until they are foamy. Add a pinch of salt and continue to beat until they are stiff.

Stir one-quarter of the egg whites into the chocolate, then fold in the rest. Fold the whipped cream into this mixture.

Pour the mousse into individual serving dishes, wine glasses, or into a crystal bowl and chill for a few hours.

This recipe serves eight.

The chocolate mousse tastes best the day it is made, but it will keep well overnight in the refrigerator.

LEMON MOUSSE

Everyone loves lemon mousse - it is the perfect ending to almost any meal. Light in taste, just tart enough to please the palate and absolutely perfect with fresh strawberries.

¼ cup lemon juice
½ cup sugar
2 Tbsp. water
3 egg yolks
1 Tbsp. Cointreau
1 cup heavy cream
Garnish: sweetened whipped cream
sliced strawberries

You can cook the base for this mousse in a double boiler or in a metal bowl placed over a pot of boiling water. You will be able to whip the mixture more easily and evenly using the bowl.

Fill the pot with just enough water so that the bottom of the bowl (or double boiler) remains above the water level. Bring the water to a boil.

Combine the lemon juice, sugar, water and the egg yolks in the bowl or pot and mix well.

Place the bowl over the boiling water and cook, whisking constantly, until the mixture is thick and light.

Remove the bowl from the heat and let the mixture cool, stirring occasionally. Stir the Cointreau into the mousse.

Whip the cream until it is stiff. Fold the cream into the cooled lemon mixture.

Pour the mousse into individual serving dishes, wine glasses, or a small crystal bowl and refrigerate.

At serving time, place a layer of sliced strawberries on top of the mousse. (Sugar them if they are very tart.) Decorate with sweetened whipped cream and serve. This recipe serves six.

Other fruits, such as fresh raspberries or blueberries can be substituted for the strawberries.

The lemon mousse can be made a day ahead and refrigerated. Do not add the berries until serving time.

LIME MOUSSE

This is a very quick and easy dessert to make when fresh limes are plentiful. Lime mousse is not green, but almost white in color. If you want to color the mousse with a few drops of green food coloring, that is up to you. It tastes like lime no matter what the color. I prefer to leave it alone.

½ cup lime juice
1 Tbsp. gelatin (1 packet)
3 eggs
1 cup sugar
grated rind of 1 lime
1 cup heavy cream
Garnish: sweetened whipped cream
lime slices

Place the lime juice into a small saucepan. Sprinkle the gelatin on top of the juice and let it sit for a few minutes to soften.

Heat, stirring, until the gelatin is dissolved. Let the mixture cool a little.

In the bowl of a mixer, beat the eggs with the sugar until they are very thick and light and have doubled in volume.

Stir the lime-gelatin mixture and the grated rind into the beaten eggs.

Whip the cream until it is fairly stiff. Stir about a third of the cream into the mousse, then fold in the rest.

Pour the mousse into individual serving dishes, wine glasses, or into a bowl. Chill until serving time.

Garnish with a little sweetened whipped cream and thin slices of lime. This recipe will serve six to eight.

This mousse will hold up well in the refrigerator overnight.

COLD APRICOT SOUFFLE

A wonderful do-ahead dessert. Serve plain or with an apricot sauce.

1 six-ounce bag dried apricots
½ cup water, or more
2 Tbsp. brandy*
½ tsp. vanilla
1½ tsp. gelatin (½ packet)
juice of 1 lemon
4 eggs plus 3 egg yolks
2/3 cup sugar
2½ cups heavy cream
Garnish: sweetened whipped cream

Place the dried apricots into a saucepan and add the water. Bring the water to a boil, cover with a lid and simmer until the apricots are very tender. Add more water if needed while cooking to keep the apricots from sticking. The finished apricots should have absorbed most of the water. Cool a little.

Purée the apricots along with the brandy and the vanilla in a food processor or blender. Reserve.

The apricots can be prepared to this point and refrigerated overnight.

Pour the lemon juice into a small saucepan. Sprinkle the gelatin over the juice and let it sit for a few minutes to soften. Then heat, stirring, until the gelatin is dissolved. Cool for a few minutes.

Place the four whole eggs plus the extra yolks and the sugar into the bowl of a mixer. Beat until the mixture is very light and has doubled in volume.

Blend the apricot purée and the dissolved gelatin into the egg-sugar mixture.

Whip the cream lightly and stir a quarter of it into the apricot mixture, then fold in the rest.

Pour the soufflé into individual serving dishes or glasses and refrigerate for a few hours until firm. The soufflé can also be poured into a crystal bowl or a soufflé dish fitted with a collar and spooned out at serving time.

Decorate the soufflé with the sweetened whipped cream and serve cold. This recipe serves eight.

The soufflé can be prepared a day ahead and refrigerated overnight. Do not decorate until ready to serve. Do not freeze.

*You can use either Apricot Brandy or plain brandy for the recipe.

MOCHA POT de CREME

This was a favorite dessert in our house when my children were young - nutritious, with a smooth texture and a wonderfully rich coffee flavor. Easy enough for a family dessert yet elegant enough, as well, for company.

3 cups light cream
2/3 cup sugar
3 Tbsp. instant coffee
6 egg yolks
1 tsp. vanilla
lightly sweetened whipped cream

Preheat the oven to 325 degrees.

Pour the cream into a saucepan and heat just to scald. Remove the pan from the heat, add the sugar and the coffee powder and stir until they are well dissolved.

In a bowl, mix the egg yolks just enough to break them apart.

Whisk a few spoons of the hot cream into the egg yolks. Mix the yolks into the cream, stirring until they are well incorporated.

Blend in the vanilla and strain the custard.

Pour the strained custard into individual pot de créme dishes or small custard cups. Enough to fill from eight to ten cups, depending on their size.

Cover the custard cups with aluminum foil or use the lids that come with the pot de créme dishes.

Place the cups into a bain-marie, adding about an inch of warm water. Bake in a 325 degree oven for about thirty minutes, or until the custard is set.

You can tell when the custard is set by shaking the cups gently. If the mixture stays firm, it is done. You can also press lightly on the surface of the custard. If it feels dry, your custard is set.

Remove the cups from the water bath. Take off the lids and cool the crème to room temperature. Then cover again and chill.

Serve cold or at room temperature topped with a dollop of sweetened whipped cream. This recipe makes eight to ten pot de crèmes.

The pot de crème can be stored for two or three days in the refrigerator, if well covered.

POACHED PEARS IN A WHITE WINE SAUCE

The wine used in the poaching liquid gives these pears just enough zing to make them special.

3 cups water, or more to cover
1 cup sugar
juice of 1 lemon
2 pieces of lemon peel
1 cup white wine
piece cinnamon stick
6 firm pears

Bring the water, sugar, lemon juice, lemon peel, wine and the cinnamon stick to a boil in a saucepan just large enough to hold the pears. Cook the syrup for five minutes.

Peel and core the pears. They can either be left whole or cut into halves. Place them in the boiling liquid. Add more water, if necessary to cover the pears.

Bring the liquid back to a boil, cover the pan and reduce the heat. Poach the pears gently at a simmer until they are barely tender. This can take anywhere from ten to twenty minutes, depending on the ripeness of the pears.

Remove the pan from the heat and allow the pears to remain in the poaching liquid until they reach room temperature.

The pears can be served warm or cold, plain or with a White Wine Sauce made from the poaching liquid.

To make the wine sauce, remove the cooled pears and reserve. Return the liquid to the heat and boil until just about two cups remain.

Strain the sauce and pour it back over the pears. Serve immediately, or chill first and then serve.

This recipe will serve six.

The pears can be stored for a few days either in the poaching liquid or the White Wine Sauce. Cover and refrigerate.

POACHED ALMOND PEARS

The pears are tender and juicy, the filling crunchy and the sauce as smooth as velvet. This combination of flavors and textures blends beautifully to make a super dessert.

1 cup sugar
juice of 1 lemon
2 inch piece vanilla bean
2 or more cups water
6 firm pears
Vanilla Sauce, page 232
¼ cup toasted almond slices

Stuffing:

4 ounces almond paste or marzipan
juice of ½ lemon
1 or 2 Tbsp. Amaretto
4 Amaretti cookies

Place the sugar, lemon juice, vanilla bean and the water into a saucepan just large enough to hold all the pears. Bring to a boil and simmer for five minutes.

Peel and core the pears, leaving the stems attached to the tops. Cut a small slice off the bottoms so that the pears will stand upright easily.

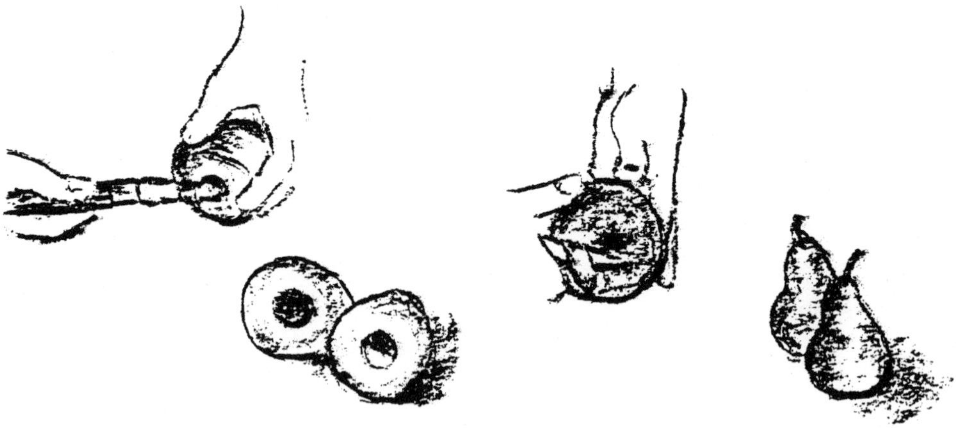

Place the pears into the simmering liquid, stem side up. Add additional water to cover the pears if there is not enough liquid in the saucepan.

Bring the liquid back to a boil, then cover the pan and lower the heat to a simmer. Poach the pears until they are just barely tender. The amount of time this takes will depend on the ripeness of the pears. Pears that have their cores removed take less time to cook than those that are left whole. If the pears are fairly ripe, begin to test after about six or seven minutes of poaching time.

When the pears are just tender, remove the pan from the heat and allow them to cool directly in the liquid.

The pears can be poached a day ahead and stored overnight in their poaching liquid. Refrigerate.

Prepare the Vanilla Sauce and let it cool.

Drain the pears well. An easy way to do this is to stand the pears, stem side up, on a wire rack placed over a pan or dish.

Prepare the stuffing. Mix the marzipan with the lemon juice and the Amaretto until it forms a smooth mixture.

Crumble the Amaretti cookies coarsely and mix them into the marzipan.

The filling can also be prepared a day ahead of time. Wrap well and refrigerate.

Stuff the hollow cores of the drained pears with this marzipan mixture.

Place the pears onto a serving dish. You can use either individual serving dishes or a platter. Pour the Vanilla Sauce over the pears. Sprinkle with the toasted almond slices and serve. Serve slightly chilled or at room temperature.

This recipe serves six.

If you do not have Amaretti cookies, you can substitute crumbled macaroons in the filling. The flavor will not be quite as good, but they will do.

The pears can be stuffed a few hours ahead of time, covered well so that they do not dry out, and refrigerated. Let them sit at room temperature for thirty minutes, pour on the Vanilla Sauce, add the almonds and serve.

RHUBARB FOOL

1 pound rhubarb
¼ cup water
¼ cup sugar, or more to taste
½ tsp. vanilla
1½ cups heavy cream whipped with ¼ cup sugar

Wash, trim and cut the rhubarb into one-half inch slices.

Place the rhubarb and the water into a saucepan and cook, covered, until tender. This should take about twenty-five minutes. Stir occasionally while cooking.

Let the rhubarb cool a little. Then place in a food processor or blender along with the sugar and vanilla. Purée. Add more sugar to taste, if needed.

Chill the rhubarb purée until serving time.

Whip the cream with the sugar until it is stiff. Layer the rhubarb and the whipped cream into four serving dishes.

Serve chilled. This recipe serves four.

APRICOT SAUCE

This is a wonderfully piquant dessert sauce that is good on almost anything. Serve with the Cold Apricot Soufflé, or even over plain vanilla ice cream.

1 cup dried apricots (4 ounces)
1½ cups water, or more
1/3 cup sugar
1 tsp. lemon juice
2 Tbsp. Apricot Brandy

Place the dried apricots and one cup of the water into a small saucepan.

Bring to a boil, then cover and simmer until the apricots are very tender. This will take about one hour. Stir occasionally and add more water if needed to keep them from sticking.

Let the apricots cool a little and then purée them in a blender or food processor. Add the sugar, lemon juice, Apricot Brandy and the remaining half cup of water to the machine and blend well.

This sauce can be served hot, cold or at room temperature. This recipe makes about one and one-half cups of sauce.

Apricot Sauce can be stored in the refrigerator for a week if well covered. The sauce can also be frozen.

CHOCOLATE SAUCE

You can use any liqueur you like for this sauce - try Tia Maria, Cacao, Grand Marnier, Sabra or even plain brandy. And of course, you can add more than one tablespoon if you desire.

For a sauce with a mild coffee flavor, add a teaspoon of instant coffee powder to the chocolate and cream mixture while it is being heated.

8 ounces semi-sweet chocolate
1 cup heavy cream
1 Tbsp. liqueur

Chop the chocolate into small pieces.

Heat the cream in a small saucepan. Add the chopped chocolate to the hot cream and stir until the chocolate is melted and the sauce is smooth.

Remove the pan from the heat and blend in the liqueur. Serve the sauce hot or at room temperature.

This recipe makes about one and one-half cups of sauce.

If you chill this sauce it will harden. Reheat carefully. The sauce can be stored for a week or longer in the refrigerator.

ORANGE SAUCE

This orange sauce is usually served warm and is wonderful over the Orange Rice Mold.

Try the sauce with fresh orange slices or strawberries - equally delightful.

1 Tbsp. cornstarch
¼ cup lemon juice
1 cup orange juice
grated rind of 1 orange
1 Tbsp. butter
½ cup sugar
1 egg yolk
3 Tbsp. Grand Marnier

Dissolve the cornstarch in the lemon juice and set aside.

Place the orange juice, orange rind, butter and sugar into a saucepan. Bring the mixture to a boil.

Once the liquid has come to a full boil, add the cornstarch mixture, stirring well. Simmer the sauce for a few minutes.

Whisk a few spoons of the hot sauce into the egg yolk. Then add the yolk to the hot sauce, stirring constantly. Cook for just a few seconds.

Remove the pan from the heat and stir in the Grand Marnier. Serve the sauce as soon as possible.

This recipe makes about one and one-half cups of sauce.

The Orange Sauce can be made a half hour or so ahead of time. Cover and keep warm in a bowl that has been placed over a pan of hot water. If you have to reheat this sauce, do so with caution. Do not bring it back to a boil once you have added the egg yolk - reheat using a double boiler. Or just serve the sauce cold, it is good that way, too.

RASPBERRY SAUCE

Fresh raspberries make a marvelous sauce, but this is one case where frozen berries will work as well.

Fresh raspberries are such a treat that I never have the heart to purée them for a sauce unless they are absolutely falling apart.

2 packages frozen raspberries
¼ cup sugar, or more to taste
1 Tbsp. Kirsch
1 Tbsp. Framboise

Thaw the frozen raspberries. Do not pour off the juice that forms as they thaw. Purée the berries along with this juice.

The berries can be puréed most easily using a food mill. The mill both removes the seeds and purées the berries at the same time. A food processor or blender can also be used to purée the berries. Strain them afterwards to remove the seeds.

Add the sugar to the purée, stirring well to dissolve. Then add the liqueurs and mix well.

This sauce will keep well for a few days. Cover and refrigerate. Stir well before using.

This recipe makes about one and one-half cups of sauce.

If using fresh berries to make the sauce, sprinkle them with the sugar first (you may need more than a quarter cup as frozen berries are usually pre-sweetened). Let the berries sit for an hour or two to allow the juices to run, then purée.

VANILLA SAUCE

This is a lovely plain vanilla sauce. Serve over poached pears or any fresh fruit.

1½ cups milk
3 inch piece vanilla bean, split
¼ cup sugar
2 tsp. cornstarch
2 egg yolks
½ cup heavy cream

Pour one cup of the milk into a saucepan. Add the split vanilla bean, scraping the inside black specks into the milk and heat.

In a bowl, mix the sugar, cornstarch and the egg yolks together. Stir in the remaining half cup of milk to form a smooth mixture.

Whisk a few spoons of the hot milk into the egg yolk mixture. Then add the yolks to the hot milk. Cook, stirring constantly, until the sauce has thickened.

Pour the sauce through a strainer. The little black specks that remain in the sauce are the true vanilla flavor - you want them to be there.

Stir the heavy cream into the sauce and chill until serving time. This recipe makes about two cups of sauce.

The Vanilla Sauce will keep well, if covered and refrigerated, for a few days.

If you do not have a vanilla bean, add a teaspoon or two of pure vanilla extract to the sauce along with the heavy cream. A vanilla bean will make a better tasting sauce.

Beverages

ALMOND SANGRIA

This is a delightful hot punch that is very quick to make. The Amaretto gives it a mild almond taste while the Apricot and Apple Brandies add a fruity flavor.

16 ounces Sangria
¼ cup Amaretto
¼ cup Apricot Brandy
¼ cup Calvados or Apple Jack

Garnish: apple slices
orange slices
lemon slices

Mix the Sangria with the Amareto, Apricot Brandy and the Calvados in a saucepan.

Heat the liqueurs just until they reach the boiling point.

Ladle the hot punch into wine glasses or mugs, garnish with the fruit slices and serve.

This recipe serves five to six portions.

ALMOND WINE PUNCH

The taste of orange with Amaretto combine to give this punch a very lovely flavor.

8 ounces white wine
1 ounce orange juice, strained
2 Tbsp. honey
2 ounces Amaretto
orange slices for garnish

Place the wine, orange juice, honey and Amaretto into a saucepan. Heat, stirring occasionally, just until the mixture reaches the boiling point.

Remove the pan from the heat and let it sit for a few minutes.

Ladle the punch into wine glasses or mugs, garnish with an orange slice and serve while still hot.

This recipe serves four.

CHAMPAGNE PUNCH

A memorable Champagne Punch with lots of zing!

2 ounces Grand Marnier
2 ounces Cognac or brandy
2 ounces Sweet Marsala
¼ cup superfine sugar
juice of 1 orange
12 ounces Champagne (1 split)
20 ounces club soda
½ orange, cut into thin slices

Pour the Grand Marnier, Cognac and Marsala into a punch bowl.

Add the sugar and the orange juice and stir until dissolved. Then pour in the Champagne and the club soda. Add ice to the bowl. Float the orange slices on top of the punch.

Serve as soon as possible - before the Champagne looses its fizz.

This recipe makes five cups of punch, enough to serve twelve drinks, three and one-half ounces each.

HOT FORTIFIED CIDER

One glass of this is enough to warm you all the way down to your toes!

2 cups apple cider
2 ounces Vodka
2 ounces Apricot Brandy
2 slices of lemon
3 Tbsp. raisins
orange slices for garnish

Place the cider, Vodka, Apricot Brandy, lemon slices and raisins into a saucepan.

Slowly bring the ingredients to a boil and simmer the cider for about three minutes.

Let the cider sit for a few minutes to settle, then ladle into mugs. Serve with a slice of orange as a garnish.

This recipe serves four.

ENGLISH BIRTHDAY PUNCH

You don't have to be English and it does not have to be your birthday in order to enjoy this punch.

1 cup red wine
¾ cup brewed English tea
¾ cup orange juice
¼ cup sweet Marsala
1 stick cinnamon
1 tsp. vanilla
2 Tbsp. sugar

Place all of the ingredients into a saucepan.

Heat them just to the boiling point. Then turn off the heat and let the punch sit for at least ten minutes.

The punch can be prepared to this point up to an hour ahead of time.

Reheat just to the simmering point when you are ready to serve the punch. Ladle into wine glasses or mugs.

This recipe will serve four.

HOT RUM AND CACAO TODDY

Hot rum, cocoa and spice - really nice.

2 Tbsp. butter
10 ounces water
6 ounces white light Rum
2 ounces Cacao
2 tsp. sugar
1 cinnamon stick
dash nutmeg

Place the butter, water, Rum and Cacao into a saucepan. Add the sugar and the cinnamon stick.

Heat slowly until the butter melts and the liquid reaches the boiling point. Boil for one minute then ladle the toddy into mugs or wine glasses.

Top each with a sprinkling of nutmeg and serve while hot. This recipe makes four drinks.

SUPER BOWL PUNCH

This punch was concocted by my husband on Super Bowl Sunday to sip while watching the big game. It is a hearty brew that is good anytime your spirits need warming.

24 ounces Claret or red wine
4 ounces brandy
4 ounces Port
4 ounces Cherry Herring
8 ounces club soda
6 Tbsp. brown sugar
12 cloves
1 or 2 cinnamon sticks
½ tsp. nutmeg
juice of 1 lemon
1 lemon, cut into slices

Place all of the ingredients in a saucepan and stir well. Bring to a boil, then simmer for five minutes.

Let the punch sit and keep warm for ten or fifteen minutes before serving to allow time for the flavors to mellow.

Ladle into mugs or glasses and serve.

This recipe makes six cups of punch, enough for eight six-ounce servings.

RED WINE PUNCH

2 cups red wine
¼ cup orange juice
¼ cup lemon juice
½ cup Vermouth
¼ cup Port
diced strawberries

Mix all of the ingredients for the punch together in a bowl. Add ice and stir until all is cold.

Serve the punch ladled into wine glasses. Make sure you get some strawberries into each glass.

This recipe serves six.

CAFE IMPERIAL

The perfect way to end a perfect meal.

2 cups strong coffee
¼ cup Cognac or brandy
5 or 6 cloves
1 piece orange peel
2 Tbsp. sugar
1 tsp. vanilla
sweetened whipped cream

Place all of the ingredients except the whipped cream into a saucepan. Slowly bring the liquid just to a boil and then turn off the heat.

The coffee can be served immediately or it can wait for up to an hour at this point.

When ready to serve, reheat the coffee and ladle it into wine glasses, cups or mugs. Top with a dollop of sweetened whipped cream and serve.

This recipe will serve four.

BRANDIES AND LIQUEURS

Flavor	Name
Almond	Amaretto Noyan de Poissy
Anise (licorice taste)	Anisette Sambuca
Apple	Applejack Calvados
Carraway and Cumin	Kummel
Cherry	Cherry Herring Kirsch
Chocolate and Cherry	Cheri-Suisse
Chocolate and Mint	Vandermint
Chocolate and Orange	Sabra
Cocoa	Creme de Cacao
Coffee	Kahlua Kona
Coffee and Rum	Tia Maria
Herb	Benedictine Chartreuse
Herb and Brandy	B and B
Mint	Creme de Menthe
Orange	Cointreau Curacao Triple-sec
Orange and Brandy	Grand Marnier
Pear	Poire
Prune-Plum	Quetsch Slivovitz
Raspberry	Framboise
Scotch, Honey and Herbs	Drambui Irish Mist
Strawberry	Fraise

WINE AND FOOD AFFINITY CHART

In selecting wines for a menu, you must keep in mind that a balance should be achieved among all of the wines you intend to serve.

As a general rule, younger wines are used earlier in the meal, with the more mature and heavier wines following, to be served with the entree and the cheese.

Full bodied wines should be selected for the more substantial courses with heavier sauces. Lighter sauces and foods require simple wines with less body.

THE FOOD	THE WINE	THE TEMPERATURE
Raw Oysters and Clams, Crab, Lobster, Prawns, Shrimp	Chablis, Pinot Chardonnay, Macon Blanc, Sancerre, Muscadet	Moderately chilled 45–50°F.
Delicate fish such as Sole, Sandab, Trout, etc.	Reisling, Pinot Chardonnay	Moderately chilled 45–50°F.
Fried Oysters and strongly flavored fish such as Salmon, Swordfish, etc.	Sancerre, Pinot Chardonnay, Reisling, Chenin Blanc, Champagne	Moderately chilled 45–50°F.
Roast chicken, Broilers, Cold Chicken and Turkey	Any of the above White Wines or Light Red Wines	Moderately chilled 45–50°F.
Lamb, Veal, Young Pork, Cold Ham	Pinot Chardonnay, Gewurztraminer, Reisling, or Light Red Wine	Moderately chilled 45–50°F.
Roast Turkey, Beef, Mutton, Ham, Tongue, Beefsteak, Hamburger, Duck, Squab, Corned Beef, Stews, Tripe, Curried Dishes, Rabbit, Pasta, Liver and Kidneys	Burgundy, Beaujolais, Zinfandel, Cabernet Sauvignon, Pinot Noir, Bordeaux	Room Temperature 68–70°F.
Quail, Pheasant, Wild Duck, Goose, Venison	Pinot Noir, Cabernet Sauvignon, Beaujolais-Village	Room Temperature 68–70°F.
Mild Cheese	Any White or Light Red Wine	Moderately chilled 45–50°F.
Full Flavored Cheese	Any Full Red Wine - Burgundy or Bordeaux	Room Temperature 68–70°F.
Sweet Desserts	Sauternes, Barsac, Champagne	Well chilled 40–45°F.

VINTAGE CHART

YEAR	Claret	Sauternes	Red Burgundy	White Burgundy	Rhone	Loire	Rhine & Moselle	Champagne	Port
1945	7	7	6	—	5	—	4†	4†	7
1947	6†	6†	5†	—	5	4	4†	4†	6†
1948	5†	5	4†	—	4	—	—	—	7
1949	6	6†	5†	—	6	—	5†	5†	—
1950	4†	5	1†	—	5	—	—	—	3†
1952	4	6	5	3†	6	—	2†	4†	—
1953	6†	6†	4†	3†	6	—	5†	4†	—
1955	5	7	3†	3†	6	—	3†	5†	7
1957	3	4	4	3†	6	—	2†	—	—
1958	3	2	—	—	4	—	—	—	5
1959	6	6	7	3†	6	—	5†	5	—
1960	2†	1	0	0	6	—	—	—	6
1961	7	5	5	4†	7	—	4†	6	—
1962	5	6	6	5†	5	—	3†	5	—
1963	1	0	1	2†	2	—	—	—	7*
1964	3/6	2	6	5†	6	4	5†	6	—
1966	7	5	5	5	6	2	4†	6	6*
1967	3	7	4	5	6	3	4†	—	6*
1969	2	4	7	5	6	5	5†	5	—
1970	7	6	5	4	6	5	4†	6	7*
1971	5/7	6*	7	7	5	6	7	7	—
1972	3	3	5	4	6	3	3	—	4*
1973	4	3	4	5	5*	5	5	6	—
1974	3	1	3	4	4*	6	4	—	—
1975	7*	6*	1	5	4*	5	5/7	7	7*
1976	6*	6*	7*	6*	5*	6	7	6	—
1977	3	3	4	4	5*	3	4	—	6*
1978	6*	3	6*	6*	7*	6	5	6	—

Champagne and Port have been restricted to generally "declared" vintage years. Certain white wines which do not improve with age have not been evaluated for as far back as 1945; hence the dash.

7—The Best 0—No Good

*Recommended for Laying Down †Tiring, Drink-Up

Menus

LUNCH AND BRUNCH

If you care to serve a wine with lunch or brunch, champagne, a good Bequjolais or a Riesling is always appropriate.

Tomato Juice
Smoked Salmon Quiche
Tossed Green Salad
Banana Bread

Melon
Hot Cheese Soufflé
Asparagus
English Cream Scones
Fresh Fruit

Salmon with Herb Butter
Plain Rice Pilaf
Cucumber Salad with Cream
Chocolate Raisin Squares

Split Pea Soup
Quick Whole Wheat Bread
Chicken Livers with Madeira
Saffron Rice Pilaf
Cheese and Pear Tart

Salad Escoffier
Fresh Tomatoes
Quick Whole Wheat Bread
Poached Almond Pears
Vanilla Sauce

Sautéed Crabmeat
Green Rice Pilaf
Tomatoes
Zucchini Bread

Shrimp Creole
Green Rice Pilaf
Watercress and Mushroom Salad
Chocolate Raisin Squares

Cream of Tomato Soup
Shrimp Quiche
Vanilla Ice Cream, Hot Chocolate Sauce
Oatmeal Raisin Cookies

Hungarian Goulash Soup
Bread
Tossed Green Salad
Noodle, Cheese and Apple Pudding

Cream of Corn Soup or Grapefruit
Broiled Shad and Roe
Layered Potato Cake
String beans with Mushrooms
Carrot-Pineapple Cake

Cheese Custard
Mornay Sauce
Asparagus
Bread, Apple and Nut Pudding

Sautéed Scallops with Parsley and Chives
Rice Pilaf
String Beans
Chocolate Chip Sour Cream Cake

QUICK DINNERS

Grapefruit
Veal Marsala
Noodles with Cream
Baked Zucchini
Chocolate Raisin Squares
Chinon

Melon
Pasta with Mushrooms and Peas
Tossed Green Salad
Poached Pears with a Vanilla or White Wine Sauce
Frascati

Cream of Lima Bean Soup
Entrecote à la Moutarde
Noodles with Cream
Spinach
Tossed Green Salad
Chocolate Raisin Squares
Margaux

Avocado and Pineapple Salad
Chicken Breasts with Bacon and Cheese
Noodles with a Mushroom Sauce
String Beans
Mocha Pot de Crème
Santenay or Graves

Chicken Livers with Madeira
Saffron Rice Pilaf
Baked Zucchini
Poached Pears
St. Estephe

Red Snapper with a Sour Cream Topping
Baked Potatoes
Spinach
Vanilla Ice Cream with a Raspberry Sauce
Vouvray

Cream of Lima Bean Soup
Scampi
Plain Rice Pilaf
Sliced Tomatoes
Brandied Chocolate Mousse
California Chardonnay

Cream of Corn Soup
Salmon with Herb Butter
Rice Pilaf
String Beans with Mushrooms
Rhubarb Fool
Puligny Montrachet or St.-Veran

Grapefruit
Piquant Pork Chops
Mashed Potatoes
String Beans
Brandied Chocolate Mousse
Cotes du Rhone-Villages

Curried Scallops with Pasta
Tossed Green Salad
Cheese, Italian Bread
Vanilla Ice Cream with Chocolate or Raspberry Sauce
Soave

Leek and Potato Soup
Rack of Lamb en Persillade
Spiced Rice Pilaf
Tossed Green Salad
Lime Mousse
St. Emilion

Curried Cream of Pea Soup
Chicken Paprikash with Potatoes
Broccoli
Tossed Green Salad
Orange Slices with an Orange Sauce
Egri Bikaver

FAMILY DINNERS

Cream of Tomato Soup
Westphalian Pork Chops
Noodles with a Mushroom Sauce
Broccoli
Apple-Pear Pecan Pie
California Petite Sirah

Mushroom, Lima Bean and Barley Soup
Entrecote à la Moutarde
Layered Potato Cake
Broccoli Salad
Poached Pears
California Cabernet

Grapefruit
Old Fashioned Beef Stew
Tossed Green Salad
Dried Fruit Pie
California Zinfandel

Dairy Noodle Soup
Broiled Shad and Roe
Beets with Sour Cream and Horseradish
Lime Mousse
Sancerre

Melon
Shrimp Creole
Rice Pilaf
Broccoli
Cucumber Salad with Cream
Mocha Pot de Crème
Croze Hermitage Blanc

Chicken Breasts with Bacon and Cheese
Stuffed Acorn Squash
String Beans with Mushrooms
Tossed Green Salad
Chocolate Raisin Squares
California Petite Sirah

Grapefruit
Roast Split Chicken with Herbs
Pommes de Terre au Gratin
Carrots with Madeira
Brandied Chocolate Mousse
St. Emilion

Chicken Barley Soup
Veal Rolls with Ham, Herbs and Cheese
Mashed Potatoes
Tossed Green Salad
Ice Cream with Hot Chocolate Sauce
Cotes du Rhone-Villages

Beef and Bean Soup
Tossed Green Salad
Light Biscuits
Noodle and Apricot Pudding
Muscadet

Chicken Paprikash with Potatoes
Baked Zucchini
Watercress and Mushroom Salad
Apple Custard Tart
Egri Bikaver

Leftover Curry
Orange and Endive Salad
Brandied Chocolate Mousse
Cookies
Beer or Reisling

Cream of Corn Soup
Meat Loaf
Mashed Potatoes
String Beans
Chocolate Chip Sour Cream Cake
Beaujolais

ONE POT DINNERS

Chiopino
French Bread
Tossed Green Salad
Cheese and Pear Pie
Hermitage

Fish Chowder
Whole Wheat Corn Bread
Watercress and Mushroom Salad
Lemon Mousse with Strawberries
Corvo Bianco

Old Fashioned Beef Stew
Romaine Salad Mimosa
Apple-Pear Pecan Pie
California Cabernet

Chicken in a Pot with Cornbread Stuffing
Orange and Endive Salad
French Chocolate Cake
Medoc

Paella
Romaine Salad Mimosa
Lime Mousse
Cookies
California Pinot Chardonnay

Coq-au-Vin
Tossed Green Salad
French Bread
Cheese
Mocha Pot de Crème
Chablis

COMPANY AND PARTY DINNERS

Fish Quenelles
Sauce Badania
Roast Stuffed Leg of Lamb
Pommes de Terre au Gratin
String Beans
Cheese
Cold Apricot Soufflé
California Reisling
St. Julien

Seafood Timbales
Beurre Blanc Sauce
Chicken with Artichokes, Carrots and Mushrooms
Romaine Salad Mimosa
Cheese
Almond Creme Tart
Pinot Chardonnay
Moulin-a-Vent

Galantine of Duck
Poisson en Croûte
Vin Blanc Sauce
Zucchini Casserole au Gratin
Pineapple-Carrot Cake
Meursault

Spinach Salad with Foie Gras
Stuffed Breast of Veal
Oven Browned New Potatoes
Baked Zucchini
Apple Custard Tart
Moulin-a-Vent

Coquilles au Gratin
Duck with an Orange or Green Peppercorn Sauce
Wild Rice with Mushrooms
String Beans
Cheese
French Chocolate Cake
Macon Blanc
Graves

Shrimp and Scallops au Gratin
Veal with Morels
Noodles with Cream
Asparagus
Cheese
French Chocolate Cake
Meursault
Bordeau Grand Cru

Rough Country Pâté
Onions a l'Orientale
Fish Quenelles
Sauce Badania
Entrecote à la Moutarde
Pommes de Terre au Gratin
String Beans
Cheese
Lemon Mousse with Strawberries
Sancerre
Morgan

Potage St. Germain
Layered Fish Terrine
Herb Mayonnaise
Poulet en Croûte
Morel Sauce
Carrots with Madeira
Asparagus
Cheese
Raspberries with a Raspberry Sauce and Whipped Cream
Saint-Veran
Pauillac

Smoked Salmon Quiche
Rack of Lamb en Persillade
Layered Potato Cake
Broccoli
Mocha Hazelnut Torte
Chablis
Chateauneuf-du-Pape

Molded Liver Pâté
Coq-au-Vin
Noodles with a Mushroom Sauce
Orange and Endive Salad
Linzer Torte
Champagne
Beaujolais-Brouilly

Sweetbread Terrine
Onions a l'Orientale
Clear Fish Soup
Croutons
Cornish Hens Farci
Morel Sauce
Carrots with Madeira
Bib Lettuce Salad or Cheese
Brandied Chocolate Mousse
Sancerre
Pomerol

Seafood Timbales
Beurre Blanc Sauce
Beef Cordon Rouge
Pommes de Terre au Gratin
Spinach
Poached Almond Pears
Vanilla Sauce
Cookies
California Chenin Blanc
Bourgueil or California Cabernet

BUFFETS

Smoked Salmon Quiche
Vegetable Quiche
Roast Stuffed Leg of Lamb
Wild Rice with Mushrooms
Zucchini Casserole au Gratin
Linzer Torte
Brandied Chocolate Mousse
Champagne
St. Emilion

Ham and Leek Quiche
Shrimp Quiche
Chicken with Noodle Casserole
Stuffed Acorn Squash
Broccoli
Romaine Salad Mimosa
Mocha Hazelnut Torte
Strawberries with Raspberry Sauce
Champagne
Sancerre

Fish Quenelles
Sauce Badania
Poulet en Croûte
Morel Sauce
Carrots with Madeira
Asparagus
Lemon Mousse with Strawberries
Chocolate Raisin Squares
Meursault
Pauillac

Curried Beef in Pastry
Walnut Mushrooms
Molded Liver Pâté
Shrimp and Scallops au Gratin
Coq-au-Vin
Rice Pilaf
String Beans
Coffee Walnut Torte
Cold Apricot Soufflé
Champagne
California Cabernet

Cabbage Strudel
Spinach and Cheese Strudel
Beef Ragoût
Noodles with Cream
String Beans
French Chocolate Cake
Raspberries
Reisling
Fleurie

Sweetbread Terrine
Paella
Tossed Green Salad
Cheese
Cold Apricot Soufflé
Almond Creme Tart
Spanish Roja

Index

C

G

H

I

L

M

N

O

P

T

W

V

Z